ABERDEEN
EUROPEAN NIGHTS

ABERDEEN
EUROPEAN NIGHTS

STORIES FROM ABERDEEN'S GREATEST
EUROPEAN GAMES

ALLY BEGG

POLARIS PUBLISHING LTD
c/o Aberdein Considine
2nd Floor, Elder House
Multrees Walk
Edinburgh
EH1 3DX

Distributed by Birlinn Limited

www.polarispublishing.com

Text copyright © Ally Begg, 2021

ISBN: 9781913538477
eBook ISBN: 9781913538484

British Library Cataloguing-in-Publication Data
A catalogue record for this book is available on request from the British Library.

Designed and typeset by Polaris Publishing, Edinburgh
Printed in Great Britain by CPI Group (UK) Ltd,
Croydon CR0 4YY

CONTENTS

This book is dedicated to my children Lennox and Harvey.
During the 2020 global pandemic they both gave me purpose after
being made redundant for the first time in my professional life.
I channelled all my energy, desire and inner strength their way.
I came out the other end a better, stronger person.
Nothing else matters – I am so grateful to have you both in my life.

ACKNOWLEDGEMENTS

I have so many people to thank for helping me ride this journey from a simple blog idea to a brand-new book. I must pay special attention to my friends Rob A. Clark, Andy Smith, and renowned Aberdeen FC author and historian Kevin Stirling who all provided me with invaluable research items, most of which would never have seen the cold light of day if it were not for their help. A big thank you goes to Mark 'Dolly Digital' Elrick for his fantastic illustrations which have helped bring the book to life. Thank you to everyone at Polaris Publishing, in particular, Peter Burns whose original idea inspired this book. His encouragement and support throughout the entire process has never wavered. My sincere thanks must go to all the players, past and present who helped contribute their original stories for my blog, there would not be a book without you and for that I will always remain grateful. To Mike Loggie and Craig Cameron at Saltire Energy Group, I thank them both for their invaluable support with my blog. I must pay special attention to my wife Miriam who first had the idea for me to start my own blog. She encouraged me, supported me and drove me to write. If it were not for her, I would not be writing these words. And finally, a huge thanks to the Red Army, your support of my blog has been incredible, you continue to inspire me. Enjoy the read.

FOREWORD

I was delighted to have been asked by Ally to contribute the foreword to this new book. Having played in the majority of the games he recalls in the following pages, I have no doubt many great memories will be stirred, not just for the fans but for those of us who were lucky enough to have played a part in these great games.

As I look back, it's a wonder that a group of guys, no older than 28, went all the way to the Cup Winners' Cup Final in 1983 and beat the mighty Real Madrid, all of which has been brilliantly captured by Ally in this book. Who will ever forget that magical night at Pittodrie against Bayern Munich and, before that, knocking UEFA Cup holders Ipswich Town out of the competition at the first hurdle, when nobody outside of Scotland gave us a chance?

It was fascinating to read all the stories from my former teammates who themselves looked back on a golden period in the club's history. As well as the great games from an unforgettable decade, I thoroughly enjoyed catching up with more recent events and Aberdeen's adventures in the UEFA Cup group stage and Europa League qualifiers.

Ally's attention to detail has come as no surprise having got to know him well over the last 25 years. His passion for our club is there for all to see and I have no doubt you will enjoy this book as much as I did.

Willie Miller

INTRODUCTION

'Aberdeen have got to find some strength in those legs to hustle for a few more minutes yet, and they've done so – Weir. That's a good ball from Peter Weir – now Aberdeen with McGhee making the break – and Hewitt waiting in the MIDDLE!!!'

Those are the now immortal words spoken by the late Brian Moore as he described Aberdeen's winning goal against Real Madrid in the 1983 Cup Winners' Cup final to a TV audience of millions back home in the UK, live from Gothenburg, Sweden. Over the years I have listened to those words more times than I can remember, and every time I hear them my emotions get the better of me. That moment is the greatest football memory I have from my childhood. That night, 11 May 1983, Aberdeen defied all the odds to beat Alfredo Di Stefano's Real Madrid side to win their first European trophy. It's the greatest moment in the club's long and distinguished history and I was lucky enough to be there as a ten-year-old boy. My own emotions around that game go far deeper than I will ever be able to express; it's a night I will never forget.

Only seven months on from that unforgettable night in Gothenburg, goals from Neil Simpson and Mark McGhee helped Aberdeen beat European Cup winners SV Hamburg over two games in the Super Cup final. For a short spell, Aberdeen, a small provincial club from the north-east of Scotland, were officially the number one ranked side in European football. It was an astonishing achievement. It was also the night that my late dad lost all control when Mark McGhee scored what proved to be Aberdeen's winner, punching the air with delight and screaming the word 'yes' at the top of his voice. In all the years we attended football together before he died, this was the one and only time he lost all control when celebrating a Dons goal. It's just another fond memory from another incredible night under the lights at Pittodrie.

Going to Pittodrie for a European game was like no other. The place had a different feel to it; there was an air of expectation. The summer months helped give Pittodrie a glow as the sun set far out at sea, the seagulls taking in the last rays before settling down for the night, their squeals echoing around the stadium as kick-off approached. Fans would stream in from all corners of the stadium, filling the place with colour and charisma – the smell of meat pies and Bovril catching every breath. In the winter, the floodlights would cast their beams like a lighthouse over moody seas; you could see them for miles. As a child travelling to the game from the outskirts of the city, the first glimpse of the floodlights from miles beyond awoke the butterflies in my stomach, the nervous tension began, and we were still 45 minutes from kick-off. Under the lights the pitch glistened; the stadium came alive, fans wrapped up tight in their winter attire with the red-and-white colours of their scarves out for all to see. Steam emanated from thousands into the night sky with every nervous breath, and the occasional rendition of 'Here we Go' or 'Stand Free' rang out across the Pittodrie sky. It was special. Nothing compares to that moment as the first ball is kicked upon the referee's whistle – all you could do was sit back and go along for the ride.

Aberdeen first entered European competition in 1967 after losing to eventual league champions Celtic in the Scottish Cup final. Thanks to Celtic's league triumph, Aberdeen entered the Cup Winners' Cup as Scotland's sole representative. Over the next five decades Aberdeen continued to enjoy their European adventures, contesting many memorable games along the way. The aim of this book is to take a trip down memory lane and recall the best of Aberdeen's European adventures – from Real Madrid to Bayern Munich, Ujpest Dozsa to, more recently Dnipro, FC Copenhagen and HNK Rijeka. Gothenburg legend Neil Simpson once said to me that 'nothing could beat Pittodrie on a European night; the stadium comes alive'. Neil is right; the old stadium has been lifted from its foundations on several occasions over the last 50 years. Nothing beats the sheer excitement and adrenaline rush of those heady moments.

In the course of writing this book, I have spoken to a host of Aberdeen players who played a key role in the Dons' triumphs and occasional disappointments over the years, as well as a number of players who faced Aberdeen in order to gain a better understanding of what it was like to be in direct competition with the Pittodrie outfit. These interviews include former Ipswich Town striker Paul Mariner, Real Madrid defender Johnny Metgod and former Waterschei striker Larus Gudmundsson, whose side was on the receiving end of a good old-fashioned drubbing in a European semi-final. As we approach a possible move away from our spiritual home, I for one hope the old lady continues to enjoy more spectacular nights under the current regime with King Street, the Beach Road and all surrounding areas capturing the roar from Pittodrie time and time again before pastures new become a reality.

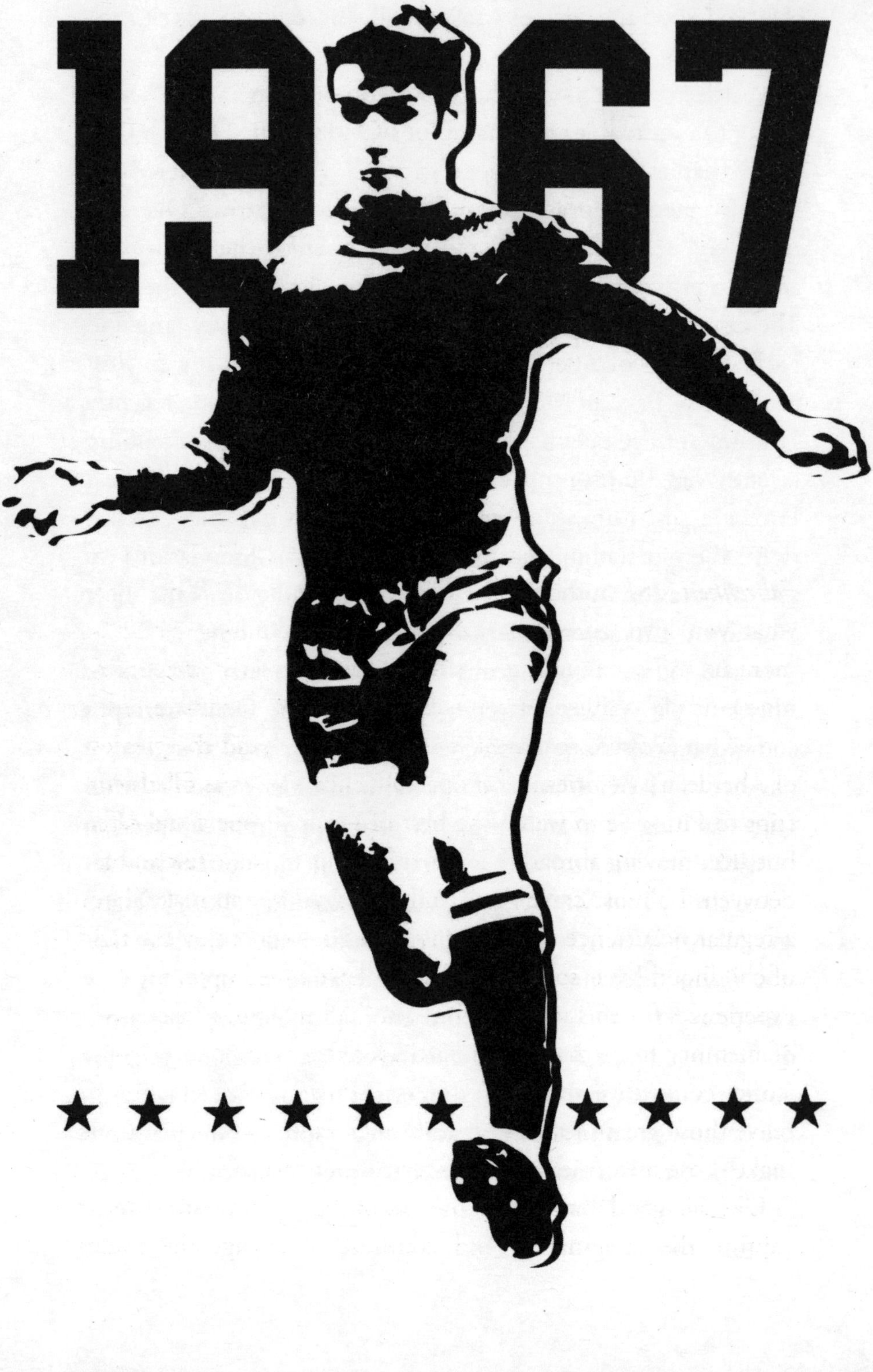
1967

ONE

FC REYKJAVIK

Fahrenheit 451 author Ray Bradbury once said, 'Write only what you love, and love what you write.' Nothing could be more apt as I start to piece together Aberdeen's most memorable moments on a European stage. I have been fortunate, even somewhat blessed, to have witnessed at first hand the greatest of Aberdeen's victories in Europe. My childhood was filled with trips to Pittodrie to watch the best of what Europe could offer, but after moving abroad in 2007 those trips became few and far between. I almost crave them and one day hope to make them a regular occurrence again so my own boys can enjoy the type of childhood I was so lucky to have. I have called upon my own experiences for this narrative but also had to employ the power of memory from those who participated in games to help the stories come alive and offer you, the reader, an opportunity to relive those great moments and through your own recollections make those memories a vivid experience once again.

Like all good narratives, the beginning of any story must capture the imagination and continue to engage the reader throughout. In sporting terms, Aberdeen's first venture into Europe did just that and a little bit more. It all began on 5 July 1967 when Aberdeen were drawn against Iceland's oldest club, FC Reykjavik, in the Cup Winners' Cup, with the first of two legs scheduled for Pittodrie on 6 September. The draw made front page news in Aberdeen. Aberdeen manager Eddie Turnbull had instructed his players to 'go all out for goals'. In European football terms the amateurs from Iceland had over the previous years failed to make any sort of impact on the European stage, losing most of their games by a heavy margin. Believe it or not the players from Iceland actually had to pay the club £4 to represent the side and in turn buy their own kits. The players' day jobs varied from being a lawyer, an accountant, a printer, a plumber and a professional driver. On the weekend prior to the big game, Reykjavik escaped relegation from their own domestic league after securing the point needed to stay in the top flight. Aberdeen were expected to progress to the next stage without too much fuss.

The Icelandic party, which included 16 players and four club officials, arrived in Aberdeen on the Monday ahead of the game. They spent the Tuesday sightseeing and having a light training session at Pittodrie before settling down for the evening in their city-centre base. The confidence among the players wasn't good, but when speaking to the local press, manager Sveinn Jonsson said, 'We will take the game seriously and we will do our best.' Full-back Bjarni Felixson, who also doubled up as the club secretary, echoed his manager's thoughts by saying, 'Although Reykjavik have not been in the best of form recently, we remain confident of putting up a good show in Aberdeen.' For Aberdeen, a disappointing defeat against Celtic the previous Saturday in a League Cup group game had left a dark cloud hanging over the home team dressing room. The Dons had been well beaten 5-1 by the current European Cup holders, but only after Celtic were awarded a controversial penalty which Tommy Gemmell dispatched at the second attempt to gain his side a valuable equaliser on the day. According to reports, one home fan who was so infuriated by that decision that he jumped the advertising boards and proceeded to chase the match referee down with his dog trailing not far behind. He subsequently received a lifetime ban from Pittodrie for his actions.

On the night of the game, local newspaper the *Evening Express* splashed an eye-catching headline across the back page – 'Pittodrie history is being made'. Aberdeen entered the European stage on 6 September 1967. A healthy 14,000 fans were in attendance that night to witness the history of the club change forever. Nineteen times winners of the Icelandic National Championship and six-time winners of the National Cup, Reykjavik were playing their fourth game in European competition, Aberdeen their first. The Aberdeen team that rewrote the club's narrative lined up like this:

1 Bobby Clark
2 Jim Whyte
3 Ally Shewan
4 Jens Petersen
5 Tommy McMillan
6 Martin Buchan
7 Jimmy Wilson
8 Frank Munro
9 Jim Storrie
10 Jimmy Smith
11 Ian Taylor

With Aberdeen's full-time professionals going head-to-head with the part-timers from Iceland, it was no surprise that the Dons settled and stamped their authority on the pattern of the game from the first whistle. On 19 minutes Aberdeen's right-half

Frank Munro, who was a doubt for the game having received a leg knock against Celtic, scored the club's first ever goal in European football when he headed home from a Dons corner. He would go on to complete a hat-trick that night. Frank only spent two seasons with the club under manager Eddie Turnbull before signing for Wolves 13 months on from Aberdeen's first European adventure. Sadly, Frank passed away in August 2011, but he will always be remembered by the club for that special moment. After the Dons took the lead, the floodgates opened. Aberdeen went into the break four goals to the good thanks to further strikes from Jim Storrie, Jimmy Smith and Tommy McMillan. The onslaught continued in the second half with the Dons adding a further six goals to their tally. Frank Munro completed a memorable hat-trick with Ian Taylor, Jim Storrie, Jens Petersen and Jimmy Smith, with his second of the night, finishing off the rout. The final score read Aberdeen 10 Reykjavik 0; Aberdeen's margin of victory set a new scoring record for a Scottish club in Europe, bettering Dundee's 8-1 win against German side FC Cologne. The back page of the following morning's *Press and Journal* read, '10-goal Dons storm into Europe' with a sub-headline reading, 'Icelandic amateurs outclassed in Pittodrie goal-fest'.

PT student and Reykjavik goalkeeper Gudmundur Pétursson was only 21 years old when he faced Aberdeen at Pittodrie. Still in excellent health, he very kindly offered me a few words for this book about that night. I wanted to know from him before facing Aberdeen if he knew much about the game in Scotland. 'We knew a thing or two about Scottish football. In 1960 some of us, including myself, went with the KR 14- to 16-year-old youth team to Scotland as guests of Drumchapel Amateurs. We stayed for one week and played some matches. They invited us to a match between Rangers and Celtic at Celtic Park, with Rangers winning 4-2. In 1961 a player from KR, Tottie Beck, became only the second Icelander to become a professional footballer when he signed for St Mirren from KR for £3,000. He was later sold to Rangers in 1965 for a record fee between Scottish clubs; we were told £20,000.'

Having some knowledge of the Scottish game, I was also intrigued to know from Gudmundur if he was acquainted with any of the Aberdeen players prior to facing the Dons. 'I seem to remember that when we were drawn against Aberdeen, we checked out the players they had, and we knew Bobby Clark the goalkeeper, who was the Scotland keeper at that time and had played against Iceland in a recent match between the two countries. Another was the centre-forward Jim Storrie who had played for Leeds United in the English First Division which most of us were quite familiar with. Then there were two younger players who were said to be very promising: Jimmy Smith who was later sold to Newcastle and Martin Buchan who went to Manchester United, and then there was a Danish midfielder, Jens Petersen.' Given the occasion and the task ahead, I asked Gudmundur if he and his colleagues felt their nerves as kick-off approached. 'Yes, we the amateurs were playing against a professional team whom we expected to be considerably better than us; we were struggling in the league back home in Iceland, but we fully expected them to be a better team than we were. But I don't think that the difference between the teams was quite as much as the scoreline might have suggested on the night.'

To gain a better understanding of what lay in wait against Reykjavik, former Aberdeen goalkeeper Bobby Clark kindly gave up his time to speak with me for this book. I wanted to know from Bobby what he recalled of the build-up to the game. 'I had twice been to Iceland, once with a British amateur team called the Middlesex Wanderers when I was 18 years old, and I went back again with the Scottish amateur team. In those days, the team was pretty much Queen's Park; we played against the full Iceland national team and beat them 1-0. I had some understanding of them and without talking to anybody about it I felt at the time we should win the game. For the game itself it was just one-way traffic, and I hardly recall touching the ball throughout the game. To be honest I don't think we broke sweat. It was very exciting though because it was our first game in Europe which made it even more special.'

FC Reykjavik were a complete unknown, so with that in mind how did the team prepare for the game? Bobby recalls, 'We knew nothing about them which made it very strange for us, and not even our coaching staff knew much about them. Eddie Turnbull, who was usually very thorough and well prepared, knew very little about them. Back then we didn't have the television coverage that we have today and therefore there was no footage to look over, so we really had no idea what to expect. I knew they had a team full of international players but that was all I knew about them.'

For the game itself Aberdeen had far too much in their locker for the amateurs from Iceland. With the goals piling up and Bobby a mere spectator, I did wonder if at any point he started to feel sorry for his counterpart in the Reykjavik goal. 'When you play in Europe, in a two-legged affair, we were happy just to get as many goals as we could because things can get turned around, but in that case, I didn't feel sorry for them. I do not think their goalkeeper was having a particularly bad game, it was just that we were dominating. There is a degree of sympathy for the opposing goalkeeper if he is having a bad game; 'there but for the grace of God go I' sometimes comes into play. There is a goalkeepers' union out there which I always supported; their keeper wasn't a bad keeper, but I just think Reykjavik caved in. The second game was a foregone conclusion but what I do remember about that game was Jim Kirkland making his Aberdeen debut at left-back. Iceland was a fantastic place; it's a lovely country.'

For the return leg, Aberdeen flew to Iceland on the Monday before the game on the Wednesday night. Manager Eddie Turnbull was adamant that his side were not there for a short break. He said upon arriving in the team hotel, 'This is no holiday, ten goals or not. We are out to win on Wednesday night. The players will train tomorrow and on the morning of the game. My players have been told to score goals. We must look ahead. The European Cup Winners' Cup tournament is, of course, important, but even more important is our domestic competition as we are due to play St Johnstone at Muirton Park on Saturday.' Included in the 20-strong Aberdeen party were the 14 players, manager Eddie Turnbull, coach Teddy Scott, club secretary Bert White and three club directors. Reykjavik coach Sveinn Jonsson, who was still feeling the pressure after his side's heavy defeat in the first leg, said, 'Don't mention our arrival back in Reykjavik. We received a lot of criticism. Icelandic football in general is being heavily criticised because we lost 10-0 in Aberdeen and the Icelandic team lost 14-2 in Denmark. People are saying that the whole set-up is wrong. There will never be professional football here, but our clubs and players must develop a more professional approach to the game. The whole question of our participating in European competitions will have to be considered by the club. But the 10-0 defeat at Pittodrie has made our players determined to do better tomorrow. But, once again I am afraid that we will be beaten because Aberdeen showed in the first game that they were so much better.'

Fifteen hundred spectators turned up to watch the game at the Municipal Stadium, paying £1 for a seat in the main stand or 15 shillings to watch the game from the pitch perimeter. The return leg was already a foregone conclusion, but it did take Aberdeen 42 minutes to break the deadlock thanks to Jim Storrie's opener. Martin Buchan made it two before the break. In the second half further goals from Frank Munro and another from Jim Storrie made the scoreline somewhat more respectable for the Dons who, according to newspaper reports, only played at half-pace – but who can blame them. The home support did have something to shout about when 20-year-old Eyleifur Hafsteinsson scored a consolation goal late in the game. Apparently, manager Eddie Turnbull was so incensed by that conceded goal he ripped into the players at full time, reminding them that more difficult opponents lay in wait. Turnbull was correct in his assumption as Aberdeen drew Belgian giants Standard Liège in the second round and went out of the competition having lost narrowly 3-2 on aggregate. Aberdeen's first venture into Europe ended before the year was out.

TWO

AUSTRIA MEMPHIS

For some, a 0-0 draw may not count as a memorable outing, but for our game against Austrian champions Austria Memphis, the result over two legs, as well as the determined display in the return leg in Vienna, made me believe that this game deserved a place in this book. For season 1980/81, Aberdeen entered Europe's elite club competition for the first time as the newly crowned champions of Scotland. In the first round, history was made as Aberdeen welcomed Austria Memphis, or as they are now more commonly known, Austria Vienna, to Pittodrie. Only two years previously Memphis had reached the 1978 Cup Winners' Cup final, losing 4-0 to Belgian giants Anderlecht. A year later they would contest the semi-finals of the European Cup, losing over two legs to Swedish outfit Malmo FF, which made Aberdeen's passage to the second round that little bit more impressive.

For the first leg at Pittodrie, Aberdeen came into the game having only lost one game since the start of the new season, which came against Rangers in the League Cup at Ibrox. Alex Ferguson said in his programme notes ahead of the game that he had impressed upon his players 'that it can be a fatal mistake to underestimate the strengths of any opposition, whatever we may have heard or know about them'. He went on to say that 'chances are likely to be rarities, so it's even more vital for the lads up front to make absolutely sure they make them count'. Nearly 19,000 fans packed out Pittodrie to watch history in the making. Despite a valiant effort and the words of Alex Ferguson in print, Mark McGhee's strike after 31 minutes proved to be the decisive goal. It was a slender lead to take to the Austrian capital, but Ferguson told the waiting press after the game that he 'was looking to take any lead to Vienna for the return leg'. He went on to say, 'The fact that we didn't concede was vital; they will need to come at us more over there so that will suit us.'

Austria Memphis striker Walter Schachner was particularly impressed by Aberdeen's Gordon Strachan, and said after the game, 'We knew all about this player Strachan and we had been warned that he was their main playmaker. We tried to close him down, but it was virtually impossible. He was all over the pitch, spreading the ball around, taking on defenders, backing up players and always making himself available. He is a marvellous motivator, always wanting to be where the action is. I rate him very highly. He is a superb striker of the ball, very clean with either foot.' High praise indeed from Austria's World Cup veteran who was marshalled carefully by both Alex McLeish and Willie Miller in the first game at Pittodrie.

Two weeks later Aberdeen travelled to Vienna for the return leg, looking rather resplendent in their official club tracksuits as they boarded the plane to Austria for the three-hour flight, 48 hours prior to kick-off at the magnificent 37,000-capacity Praterstadion, or as it's now known, the Ernst Happel Stadion. A handful of Aberdeen fans also made the trip across Europe to the ancient Austrian capital, spending just less than £5 for a match ticket. Ahead of the game the Dons faced two games in the space of three days against either side of the Old Firm; Rangers were dispatched with ease in the League Cup 3-1 to progress over two legs and despite going behind against Celtic at Pittodrie, two goals in the space of two minutes earned the Dons a vital point in the league. The form was good. Fergie made two changes from the Celtic game, Willie Garner replacing the injured Alex McLeish in the centre of defence and Derek Hamilton missing out with Doug Rougvie reverting to his normal left-back role. The ever-dependable Ian Scanlon was given the nod in place of John Hewitt on the left side. For this chapter I spoke with former Aberdeen defender Willie Garner who was making his first start of the new campaign that night, one of only four appearances he made that entire season. Willie recalls the games fondly.

'I am not going to say we were lucky, but they had a really good side at that time. They were not competing in the European Cup for nothing. Mark McGhee scored what proved to be the winning goal on the night, but I do recall the Austrians missing plenty of chances. They were big and athletic, and we have wee Gordon Strachan running around the park. All I was thinking about was what great athletes they were plus the fact they had many international players playing for them. The build-up to the game was all about how fit they were and how athletic they were and that they have good players, but Fergie made sure we understood that we had the better players. He was exceptionally good at turning the mentality. We also had a few international players in our team, so Alex drummed that message home. There was certainly a sense of relief after the game that we had won and Alex was delighted to be able to go away in Europe for the second leg with some sort of lead. He was satisfied with the 1-0 win, but he also knew the second game was going to be a difficult match. It's difficult to say if 1-0 is enough, but we always had the confidence that we could score away from home. We knew if we could score in Vienna, Memphis would be right up against it; we knew we were heading over there, and the pressure would be on.'

Willie was in his sixth season with Aberdeen, and he was a league championship winner and a League Cup winner, but he knew with the young brigade knocking on Fergie's door that his appearances would be few and far between. That said, he was always ready if the call came which it did in Vienna. He explains. 'Despite being injured, Alex McLeish travelled with us to Vienna. He wasn't ruled out of the game until late in the day. Fergie and Roland Arnott [club physiotherapist] gave Alex as much of an opportunity as possible to prove his fitness to play; knowing this I was pulled into the travelling party. I had no idea that I could play during the trip over. We trained at the stadium the night before the game and it was then that I was told that Alex had failed a fitness test and I would start the game. To be fair, that wasn't a problem for me at all because it was just a case of going out and playing the game. During this time there was an inevitability that I was on my way out of the club, plus there had been a couple of offers for me. It was obvious that Alex McLeish had very much established himself in the team and I would only play for the first team when required as opposed to playing all the time. I did want to leave but to be fair to Fergie he didn't banish me away to train with the reserves even though I was playing mainly reserve-team football; I was still very much part of the first team training set-up. I was ready to play, but getting thrown into a European Cup tie when I had not played that many games beforehand wasn't ideal. To be honest I didn't overly think about it, I just got on with it. I was more than experienced enough to just go out and play and deal with the situation.'

Ahead of the game, Alex Ferguson set out his game plan with the lads. He knew the stadium's pitch was a big one, so he demanded ball retention as well as instructing the lads to 'keep their heads' during the game. Willie recalls the pre-match routine. 'Alex had done his homework which I know was very intense in terms of knowing all he could about the opposition. He had them watched again before we flew to Vienna to see if there were any changes in their line-up or tactics after the first game at Pittodrie. On the day itself it was a very normal day. We got up, did a short and easy training session, went for lunch and then got our heads down for the afternoon before getting on the bus to the stadium. Alex wasn't bothered if we slept or not, but he did insist that whatever we did late afternoon, we were fresh enough for the game. His team talk was very much like any other team talk. He took us through the opposition and pointed out their strengths, but mainly he would talk about our strengths and how we should go out and play against them. That night, he changed the team from the first leg. I came in for Alex McLeish and Dougie Bell came in for Drew Jarvie. Dougie had a specific role which was to do exactly what Dougie Bell did – collect the ball and run at the opposition. There was a lot of emphasis on that tactic because at Pittodrie we played two up front, whereas in Vienna we played five across the middle with Mark McGhee being the lone striker. Dougie was given the freedom to roam the pitch. Their tactics suited us that night as Fergie wanted to keep us intact, Gordon Strachan and Ian Scanlon playing out wide, with Dougie Bell, Andy Watson and John McMaster playing in midfield. I partnered Willie Miller with Doug Rougvie at left-back and Stuart Kennedy at right-back. That allowed Gordon and Dougie to do whatever they wanted to do. Dougie did that all night; he just picked up the ball and ran at the Memphis players because he was so good at it. All we had to do at the back was keep things tight and intact as per Fergie's instructions. We were under some pressure during the game, but we defended well that night and thankfully got the result we needed to progress.'

15

The scenes at the end of the game epitomised the effort that was put into the game, and Willie was quick to recognise the significance of the performance and result by saying, 'It just goes to show how much that result meant, because at full time we celebrated almost like we had just won the cup. It was a big deal for the club at the time as it was the first time the club had competed overseas in the European Cup, so to get a result was important for the club. I do not think many people expected us to go over to Vienna and get any sort of result because first and foremost Aberdeen have no history in the competition, so it was a big test and a big step; it was also a big statement for the club to get a result like that away from home against a very decent side in Austria Memphis. If you take a closer look at the Aberdeen team who played that night, it was only me and Ian Scanlon who were not involved in the winning Cup Winners' Cup side; all the others were involved in some capacity. We stayed over for the night before flying back to Aberdeen; we went out for a meal where Alex allowed us one drink each – it was a good trip!'

After the game, a very content Alex Ferguson met the travelling press and had this to say about Aberdeen's progression to the next round: 'We were always worried about the Memphis attack because they have dangerous players in Felix Gasselich and Walter Schachner, but we did just what we wanted to do. The pattern was to withdraw to our own half, try to win the ball and counter-attack, and that was how it worked out.' Austria Memphis coach Erich Hof was very complimentary about Aberdeen's style of play. He observed, 'The Aberdeen defence played very well. They had nine players in defence but that is normal, and we would have done the same in a similar situation. Our main problem was that Aberdeen had superiority in the air. We did have enough chances, especially in the first 20 minutes, but the longer the game went on the more our system broke down.' Next up for the Dons, English champions and two-time former winners, Liverpool.

1980

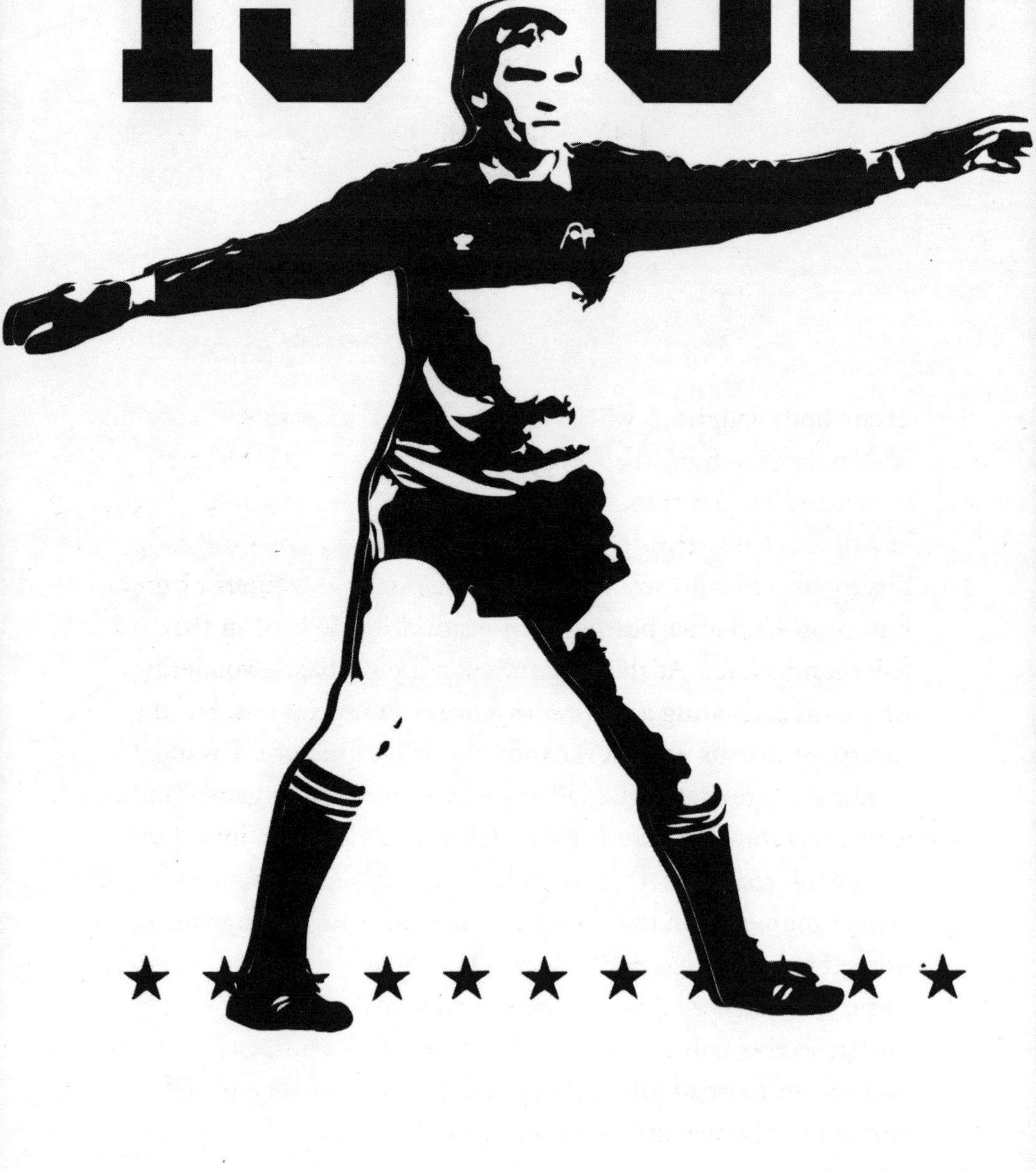

THREE

LIVERPOOL

'If anybody laughs, I will fine you £10.' Those are the words of Alex Ferguson on the team bus as the squad made their way back to Aberdeen from Liverpool after a night of humiliation at Anfield. Over two legs Aberdeen had been beaten 5-0 by a Liverpool side who would become the eventual winners of the European Cup after beating Real Madrid in the final in Paris a few months later. At this juncture you are probably wondering why I am dedicating a chapter to a heavy European loss, but the Liverpool defeats are relevant for the bigger picture. I wanted to know more about the lessons learnt from those games and why Ferguson used the hurtful defeat at Anfield to introduce a type of resilience that would eventually lead Aberdeen to greater moments on the European stage. He made many mental notes. He knew Liverpool had the extra quality when it came to game mentality, which at the time may have given him a sense of perspective going forward. He knew he had just been given a lesson in football and he was determined that type of defeat would not happen again under his watch.

Ahead of the first leg at Pittodrie, Alex Ferguson was unhappy with his side's form coming into the game, and he believed the hype generated from such a high-profile game had played its part in distracting not just the club, but the city as a whole. That all said, the Dons had still only lost one game since the season started back in August. For the game itself Fergie decided to match Liverpool tactically by playing a 4-4-2 formation. He named an unchanged team from the side that beat St Mirren 3-2 in the league only days before. Fergie was determined that the game would be played on Aberdeen's terms and not play into the hands of their illustrious visitors, so he demanded from his players that they 'keep their heads, be disciplined and controlled and be prepared to spend time away from the ball'. In the subsequent weeks after the draw was made, Fergie had Liverpool watched four times, so he and his assistant Archie Knox fully appreciated their strengths, and Fergie publicly admitted in the days leading up to the game that his side 'must resist any temptation to charge at them and lose the head because if we keep our composure, I am convinced we can get a famous result'. He also said, 'A 1-0 win would suit us. Anything more would be a bonus. Whatever happens we will play a different game in the return at Liverpool. I have players who are capable of changing the tactics completely. This is necessary at European level.'

Alex Ferguson's assistant Archie Knox spoke to me for this book and recalls the time he and Alex visited Anfield while on a scouting mission, 'Before the first game at Pittodrie, Alex and I travelled down together to watch Liverpool play on a Wednesday night and who is sitting one along from me – Bill Shankly! The following Saturday I travelled down to Liverpool alone to watch them again! Before the game I was standing in the boardroom and Mr Shankly came over to me and said, "Aye son, you're down to watch our team again." I was so nervous that I didn't know what to say, so I started saying to him that I was down to see if there were any changes in the Liverpool team and changes to the formation. I told him I had taken some notes from the first half and he said to me, "Aye son, they've all tried that!" For the second half he was sitting two along from me and I swear I didn't take my notebook out at all for the second half! I kept it in my pocket! Mr Shankly wasn't belittling me or anything like that, it was just the way he was.'

Liverpool manager Bob Paisley fully expected a difficult game, telling the English press that he believed Aberdeen were a good side and that he had noticed they had a good result in Vienna. Paisley noted, 'We rate Aberdeen highly. It will be a really testing struggle for the both of us over the two legs. You have to win the European ties at home, so we won't be taking any risks at Aberdeen.'

Like his counterpart Alex Ferguson, Paisley also had Aberdeen watched on numerous occasions prior to the first leg at Pittodrie. The stadium that night was packed to the rafters as a capacity crowd of 24,500 waited in anticipation of what was billed as Britain's biggest club game of the year. The demand for tickets was that great that the club could have sold the game out three times over; those who were fortunate enough to attend paid between £1.50 and £3 for a ticket, depending in which part of the stadium they watched from. All the tickets sold out within 45 minutes. Hundreds queued, some overnight, but many loyal fans were left disappointed, which prompted the club to change the ticketing system and introduce a new voucher system which helped ensure loyal fans always received tickets for big games; the new initiative worked wonders.

To the game. Within five minutes of kick-off, Ferguson's best-laid plans were undone. John McMaster was off the pitch receiving treatment for a nose injury, and while the Dons played on with ten men, Liverpool broke down the park and, after a fine move involving Kenny Dalglish and David Johnson, Terry McDermott scored a quite brilliant chip to put Liverpool ahead.

It proved to be the only goal of the game. For the remainder of the match Aberdeen huffed and puffed but were unable to break down a solid Liverpool rearguard. Much of the English press who were at Pittodrie that night praised the Dons' determination and spirit, but believed the task ahead was a nigh-impossible one. Alex Ferguson said after the game, 'Liverpool are a great side and they have given us a mountain to climb in the second leg. If we had kept the tie level at the break, we could have afforded to gamble by sending extra men forward, but their goal made that impossible. However, I am pleased with our attitude and discipline.' Liverpool manager Bob Paisley came away from Pittodrie content with his side's showing, saying, 'The performance was a very good one as was the goal. We are particularly pleased because Aberdeen are a good team. We knew that before we played them, and nothing happened tonight to change our minds. The biggest tribute I can pay them is to say that we played exactly the kind of game we would have against the top sides in Europe.'

Even before the game had kicked off, Paisley lavished praise on Gordon Strachan in his pre-match press conference – was this an attempt to soften him up? Did that exercise in reverse psychology mean trepidation or excitement for Gordon himself? He explains more. 'Definitely excitement because we had just beaten the Austrian champions Austria Memphis. We had won the league the previous season by beating an excellent Celtic side on the way. We had a decent side, but we knew within a couple of minutes that we were not as good as we thought we were. The problem was it wasn't just a normal goal they scored; it was an extraordinary goal they scored so, from then on, we played with total respect towards Liverpool. In the build-up to that game, we didn't have video analysis like you do today, so Sir Alex had three team meetings and each one was about 90 minutes long. We believed we had everything covered, but what Sir Alex didn't do was tell us about this goal that Terry McDermott was going to score very early in the game. That game was a reality check, not that we were big-headed or anything like that, but we did have a belief in ourselves. That game, as well as the second leg at Anfield, helped bring us back down to earth, that's for sure.'

That defeat was Aberdeen's first loss in a competitive game at Pittodrie in more than nine months, but they headed to Anfield knowing Liverpool had not lost a home game for 75 matches. The Everest of football awaited them. Aberdeen's task was compounded by a key injury to right-back Stuart Kennedy two weeks previously, which forced Fergie to field 17-year-old Andy Dornan at full-back for what was only his second start of the season. Walker McCall, who had scored a hat-trick the previous Saturday against Airdrie, was ineligible for the game, so Fergie replaced him with Dougie Bell who came in to help protect young Andy Dornan with Gordon Strachan playing central midfield. Ahead of the game during his pre-match press conference, Alex Ferguson was in optimistic mood, telling the gathered journalists, 'I feel less worried about this game than I was about the first leg, and the players feel the same.' He went on to say, 'The pressure is now off, as we are not expected to win, whereas the whole of Scotland was looking for us to do something special at Pittodrie.' He finished off by saying, 'All I want is for my players to go out and enjoy a great occasion and play to the best of their ability. If they do that, I will be a happy man.'

For the first 38 minutes Ferguson must have been delighted with his side's application as they stood firm while holding Liverpool's front men at bay. It could have been all so different on 23 minutes if Mark McGhee had been able to convert Aberdeen's best chance on the night when he quite brilliantly turned Phil Thompson inside out and bore down on the Liverpool goal. His shot from 18 yards though was easily saved by Ray Clemence; the warning signs were there for the home side. On 38 minutes Aberdeen's European ambitions for that season ended when the unfortunate Willie

Miller sliced a clearance into his own net to put Liverpool 1-0 up. The task was made that bit harder as Aberdeen went into the break 2-0 down on the night and 3-0 down on aggregate after Phil Neal scored a brilliantly worked goal just before the break. It was a killer punch. At half-time, while forever the optimist, midfielder Drew Jarvie decided to give the boys a vote of confidence as they headed out for the start of the second half by shouting the now immortal words, 'Right, lads, three quick goals and we are right back in this.' Drew explains the reasoning behind his thoughts. 'I was still feeling quite confident because we had chances in the first half. Mark McGhee had an excellent chance and if he had taken it that would have been the tie level. Just on half-time we lost a second goal from a corner kick and that put us 3-0 down in the tie; I appreciate Liverpool had not lost many games at home, but I just felt if we could get a goal back, we were right back in it. It was just a small thing really as we went back out on to the park. I just wanted to gee the lads up a bit, so I just started saying, 'Come on, come on, three quick goals and we are right back in this.' That is just the way I was; I had that belief that Fergie had. I appreciate we were three down in the tie, but I really believed we had a chance. Liverpool didn't really create many chances in the first half. I was up directly against Graeme Souness in midfield and wasn't overawed by that at all; we had a couple of scuffles which I was quite enjoying. I certainly don't regret saying that as I still believe to this day that if we had scored a goal early on, we had a particularly good chance.'

The second half showed the gulf in class between the two sides as Liverpool stroked the ball around the park with charming grace. Aberdeen offered little back in terms of attacking football and did their best to contain Liverpool's quality, but further goals from Kenny Dalglish and Alan Hansen finished the Dons off in style. Aberdeen had lost 4-0 on the night, 5-0 on aggregate. It was a sore one to take for Ferguson, who admitted later that he had never been so happy to get a game out of the way in his whole life. To sum up the experience, Alex Ferguson said this of the game: 'Perhaps we were asking too much from a young side against a team with experienced internationals that have done it all. We were holding them well until the first goal which pushed us over the cliff and the second one just before half-time finished us.' He went on to say, which for future endeavours was far more telling, 'Nevertheless, we will learn from this, no doubt about that.'

So, what did Alex Ferguson learn from those Liverpool games, the first element of this project being to observe the recovery and learning process? In the very next game Aberdeen faced a tricky afternoon in Glasgow against Celtic. With the injuries now adding up, including captain Willie Miller who was nursing a hamstring strain, Fergie deployed a young Neale Cooper at centre-back while calling upon the services of Walker McCall to take his place up front. Walker made all the difference as his brace was enough to send the Dons back up the road worthy 2-0 winners. Going forward Ferguson made sure that no more distractions should be allowed to happen ahead of big European games. The lads and the club had to stay focused on the task at hand; take one game at a time and let the big games take care of themselves. He was adamant that no more damage would be done domestically as he believed the Liverpool games dominated and interrupted everything. In Fergie's mind this was the one and only time this would happen. To finish this chapter off I will leave you with a line from Liverpool manager Bob Paisley when speaking to journalist Alex Cameron not long after the second leg: 'Aberdeen will mature and soon become one of Britain's best teams.' How right he was.

FOUR

IPSWICH TOWN

Before Aberdeen entered the 1981/82 UEFA Cup, the club had failed to get past the second round of any European competition in ten separate attempts since first venturing into Europe in the 1967/68 season. In the 1970/71 campaign, Aberdeen created their own piece of unwanted European history by becoming the first club to be knocked out of a European competition on penalty kicks, losing the shoot-out 5-4 against Hungarian side Honved after drawing 4-4 on aggregate over two legs. Jim Forrest was the unfortunate player to have missed his penalty for the Dons. Aberdeen welcomed Italian giants Juventus, who included a very young Fabio Capello in the side, to Pittodrie the following season, but the 'Old Lady' had too much for the Dons, winning 3-1 on aggregate. For two successive seasons Aberdeen were given a lesson in how to play expansive football, having lost heavily to both Borussia Mönchengladbach and Tottenham. In the four games played, the Dons conceded a total of 14 goals. German opposition would continue to haunt Aberdeen in the late seventies when both Fortuna Düsseldorf and Eintracht

Frankfurt spoiled Alex Ferguson's first adventures in Europe as Aberdeen manager.

Dons goalkeeper Bobby Clark played 23 European games for the club between seasons 1967/68 and 1979/80. Bobby was there right at the beginning and played his final game in Europe against Eintracht Frankfurt in a narrow 1-0 defeat in Germany in October 1979. Bobby kept goal for Aberdeen in nine separate European campaigns but was unable to help the Dons go beyond the second round. Bobby and I looked back on the 1970s, an era which still remains vivid in his mind. He takes up the story of Aberdeen's adventures in Europe during that decade: 'We had a good result against Slavia Sofia and then we lost to Real Zaragoza who were a good Spanish team, but I would not say brilliant. That was a game where I felt we never got started; we knew nothing about them before the first game. The other Spanish side we played was Celta Vigo and we had a great result against them in front of 35,000 spectators. We played really well that night. I remember the Spanish newspaper the next day asking, "Where would Aberdeen be if they played in the Spanish League and could Aberdeen be a top team in the Spanish League at that time?" I tore my medial ligament in that game and missed the return leg. Joe Harper scored a brilliant goal for us at Pittodrie.'

In the 1970/71 season, Aberdeen created their own piece of unwanted history when they became the first team to be knocked out of any European competition on penalty kicks, going down 5-4 to Honved after both games finished 3-1 in favour of the home sides. For Bobby, there was a sense of frustration about those games. 'I felt the Honved game difficult; it was a game I felt we should have won. The trip to Budapest was a difficult trip because if my memory serves me well, we didn't get to train at their ground before the game. We had an issue with our travel because to fly behind the Iron Curtain wasn't so easy in those days. We had to fly from Aberdeen to London and then stop for a night in Prague before flying on to Budapest. Honved scored very quickly. I remember the linesman flagged for offside and we all stopped, but the referee waved play on and the boy ran in on goal and scored; it was a strange goal to get them off the mark. It wasn't so easy for us back then because we kept drawing difficult teams in the first or second round. Juventus springs to mind immediately. Juventus back then were one of the top teams in Europe of that era; they were an amazing team full of top-class international players.'

Bobby continues: 'To be honest if we had been smarter in that game, I think we could have done better. The first game was in Turin and it was one of those games which reminded me of playing at either Ibrox or Celtic Park where they would pummel you right from the start, but in this game the Italians sat back and played a medium-pressure style of game and let us come out with the ball. Whenever we played the ball in, they pressed it and they won it and they counter-attacked us. We thought we were doing OK for the opening period, but we weren't going anywhere, just playing balls around the back, so as soon as we played it forward, they pressed us down. We got away from Turin with only a 2-0 defeat. At Pittodrie we played so well; we were very good that night. Joe Harper equalised for us to make it 1-1, but it was a big ask; it would probably have been the equivalent of Aberdeen beating Bayern Munich in 1983 all those years later. I think that is a fair comparison. Juventus made it to the semi-final where they lost to Wolves over two legs.'

In the 1970s Aberdeen faced German opposition on three different occasions, the first coming way back in the 1972/73 season against Borussia Mönchengladbach. In what was a highly entertaining game at Pittodrie, the Dons lost 3-2. It was their first European defeat at home in seven games. Bobby looks back: 'Borussia Mönchengladbach were a phenomenal team back then. I was injured for the first game and came back for the return leg. I felt we almost had them in the second game. We had to play that game in Nuremberg because of crowd trouble in their previous game. We had a goal disallowed right on half-time which would have put us up 6-5 on aggregate. We were right in that game but they ended up getting two penalties, and after that we fell away. We did play well that night, especially in the first half, so if that disallowed goal had been given, who knows what would have happened.

'We got cuffed by Tottenham down in London, but it was a good game against them at Pittodrie where we played well against them. I think that would have been a better game for us if we had played the first leg at White Hart Lane.

'Before the Düsseldorf games I had broken my hand in a pre-season friendly, and that's when Jim Leighton came in for me. We lost 3-0 in Germany and for the return game I had only just had my plaster taken off on the Friday. The following Tuesday Alex Ferguson played me in a combined Reserve League game down in Arbroath, which was my first game back after injury, to get a feel for the ball. I came in the next morning just to train with the reserves as the first team had their game that night. Alex called me into his office and said, "You're playing tonight!" I did explain to him that I had played against Arbroath the previous night which he knew, but he went on to say, "It will give the crowd a lift to see you back and I doubt if you will have much to do." That's how I came back for that game. Alex was right, as I had very little to do in that game. Before we played Fortuna, we played Marek Dimitrov in the first round. I was still injured and couldn't play in those games, so Alex sent Pat Stanton and me to go and scout them in Bulgaria which was a great experience.'

Bobby's final expedition on European shores took him to Germany once again. For the first leg against Eintracht Frankfurt at Pittodrie, he was, by then, a seasoned European campaigner. Aberdeen were competing in their 14th home tie since 1967 and came away with a rather disappointing 1-1 draw. The Dons had a mountain to climb for the return leg and put up a spirited performance, but despite all their efforts lost the game 1-0. The Dons though had gained the respect of the Germans for their narrow aggregate defeat. 'I remember reading somewhere that the manager of Eintracht Frankfurt at that time had said that their hardest game in the tournament came against Aberdeen. Both games were very tight; they had some top players in Jürgen Grabowski, their captain and Bernd Hölzenbein and the big Austrian international centre-back Bruno Pezzey who was an excellent player. They also had South Korean international Cha Bum-Kun who was very fast and strong. Eintracht went on to win the UEFA Cup that season and we went on to win the league. We had a very good team back then. That was the beginning of a very special period for the club.'

Aberdeen lost to Frankfurt on 3 October 1979. For the remainder of that year the Dons only lost three more games, two in the league and more frustratingly a heavy 3-0 defeat to Dundee United in the League Cup final replay at Dens Park. The seventies was ending and the eighties was upon us. There was new hope, a fresh hope. The 1980s would bring unparalleled joy, and it was a decade never to be forgotten – the greatest in the club's history.

Ipswich Town

Microsoft billionaire Bill Gates once said, 'It's fine to celebrate success but it's more important to heed the lesson of failure.' Nothing could be more apt as Aberdeen entered the European stage once again 11 months on from that hurtful defeat against Liverpool. The Dons were paired with English opposition for the second successive season in the form of UEFA Cup holders Ipswich Town. Not surprisingly Ipswich went into the tie as red-hot favourites with the English press in particular writing off Aberdeen's chances even before a ball was kicked. Aberdeen went into this game knowing their illustrious opponents had only conceded seven European goals at Portman Road in their entire history. What Ipswich manager Bobby Robson and co. may have underestimated was the amount of hard work and dedication that Alex Ferguson and his staff had put into righting the wrong of the now infamous Liverpool defeats in the past few months. Fergie was driven by that result; you could argue he was inspired. Saying that, the late Bobby Robson was full of respect for Aberdeen in his programme notes ahead of the game when he said, 'It has taken them some time to find their feet at the start of the Scottish League programme, but we will be treating them with every respect and are expecting two very competitive matches. These Scotland–England clashes are a bit special, and I know Aberdeen were disappointed with the way they played against Liverpool in the European Cup last season. It goes without saying that they will have learned a few lessons and will be determined to put up a better show against us.'

Ferguson was determined nothing would distract the team as the game edged ever closer. The form of the side in the league was already of concern with the Dons beginning the new campaign with back-to-back defeats against Dundee United and Celtic respectively, but gained confidence by beating Partick Thistle 2-0 at Firhill on the Saturday prior to the first leg at Portman Road. Ferguson admitted some work had to be done. 'It's been a nightmare start but I am sure we will soon recover. Some of the goals we have conceded have been real comic-cut stuff and it's so out of character. The lads who have made mistakes are normally so dependable. They're good professionals and between us we'll put it right. It will be a good test for my team to meet a side like Ipswich. Last year our season went to pieces after we lost to Liverpool, but I think we've learned a few lessons from that.'

When the sides were drawn together for the opening round, winger Peter Weir recalls the reaction of the draw from the lads. 'We knew they were UEFA Cup holders, and drawing them was huge for us. I was able to name all their players without even looking them up. That is the type of quality they had, all great players. There is no doubt they were the favourites, but we were determined to do our best and try and get some sort of result down there. After John Hewitt scored from my corner to make it 1-1, we knew then what a great chance we had in the second leg back at Pittodrie. You must remember we were just a young team getting together, so to hold them to a draw down there was a great result. Alex Ferguson and Archie Knox always instilled a belief in us to go out and give our best which we always did. If we followed their instructions during games with the quality we had in the side, we knew we had the ability to beat anybody on our day.'

Ferguson had Ipswich watched three times prior to the first leg which gave him confidence to play a 4-4-2 formation with Gordon Strachan and Peter Weir playing wide and deep. Portman Road was full to capacity with each fan paying on average £4.50 for a ticket. On what was a good night for the Dons, John Hewitt's equaliser six minutes after the restart meant the lads came away with a very creditable 1-1 draw, but more importantly an away goal to take back to Pittodrie. In fact Aberdeen could have come away with a historic victory if it were not for Andy Watson passing up two good chances in the final six minutes of the match. Nevertheless, a draw against the UEFA Cup holders on their own patch made the English press start to think that the gulf between English and Scottish clubs wasn't as wide as first expected. In his post-match interview, Bobby Robson claimed Aberdeen 'will never play as good as that again' – how wrong could he be.

Second leg

Aberdeen had to wait exactly two weeks for the return leg at Pittodrie. In between, the Dons navigated their way past Hibs, Berwick Rangers and Airdrie without conceding a goal, so their form was encouraging. Alex Ferguson called upon the solid showing in the first leg to help galvanise his troops, but the defeat against Liverpool still niggled away at him. This was all epitomised in Fergie's programme notes on the night of the game when he said, 'The great performance at Ipswich did Aberdeen good in respect of last year's showing in the second half of our European clash with Liverpool at Anfield. Those kinds of memories burn deeply, and they hurt. The kind of night you do not wish to suffer again. To avoid it, there is only one answer: be prepared to battle with all the traditional passion and aggression for which Aberdeen and Scottish football are renowned.'

Fergie went on to add, 'Such defeats as we suffered against Liverpool brings out all the dedication and fight to survive at this high level. The memory of Anfield floods back as kick-off time approaches and must act as a trigger of inspiration.' It wasn't just Alex Ferguson who took inspiration from the Liverpool defeat, because captain Willie Miller also used that game as a tool to do better. He said, 'We are going into tonight's game particularly keen to wipe out the memory of that horrific night at Anfield last season when we lost to Liverpool. I believe we have come a long way in atoning for that result by the way we played against Ipswich in the first leg.'

Ahead of kick-off Ferguson's assistant manager Archie Knox had come up with an imaginative way of understanding the tactics that Bobby Robson would deploy that night at Pittodrie, and he takes up the story. 'Inside Pittodrie, there is a vent which comes from the away dressing room and I knew where the vent ended up. I would stand beside the end of the vent and I was able to hear every single word coming from that dressing room. The only person I talked about this vent to was Alex; I didn't tell any players or any members of staff. All I would do is place myself beside the end of the vent and listen to the team talks coming from the away dressing room. I could hear every single word that Bobby Robson was telling his players; it was absolutely amazing! No matter the game, be it Airdrie or Celtic or a big European game, I would always stand there and listen to their team talks. I guess that isn't very fair but that's just the way it was. That was my excuse for being a tactical genius!'

Thousands of fans streamed down the Merkland Road and across the beach links in the hope that the Dons could pull off a famous victory. The scene was set, and all eyes were on Pittodrie. With the lads securing the draw at Portman Road, Alex Ferguson quietly told his closest confidants of his belief that his young Dons side could upset all the odds and triumph over their English adversaries in the return leg. Ferguson came to the fore when pitted against Bobby Robson, and the apprentice outsmarted the master, which in turn led to new-found fearlessness in his players. When talking to Peter Weir I asked him to elaborate on Fergie's spirit. 'The confidence in the team was good, incredibly positive in fact. I was still getting to know the lads as I was just through the door a matter of months, but their confidence was rubbing off on me. You must remember Aberdeen had won the league title in 1980 and were a very self-assured bunch. We were not over-confident, but we realised that the hard work had been done down at Portman Road. We knew we could welcome any team back to Pittodrie and had the capabilities of beating them, but that didn't stop folk still making Ipswich firm favourites. They finished second in the league that season just behind Aston Villa, so it was a huge shock for a club like Aberdeen to knock the holders out of the UEFA Cup.'

Ipswich manager Bobby Robson was a man of class, and he openly applauded the Dons' first-leg efforts, but was quite vocal in his belief that potentially all the hard work had been already exhausted from the first leg. He was unsure that the Dons' exploits could be repeated. There is an argument to suggest he underestimated the collective strength of character when plotting Aberdeen's downfall in the return game. For the Aberdeen players, including Peter Weir, all that concerned them was the game plan. 'Nothing really inspired me, but the Scotland–England rivalry did play its part, because Scottish football wasn't as bad as it was made out to be back in those days. Ipswich had a great side with two Dutch internationals in Arnold Mühren and Frans Thijssen, and a host of players who played for both Scotland and England. The goals came at the right time, and it was a fantastic result which led to many a great European night, which obviously culminated in us winning the Cup Winners' Cup. It gave us great confidence beating Ipswich, because we knew we were on to a good thing. I have watched the goals once or twice over the years, and I love both to be honest. It was a great night for me personally, what with the big fee and signing for Aberdeen, and then attempting to break into the team which thankfully I was able to do. I took so much confidence from that; it helped me enormously. I cannot say which one was better than the other, but it was just a fantastic result for the club. What you must remember is that the result came from a great team performance, not just Peter Weir. It was a collective effort from all the players who played that night; all of the guys played to their maximum to beat a top side like Ipswich.'

Aberdeen midfielder Gordon Strachan bossed the midfield that night – his performance was simply outstanding. Gordon recalls the game well. 'It's only when I look back that I say, "Yeah OK, we did really well there." As far as I was concerned it was just another team to beat. Ipswich were top of the English First Division at the time. They were a brilliant side, a top side in fact, and we went to Portman Road and came away with a very comfortable 1-1 draw. Then we beat them 3-1 at Pittodrie. We were really coming on as a team at that time, and we were all getting better, individually and collectively, so yes, I believe those games against Ipswich were a real turning point.'

Ipswich Town, under the stewardship of Bobby Robson, were renowned for playing an expansive style of football which would lead them to eventual European glory. Their strike force put the fear of God into many a centre-back pairing domestically and on the European stage. One such player was the late Paul Mariner, who in 1981 was a regular in the starting line-up and a full England international. He was a no-nonsense type of player with an obvious eye for goal. Paul missed the first leg at Portman Road due to injury, but recalls the Aberdeen games vividly. 'I recall thinking the away leg will be slightly difficult, but we believed, over two legs, we would have too much quality for Aberdeen. We fully expected to take care of business. The first thing that came into my mind is the fact that we were facing a Scottish team. Scotland, over the years, had produced some good sides with some excellent players. When we used to play the Home Championships in the late seventies and early eighties, Scotland had a really good side so, in regard to Aberdeen, if I'm being perfectly honest, I knew it would be challenging, but I think we took them too lightly. We believed we could turn it around going up to Aberdeen. It's easy to dwell on the result, but we had to get past it as we were playing an important league game a few days later. Good professionals can put bad results to one side; we simply had to get on with it despite the poor performance. We had to bring our 'A' game to Pittodrie. We anticipated a hostile atmosphere and were under no illusions that the task in hand was going to be an extremely difficult one, knowing Aberdeen had their away goal. We knew if we could score an away goal early on that may change the face of the game.'

That day – 30 September 1981 – is the day that Aberdeen announced their intent on the European stage. On a crisp night, Pittodrie creaked under the weight of expectation, and the floodlights cast their beams for miles to see. The home dressing room was set, studs clicking away on the cold tiled surface; the smell of Deep Heat catching every breath; Archie Knox parading around each player, reminding them all one last time of their duty that night. Ten minutes into the game Ipswich midfielder John Wark, in an uncharacteristic move, sold himself and gave away a penalty. It was the worst possible start for the away side. Paul Mariner recalls, 'It was a sloppy penalty; John should have put the ball in the crowd. He hesitated slightly which, in turn, meant he clipped Gordon. Gordon scores the resulting penalty and now we know we are right up against it. We had a little coming-together to say, "Come on, lads, we're all right," and then, thankfully, we managed to get back into the game. Going into the break level, we knew then it was only a 45-minute game.'

The sides went into the break level on all fronts – on the night and on aggregate. It was all to play for. Paul took me into the Ipswich dressing room to recall that moment. 'During the break it was as calm as it could be. We knew after we equalised it was game on. We knew we had quality in the dressing room, and we knew the next goal would be so important. The next goal would be massive for confidence. We were away from home dealing with a passionate home support, so we knew if Aberdeen scored the next goal, we really were up against it. If we scored the next goal, we knew we could take control of the game, keep the ball, pass it and make Aberdeen run around but, obviously, that didn't happen.'

With the half-time instructions still ringing in their ears the Ipswich players went into the second half full of hope. Ten minutes later all those hopes were dashed. Peter Weir produced a majestic drop of the shoulder and a clean strike from 20 yards with his right foot which resulted in the ball nestling comfortably in the back of net. It's a moment Paul has not forgotten. 'When I saw Peter pick the ball up over on the right-hand side and drive at Mick in the final third of the pitch, I still believed Mick would be able to get a tackle in or, at the very least, our central defenders would come across and block any attempt at goal. Even with Peter being able to get his shot away, I still thought our goalkeeper Paul Cooper would be able to save it because he was a very agile keeper. Peter's shot wasn't what we would call a screamer, or worldy, but take nothing away from him, it was still a good finish. All I'm thinking at this point is that we now have our work cut out.'

Aberdeen, and in particular Peter Weir, put the game to bed in the closing stages to record a famous 4-2 victory on aggregate. To knock the UEFA Cup holders out of the competition at the first hurdle made everybody sit up and take notice. Alex Ferguson had outsmarted Bobby Robson and laid to rest the ghost of Liverpool past. Paul offers nothing but credit for Aberdeen's performances. 'Over two legs the result does not look good, but let's give Aberdeen some credit. Without knocking us too much we didn't play to our level. We were a hell of a good team but take nothing away from Aberdeen. The spine of that team was excellent, there is absolutely no doubt about that. So, when you get players like Peter Weir, who was having an absolute stormer of a game, that puts a question mark in the full-backs' heads because Peter had pace, had a good touch and could go down both sides. For a full-back coming up against that style of player, that is a recipe for disaster. As a collective we didn't help Mick [Mills] out enough.'

For many Aberdeen fans the second leg game against Ipswich was arguably Peter Weir's finest performance in a Dons jersey. He ran Mills ragged that night but, for Paul, not one individual is to blame for their exit from the competition. Football is a team game, and he is quick to defend the honour of his former captain at both club and international level. 'We had a game intellect which was absolutely lights out. We knew every single position at set pieces, where every other player should be. We knew if we were a yard out of position, or not doing the job we were supposed to be doing, the players on the pitch had enough about them to sort it out themselves. We didn't need the gaffer to tell us this. Look at how many players from that Ipswich side went on to become managers. They were all responsible people, and we were the type of characters that didn't like to get beaten. When you have players of the ilk of Peter Weir playing towards our central defenders, you must wonder why this was happening. Did our midfielders not track back? Did they get drawn out by movements from other Aberdeen players in the middle of the park? If somebody is having a good game against one of your mates, you help your mates out and, on the night, we obviously didn't do that. I am not one for criticising my former teammates but, when you look at Peter Weir who went on a couple of incredible runs and managed to score two brilliant goals, we just didn't deal with him. I had never seen that before, where our defence was losing goals to a guy who was going at them with the ball at his feet and beating them with skill. It was just one of those nights, horrendous for us but, obviously, a superb night for Aberdeen. We didn't do our job; it's as simple as that. I have to be honest and tell you – there is no doubt about it; over the two legs we underestimated Aberdeen.'

The journey from Aberdeen to Ipswich by car is 550 miles which, at a steady pace and within the limits of the law, should take about nine hours to complete. Thankfully, that was one journey deemed too long for the Ipswich Town squad to partake, so the relatively short hop by plane was gratefully received by the travelling party. Paul recalls the journey home and whether, at any point, voices were raised in the immediate aftermath of their disastrous exit from the competition. 'There was no inquest; we never did that because all you do is end up fighting or getting in a scrap. That is plain stupid. When you talk about top professionals, nobody needs telling they have had a shocker; nobody needs to be told as a collective we have had an absolute shocker over two legs, and we are out of the tournament. It had to be onwards and upwards. We could argue until we were blue in the face to find out whose fault it was, but you have no choice but to dust yourself down and get ready for the next league game at the weekend. It was a massive disappointment losing to Aberdeen, but you cannot dwell on it as a professional. We had no choice but to crack on. It was a great night for Aberdeen but, over two legs, we had a shocker.'

Over the years, much has been said of the late Bobby Robson's comments ahead of the second leg as well as those of former captain Mick Mills, who allegedly made some disparaging remarks not long after the game. In the days after Aberdeen knocked Ipswich out of the competition, the club's very own Public Relations Officer, Mel Henderson, penned this letter to Aberdeen Football Club which was published in the match-day programme ahead of the Dons' UEFA Cup third round first leg against SV Hamburg, in an attempt to set the record straight. He wrote:

I am writing to say how delighted everyone at Portman Road was to see the Dons advance into the third round of the UEFA Cup. From the volume of mail we have received following our first-round knockout, it is obvious a large number of Aberdeen supporters were given entirely the wrong impression of the manner in which we accepted defeat.

Both manager Bobby Robson and captain Mick Mills were quoted at great length in the Evening Express, but they strongly deny many of the quotes attributed to them. While naturally disappointed at going out of the competition as holders at the first hurdle, I think I would be right in saying that everybody at Ipswich wishes Aberdeen every possible future success.

Unfortunately, it has not been possible to reply to each and every supporter who took the trouble to write, but hopefully this letter will go some way towards explaining the confusion that seems to have arisen. Let me repeat, there is no question of sour grapes at this end. Mick Mills has made his REAL thoughts known in our official programme and I seem to recall Bobby Robson congratulating Aberdeen on their victory and wishing them 'all the best in the next round'.

The two clubs were on very friendly terms before the tie and, no matter the final result, it was obvious from the outset that being paired together would only cement relationships. At every level – directors, management, officials, players and supporters – we hope the friendship will remain and before our next meeting I sincerely hope Alex Ferguson will have led his team to the major honour they so richly deserve.

Our best wishes to everyone for the tie against Hamburg and for the remainder of the season.

Mel Henderson, Public Relations Officer, Ipswich Town FC

To clear up any confusion, Bobby Robson entered Aberdeen's dressing room after the game and firmly shook the hands of Alex Ferguson and Willie Miller and offered them both nothing but the very best of luck going forward in the competition, even joking with them both that Aberdeen will go on and win the cup, now that Ipswich had been knocked out. He told the waiting press after the game, 'Aberdeen are a fine team, and they showed a lot of aggression as well as a considerable amount of skill and I take nothing away from them.'

That night Aberdeen came of age, and they sent out a message which reverberated across the entire continent. Alex Ferguson had drawn on that game against Liverpool and used it to drive his men on. They didn't just beat a side who at the time were leading the old English First Division, it was also a side which contained nine full internationals. It was Aberdeen's finest result in their 78-year history. Alex Ferguson beamed afterwards knowing his side had learned their lesson from the Liverpool games, suggesting they had grown in stature but more importantly had matured since the Anfield defeat. He was particularly pleased how the lads showed a new-found patience during the game and kept possession of the ball better. He said after the game, 'The fact that we knocked out a team like Ipswich, the holders, must be a tremendous morale booster for everyone at Pittodrie, but the most important thing for us now is to get our game together consistently.' Just for the record, Aberdeen beat Arges Pitesti 5-2 on aggregate in the second round, but succumbed to West German giants SV Hamburg, who included legendary figure Franz Beckenbauer in their ranks, 4-5 over two legs in the third round.

FOURTEEN

BEHIND THE IRON CURTAIN AND BEYOND

Over the years, Aberdeen have visited many of Europe's finest cities while facing some of the Continent's best teams. Willie Miller's passport for one must have a very impressive collection of stamps from Reykjavik in Iceland to Tirana in Albania and that isn't taking into consideration a host of countries he visited while on Scotland duty. For this chapter I have looked at some of the more remote and unusual places where the team have competed while playing on the European stage – some of which proved to be a logistical nightmare for the organisers. During Aberdeen's trip to Poland to play Lech Poznań in November 1982, Aberdeen fan and former club historian Kevin Stirling remembers well the anti-aircraft gun parked not far from the runway upon arrival and, after departing the aeroplane, seeing nothing but soldiers patrolling the airport. Martial law was in force back then, which meant that while out for a walk he was soon followed by soldiers who monitored his every step. The city was under curfew which meant that nobody was allowed on the streets after 8 p.m. He described the trip as a scene out of the Hollywood movie *Tinker, Tailor, Soldier, Spy*. In September 1983 Aberdeen faced Akranes of Iceland in the European Cup Winners' Cup, and goalkeeper Bryan Gunn described the approach to Reykjavik Airport as 'like landing on the moon'.

Former Aberdeen striker and coach Drew Jarvie recalls a club trip to Bermuda with a great deal of fondness: 'In 1974 we had organised a close-season trip to Australia and New Zealand to help promote football in those two countries. On our way we stopped over in Bermuda for a few days. We had organised to play two games while we were there, and one of the players who guested for one of the sides was Clyde Best who was from Bermuda and played for West Ham United at the time. Bermuda is a beautiful island, and we were very well looked after by the local police who so happened to originate from Aberdeen.'

On 2 October 1981, Aberdeen were drawn against little-known Romanian side Arges Pitesti in the second round of the UEFA Cup. History would be made as never before had Aberdeen faced Romanian opposition in a European tie. The same can be said for Pitesti, who were facing Scottish opposition for the first time. The first leg was scheduled for Pittodrie on 21 October 1981 with the return in Romania two weeks later. For his programme column Alex Ferguson had this to say about the home leg: 'This second round UEFA Cup first-leg tie is a situation where, on one front, we must not give the opposition any opportunity to strengthen their position for the return and, on the other hand, achieve a result that will have us in front against the Romanians on their home ground in a fortnight's time. Playing at home will give Aberdeen the only real chance to assess the opposition and from that point perhaps meeting them first at Pittodrie gives us a first-hand opportunity to be properly geared for the return. In these double leg ties a team must do their business in the first round, whether home or away. I believe that is the foundation that we must have.' Aberdeen did just that by winning the game 3-0 thanks to first-half goals from Gordon Strachan, Peter Weir and a peach of a header from John Hewitt. The only disappointing factor on the night was that Aberdeen were unable to add to their three-goal tally, and this could be attributed to the fact that the Arges head coach selected their back-up goalkeeper Daniel Ariciu for the game but replaced him at half-time with Romanian international and regular number-one goalkeeper Cristian Gheorghe who, at 6 feet 2 inches tall, towered above most! You will not be surprised to learn that he did start the second leg.

At the beginning of the 1980s, Romania was fast becoming a declining country under the dictatorship of leader Nicolae Ceaușescu. Living standards were poor, food rations were in operation for large parts of the population and the nation's economy was chaotic at best. Poverty was everywhere. It was rare for citizens to leave the country and those that attempted to leave faced the possibility of severe punishment. One such example of this involved Arges Pitesti's most experienced campaigner, midfielder Nicolae Dobrin, who, according to reports had a life-changing opportunity to move to Real Madrid in the early seventies but the Romanian Football Federation blocked the move! Today, Arges Pitesti's stadium is named after him in recognition of his 22-year service to the club. Television stations only broadcast for two hours a day and that mainly consisted of speeches from the state's national leaders. Only two radio stations broadcast news from foreign shores: 'Free Europe' and 'Voice of America'. Despite the obvious difficulties, the city of Bucharest remained one of the most stunning cities in the world, and all in the travelling Aberdeen party had nothing but good words to say about their historic surroundings. The club planned for the team to stay in the capital as the hotels closer to Pitesti's stadium were not up to standard, plus it was a very agricultural part of the country. Aberdeen midfielder Neil Simpson recalls the build-up to the game. 'We stayed in Bucharest and faced a two-hour drive through the Romanian countryside to reach Pitesti to play the game. The day before the game Fergie and Archie allowed us to go out and explore the city. I appreciate the revolution was still a few years away, but even then, the place had a communist feel to it. The local people appeared quite regimented. There wasn't a lot of smiling going on so you could sense that they were constantly under the rule of being told what they could and couldn't do; there was no emotion to their expressions.'

Aberdeen striker Mark McGhee remembers Bucharest well, describing it as, 'a beautiful city, very normal just like an Edinburgh or a Glasgow'. Neil Simpson continues: 'We all decided to go into the big stores and buy some gifts and things. When we went to pay, the cashier would not accept the local currency, so we had to pay in US dollars! It was obvious they knew we were foreigners. The currency in Romania at that time was called Romanian leu and when I tried to order a soft drink at the bar in the hotel the barman asked me if I needed some leu; he told me he would convert the dollars I had into leu. He offered me 30 leu for 1 US dollar, so I thought I was on to a winner and told him to give me 20 dollars' worth of leu. So now, I have bundles of Romanian leu in my hand and wherever I went and attempted to pay in the local currency, nobody would accept my notes!! Afterwards, I went back to the bar to order more drinks and the same barman who had just converted my dollars into leu now refused to accept my money!! He would only accept US dollars! I couldn't believe it! I now have a wallet full of Romanian leu and the boys gave me such a hard time for that. I was the butt of their jokes for hours! I can also recall while we were on the bus after the game going back to the airport that Fergie had a wad of Romanian leu notes in his wallet and offered all his money to the local guy who was looking after us, but he refused to take it! Fergie had hundreds of notes and the guy was quite adamant – he would not take it! Fergie was gutted!'

The town of Pitesti sits at the foot of the hills in the Arges region, about 80 miles north-west of the capital city Bucharest. The team bus had to set off in plenty of time for the drive through the countryside to the Stadion 1 May because back in 1981, under communist rule, playing football under floodlights was banned, hence the two o'clock kick-off. The early start though didn't stop nearly 9,000 fervent home fans from getting behind their team. A handful of Aberdeen fans made the trip via the official flight, leaving Dyce Airport on the Sunday morning before the game on the Tuesday afternoon, while others made their own way there. Unlike Tirana no visas were required for the trip, but fans were subject to constant checks during their stay. There were no tickets available for the game, so the small band of Aberdeen fans had to make their way into the stadium via the press entrance which sat directly behind the technical area.

For the game itself Alex Ferguson made two changes from the 1-1 draw against Dundee United the previous Saturday – Eric Black, who scored on his competitive debut for the Dons that day, missed out as did Neil Simpson who had to be content with a place on the bench. Fergie brought in Alex McLeish to shore up the centre of the defence and Andy Watson to bring some steel to the midfield. Whatever the game plan was it didn't work as the Dons soon found themselves 2-0 down. Then came the infamous tea urn/Alex Ferguson incident. Fergie was so enraged by the team's first-half performance that he let them all have it during the break, especially Gordon Strachan. He swiped at a tray of teacups which almost hit Gordon. Thankfully they all missed but smashed above the heads of Alex McLeish and Willie Miller. He then turned his attention to the urn. He was giving it both barrels which is the moment Neil Simpson has never forgotten. 'I was a sub that day. We were 2-0 down and I came on for the injured Doug Rougvie just after they had scored their second goal. At half-time Fergie had what was the major of all crack-ups. We had taken the tea urn from Pittodrie with us on the trip; it had a good five-inch core of iron to it and he absolutely whacked it with his left forearm while ranting at us and this urn didn't budge an inch. I do not think he realised it was full of hot water and absolutely solid. We could all see that he had hurt himself which in turn made him even madder! None of us dared move or even worse laugh! He tore into Gordon Strachan during the break but decided to keep him on for the second half. We were still winning 3-2 on aggregate but Fergie was furious with us. I had never seen him like that before. Thankfully, we managed to get the scoreline back to 2-2 and go through 5-2 on aggregate.'

Striker Walker McCall, who was part of the travelling squad and a non-playing substitute, also remembers well the 15-minute break between halves. 'As we walked back to the dressing room for half-time, I could see Fergie ahead by the entrance, holding the door open. I knew immediately this wasn't good! We knew this wasn't just going to be a talking-to – this could be a full-blown explosion. He started going round the lads giving them what for and he stopped at Gordon Strachan and tore into him. Once he had finished, Gordon said something back and that was the catalyst for him to explode. Fergie by this point was still walking around the dressing room and in the middle was a table full of teacups and the tea urn. Upon hearing Gordon's comment, he literally swiped all the teacups from the table – they all flew everywhere – and he then smashed the tea urn with his arm! All the tea flew over Willie Miller's and Alex McLeish's suits which were hanging up on the pegs and Willie told Fergie he was going to bill him for the dry cleaning, which enraged Fergie even more and he went up another level! All of us got it that day from Fergie!

'I was a non-playing sub but if I didn't jump up off the bench quickly enough to retrieve the ball for a throw-in, he would give me pelters, not just me – all of us! Before the start of the second half I was in the toilet, and I was the only player left in there, but I heard Archie Knox say to Fergie, "My God, you really went off on one then." Fergie said to Archie that he was aware but he had to get it off his chest. He said to Archie that he was so annoyed because he knew the lads were capable of playing so much better and that the lads were not playing to their best. I heard the two of them discussing this, so I decided to wait because there was no way I was stepping out of the toilet while they were in mid-conversation. As I got back to the bench, Fergie barked at me, "Where have you been?" and I just told him that I needed to go to the toilet but got lost and ended up somewhere down the corridor! There was absolutely no way I was going to tell him I was in the dressing room and overheard his conversation. I had to lie to him because if I had told him the truth, he would have sent for the firing squad.

'Straight after the game we jumped on the bus and headed back to Bucharest Airport. Inter Milan were in town and had just finished their game with Dinamo Bucharest. They were all dressed resplendently in their designer suits. They were all looking like male models and here we all were dressed in our club tracksuits, looking like we had been dragged through a hedge backwards. They all looked incredible with their slicked-back hair and tanned complexions! It was like they had all turned up for a catwalk show and we were the audience.'

In one alleged amusing anecdote, Alex McLeish was talking to a host of Inter fans, and big Eck was deep in negotiations over the purchase of some souvenir badges. Unbeknown to the Inter fans, they were dealing with a Scotland international and when this was pointed out, one of the fans said, 'Ah, Gordon McQueen, nice to meet you!'

Today, sports broadcasting is a multi-billion-pound industry. We live in an age of breaking news and on-demand media.

Consumers now expect, at the click of a mouse or the swipe of a phone, to receive the very latest updates from their clubs or organisations almost immediately. The need for 24-hour sports news has become all-consuming. In the modern world this has become more achievable mainly thanks to technologies which are readily available to broadcasters to help ensure 'the news' isn't far away. Technologies have advanced that much in recent times that sending a live report to a studio on the other side of the planet now only requires a strong Wi-Fi connection! Back in the 1980s it wasn't so easy!

Renowned sports broadcaster Frank Gilfeather accompanied Aberdeen many times to cover big European games for local TV station, Grampian TV. He faced many challenges as he reported on Aberdeen's adventures in Europe, none more so than when he joined the team for the trip to Romania. Frank had vast experience working in the industry and was an instantly recognisable face on many of Aberdeen's away journeys. He very kindly recalled his memories of that adventurous trip for this book. He takes up the story: 'Grampian TV was the first of the ITV network of stations to introduce Electronic News Gathering (ENG) before which everything was shot on film with a separate soundtrack which later had to be married up in the edit. Grampian pioneered ENG and, with the Dons doing so well under Fergie, it was decided I would take a cameraman and sound guy to Romania for the game against Arges Pitesti. We had all the gear which had to go through a booking-in system, done two or three days in advance. It's called a carnet (pronounced carny) and means you can take stuff like cameras, sound equipment and all that gear into another country duty free.

'All the pre-trip stuff was done at Aberdeen Airport with a crew from the newsroom. It went on to *North Tonight* that night while we were en route to Bucharest. As a boxer, I had picked up some tips when travelling behind the Iron Curtain. I had boxed in Sofia, the Bulgarian capital, and the country's second city, Plovdiv, in 1964 and then in East Berlin the following year for the European Championships. Knowing the influence a packet of fags can bring you, I took 200 duty-free Camel ciggies and had to burst the pack open on arrival at the Intercontinental Hotel where an armed soldier greeted our arrival. A packet of fags placed in the hand of the soldier somehow changed his mind and we parked right in front of the hotel for as long as we wanted. The car was what had been an old Renault 4. Renault, who had moved on from that shape years earlier, sold the design to the Romanians. So, just about every car in Bucharest was essentially a Renault 4.

'Weeks earlier, we had arranged with the state broadcaster to beam our pictures from their studio, but payment would have to be made in cash and with American dollars. We had also arranged for a driver/interpreter to be with us for the duration of the trip. He was as essential as the dollars that can bring you a better rate of exchange than the pound. It was incredibly hot on the day of the match with Pitesti 120km [75 miles] from the capital. It was an afternoon kick-off, so how to race back to Bucharest to beam the pictures back to Aberdeen after writing a script and recording a voiceover and a little intro piece to camera, in time to catch *North Tonight* at 6 p.m.? And remember, the sequence had to be edited in Aberdeen. The only way was to leave the game early, praying there would be no change in the scoreline and that we would not miss an important incident.

'Pitesti is in the heart of Transylvania and I felt as though Dracula himself had sucked the life from me as my mind raced with worry en route back to Bucharest. A quick piece in front of the giant state broadcaster's HQ, then inside to put together a script and record it. "You need to record a voiceover?" asked the studio manager. "That'll be an extra $300." He insisted that had not been part of the prearranged deal of $1,500 to squirt the pictures back. My past experience of the corruption in the Eastern bloc countries before the Berlin Wall came down and the tyrants were removed to be replaced by other tyrants, meant I had plenty of spare dollars. I paid the guy $1,800, and I suspect he stuck the additional $300 into his back pocket.

'Next day, our driver rushed us to the airport. We gave him all the local currency we had between us as we couldn't exchange it back home, and he was extremely grateful; like "I've won the lottery" grateful. There was no booking in of equipment at their side, so we boarded and waited . . . and waited . . . Why? Because the pilot was told the Romanians would not refuel the plane unless the money (I think a figure of £25,000 was mentioned) was paid up front. Dick Donald swung into action and a flurry of telephone calls later, the money was transferred into the appropriate account and we took off.'

You can watch Frank's actual report from Romania on YouTube, and trust me, it's a fascinating watch.

Just one final thought from that trip. With the team flying home directly after the game, the captain of the charter flight had a 10 p.m. landing schedule to meet as Dyce Airport closed at that time. With strong winds buffeting the flight path, the captain announced the plane would have to divert to Edinburgh as they would miss their 10 p.m. cut-off time in Aberdeen. Upon hearing this Alex Ferguson left his seat, marched down the aisle and disappeared into the cockpit. A minute later he reappeared and took his seat, and a few seconds after this the captain announced over the tannoy, 'We will be landing at Aberdeen Airport at approximately 10.20 p.m.!' The plane did and the waiting ground crew were none too pleased as were the customs officers who had to hang around an extra half an hour to welcome home the travelling party!

Before Aberdeen's trip to Poland, in late September 1982, the Dons travelled behind the Iron Curtain to face Albanian Cup winners Dinamo Tirana. The Dons held a slender 1-0 advantage from the first leg at Pittodrie, the only goal of the game aptly scored by super-sub John Hewitt. What made the victory even more interesting was the fact that neither Alex Ferguson nor any of his scouts could travel to Albania to scout the opposition ahead of the first leg. The match-day programme for the first leg at Pittodrie, which usually lists the away team squad, had nothing but a blank page as nobody knew anything about the Albanian players. Fergie, after the first leg victory was secured, even confessed that he had never entered a game so unprepared when it came to knowing and understanding his opposition. Thankfully, he did gain some knowledge by talking to the Yugoslavian referee who officiated in Aberdeen's away game in Sion who informed Fergie that the Albanians will be a much stronger side than Aberdeen's first victims in the competition.

In 1982, Europe remained divided after the end of the Second World War and then up until the 'Cold War' ended in 1991. The Iron Curtain was a well-known term used to describe the effort of the old Soviet Union to blockade itself from their Western counterparts. In the East, many countries had connections to the Soviet Union while in the West most countries were connected by NATO or remained neutral. Albania was one such country that remained hard-line communist. It was a trip not without its dramas and difficulties! The club quickly prepared the players and staff for a foray which proved to be a logistical nightmare. Ahead of the game, Alex Ferguson spoke at length with Celtic manager Billy McNeill, whose side three years previously had contested a European Cup game against Partizan Tirana. Billy was able to offer Fergie ample advice in terms of where to stay and how to prepare his side off the field of play in preparation for the return leg in the Balkan country. His advice was invaluable!

Like it was for many years under communist rule, Albania was a closed country. According to reports, only 30 visas were granted for Aberdeen's trip to Tirana including the playing staff and members of the press. This issue had been raised more than once with UEFA by several journalists, but Albania had always discouraged, in their own words, 'spies' from entering the country. *Press and Journal* journalist Alastair MacDonald was one such sportswriter who was lucky enough to be granted a visa. He recalls the trip to Albania with much fondness in his popular column in Aberdeen's match-day programme. 'The Don' Alastair explained that with Albania only maintaining diplomatic relations with two European countries – France and Austria – he had to apply for his visa via the Albanian embassy in Paris. He had to wait a nervy two weeks before the visa was confirmed.

If you ask any journalist of that era, they will tell you that there was one vital piece of equipment which was required for them all to be able to do their job – a telephone! There was much concern among the group of six journalists that problems accessing a phone would cause major issues, but Alastair and his colleagues were delighted, if not a little relieved, that the stadium provided two telephones for the writers to call in their reports to their respective newspapers after the game. Alastair did though confess that their hotel offered one or two 'irritations' including the lack of a toilet seat and a lack of bath plugs that fitted an actual bath! He did, however, note towards the end of his column the 'friendliness and hospitality' of the Albanian people.

It wasn't just the sportswriters who encountered one or two issues at the hotel. Having arrived at the team hotel, Dougie Bell swiftly requested a change of room; an army of cockroaches had already taken occupancy before Doug's arrival! With the food an unknown quantity coupled with the slight concerns about hygiene, Teddy Scott packed a hamper full of food to accompany the lads on the trip. Physiotherapist Roland Arnott and club doctor Mr Catto made sure the necessary medical supplies were aplenty including a bundle of salt tablets! What the Aberdeen party wasn't expecting though was a military coup which swept through the Albanian capital on the day of the match! Neale Cooper once said with a wry grin on his face for a BBC Scotland documentary that 'some of the lads thought that meant a local "cow" had escaped!' Aberdeen striker Eric Black recalls several tanks arriving in the square, commenting that the scene was nothing but chaotic. In a report credited to the National Press International on the day of the match, 29 September 1982, the exiled King Leka of Albania was 'extremely upset' after a failed military coup by members of his National Liberation Army to overthrow the communist government of his native land. Thankfully, the attempted coup had no effect on the game which went ahead without incident at the Selman Stërmasi Stadium.

Former Aberdeen striker Mark McGhee recalls the trip vividly. 'One of the things I remember about that time was the amount of communist or Eastern bloc countries we visited. In the West we had a preconceived vision that all Eastern bloc countries had a uniform and that's what the whole point of communism was about, that everything was standardised and that everybody lived the same life. Whereas what we actually saw was a great sense of normality. For example, Budapest was like Edinburgh – it was a beautiful city! The place went about its business the same way as Glasgow or Edinburgh. Even when we went to Poznań in Poland, after getting through it was a little more of an unknown city, but the place was just like an Aberdeen or a Birmingham; it was a civilised place. Tirana for me personally was almost like another world!'

Mark joined Aberdeen from Newcastle in March 1979 and was already well travelled with the Dons before the trip to Albania came around. Having already played in Romania against Arges Pitesti, Mark had an inkling the surroundings in Tirana would be similar to those he experienced in Pitesti. He was wrong! 'It was like nothing I had ever experienced before. Even before we arrived in the city, we had been told we would not be eating the food over there. When we landed at the airport we were fed on the plane before we disembarked! When we did get to the hotel, we were only allowed to eat the Cornflakes with the milk that had been packed in the club's hamper and various bars of chocolate; we were not allowed to eat the food over there. The hotel was poor, and it was certainly different to many of the other hotels we used to stay at, but it was what it was. On the way home, even before the plane took off, we were served another meal while the plane stood at the gate! The meal had been pre-prepared on the plane, so as soon as we arrived after the game, Aer Lingus served us all the meal before take-off. What I do recall is staying in a hotel in the city centre and Fergie instructing us all to stay in the hotel because there was a curfew after six o'clock. Nobody was allowed out on the streets after this time. There is a huge square in the centre of Tirana and while we were all cooped up in our rooms, I remember looking out of the window and seeing thousands of people gathering in the square. Everybody was promenading so the club had obviously received the wrong information because it looked like all the folk in Albania turned up in the square after six o'clock!'

Twenty thousand fervent home supporters packed out the compact Dinamo Stadium in hope of their team overturning the 1-0 deficit from the first leg at Pittodrie, but Aberdeen were stubborn in their tactics that night. Alex Ferguson took the unusual step of playing just one striker up front, hoping to pack the midfield and retain possession of the ball for long periods. Mark was tasked with that role. 'I remember in the game itself,

I played up front on my own which is a tactic that Fergie didn't use very often, and I felt quite isolated because I had always been so used to my teammates being close to me. It was a hard game for us because there was a partisan support that night for Tirana. The stadium was packed, and they didn't half support their team, so it turned out it was a very close game. I remember just running my nuts off before Fergie took me off, which I wasn't surprised by because I had run myself into the ground, but thankfully, we came through.'

Alas for the home support it wasn't meant to be as Aberdeen held the plucky Albanians to a scoreless draw and progressed through the tournament to reach round two. After the game, a delighted Ferguson told the waiting press, 'We decided the way to play this game was with two wide men in Gordon Strachan and Peter Weir. Tirana's pitch was big and in splendid condition which suited our tactics perfectly. Because of the heat (92°F), we decided the best way to handle our opponents was to keep possession and let them tire themselves out by chasing the ball. With a two o'clock kick-off that made it extremely uncomfortable for them. Our performance was excellent and though we didn't win, 0-0 was a good result and we did the job.'

In the 1990s everything became that little bit easier for the written press when planning and preparing for big European games. Former *Evening Express* sports editor Charlie Allan started accompanying the Dons on their trips when he took up his role writing about Aberdeen's European escapades in 1991. I began our chat by asking him about the logistics of planning a trip abroad, and Charlie explains: 'I was fortunate that I tended to travel with the Aberdeen team, so the club organised the hotel, transport to and from the stadium and of course press accreditation for the games. Regarding visas, I was very fortunate on that front, as it was mainly a case of filling out a form and supplying passport details to the club.'

I wondered if Charlie ever had to book his own telephone and seat in the stadium's press box, and he explains: 'My deadlines meant it was less necessary than if I had been working for a morning newspaper. The normal routine would be to return to my hotel room and file copy using the hotel phone. It was only much later when we flew back immediately after games, we tended to have one more night at the away city then flew home in the morning. The biggest worry was that the Tandy and telephone ear coupling system didn't work. It involved attaching the small ears to the phone then hoping you could hear the screech as copy was fired down the line. If not, it was a case of getting on to a copy girl and dictating it via telephone, which our bosses weren't keen on because it was more expensive.'

It's very unusual in this day and age for copy not to be received by newspapers and online platforms, because the technology is so advanced that only an unmitigated disaster would stop reports ending up in an editor's inbox. That didn't stop me asking if Charlie had ever been in an awkward situation where not enough phones were on hand in any given stadium. 'I have seen it happen to plenty of press colleagues, but like I said it was never a panic for me because I was planning to file copy back at the hotel.

'By the time we moved into the modern age, we had equipment that allowed you to bypass the need for a phone, and I would either send it direct through the internet or piggyback for a connection through my phone. Thankfully, most clubs had very good internet connections.'

So, if phones and a good Wi-Fi connection were readily available when travelling abroad, did that stop Charlie from having any issues when filing his copy? 'The closest I came to that was when I travelled with the Dons to Kazakhstan in 2015 for their Europa League qualifier against FC Kairat Almaty. I was fortunate to be one of only three journalists permitted to fly in the luxury jet the Dons had hired for the marathon trip to Almaty, which is about 100 miles from the border with China. The total distance was more than 3,400 miles, which was crazy for a European tie. The club had warned us beforehand that the plan was to get back to the plane as soon as possible after the game because they had to start their league campaign away to Dundee United on the Sunday. I was still typing away, writing the reaction and other stuff needed for the next day on the bus to the airport . . . then disaster. I couldn't get any sort of internet connection, not even on my phone, in the few minutes I had between arriving and going on the plane. I was in a panic because I knew my office still had not received a word of my main copy, just the match report for the inside spread. Salvation came from the captain of the aircraft, who assured me I would be allowed off the plane to file my copy when we stopped in Estonia to refuel. It was a nervous seven hours or so, but I was indeed allowed to sit on the steps of the plane, on the runway, and log into the airport's Wi-Fi to send the copy over, which because of the time difference meant it would be at the office well ahead of my deadline. That was the only stop the plane made on the way back, so I was very lucky on that occasion.'

Charlie has seen it all in his privileged position as the former sports editor of the *Evening Express* and was happy to share some of his more amusing anecdotes for this book. 'The daftest tended to be in Spain, South Africa and Egypt, during pre- or mid-season with the Dons. In Spain, I will never forget the sight of the late Hicham Zerouali racing off the pitch to shelter under a tree when there was a freak hailstorm . . . Hicham asked us what the white stuff was – he had never seen it before! In South Africa, Rangers were on the upper floors of the same hotel the

Dons stayed in and their French manager had placed a huge blackboard right outside the lift with a list of itineraries for the players for the next day.

'Just before retiring to bed, I went up with a certain player, whom I shall not name, who rubbed out the "8 a.m., breakfast meeting" and replaced it with "8 a.m. Mass . . . all non-Catholic players MUST also attend." Rangers were not overly pleased! In Egypt, we went with the players on a tour of the pyramids. Inside one, which was very dark, Darren Mackie scared the living daylights out of some of his teammates by lying down inside a deep stone coffin . . . and jumping up at them when they walked past. Once, we hired a fancy horse and cart to take me, Willie Miller and three other journalists for a pint along the beach front in Alexandria, and we were on the bloody thing for two hours because of traffic; Willie wasn't amused! When travelling out of Aberdeen to Iceland I was stopped by a very nice elderly lady at the airport who praised me for my coverage of football and said I was her favourite. When I thanked her she replied, "No problem, Archie" . . . she thought I was Archie Macpherson!'

SIX

BAYERN MUNICH

'Aberdeen are technically inferior to Bielefeld. I expect Bayern to outplay them. As soon as the Scots step outside their country, they are only half as good as they are at home.' Those are the words attributed to Germany legend Franz Beckenbauer after he watched Bayern Munich beat Bielefeld 5-0 ahead of Aberdeen's stiffest of European challenges against West German powerhouse Bayern Munich in the quarter-finals of the 1982/83 Cup Winners' Cup. Just two weeks later the 'Kaiser' would come to regret those very words as Aberdeen produced two sublime performances, home and away, to knock the West German giants out of the competition. To be fair to the German legend, he did admit afterwards that he 'sold Aberdeen short'.

Aberdeen had already produced three workmanlike performances in Switzerland, Albania and Poland respectively to quietly progress their way through the early stages of the competition. The Dons had only conceded one goal during that time, so it came as no surprise to those who followed the Dons closely that a performance as sublime as the one on display in the Olympiastadion was delivered. It was a performance believed to be way above their normal standard. The work and preparation began three months previously once the draw in Zurich had been finalised. The draw for the quarter-finals was made in December with the first leg planned for 2 March 1983, plenty of time for Alex Ferguson and Archie Knox to plot their opponents' downfall. Aberdeen were entering uncharted territory as never before had they played European football post-Christmas; history had already been rewritten.

Archie Knox was in attendance for that Bielefeld v Bayern Munich game and wrote a detailed player-by-player dossier for the Aberdeen players to study. Archie was particularly impressed by big centre-back Klaus Augenthaler whom he called a commanding figure at the back, and he went on to report, 'An aggressive tackler when looking to win the ball but didn't commit himself in 1 v 1 situations. Good long user of the ball and tried a few times to hit long passes for Rummenigge to run in behind them.' Archie also noted that Augenthaler 'broke forward only occasionally and did so only when the ball was in front of him'. For corner kicks, Archie observed that Augenthaler 'came forward into the back post area'. Archie also paid close attention to West Germany international Paul Breitner by saying, 'Midfield schemer and the biggest influencer on the team in terms of linking the play. Great control and composure on the ball. Operates mostly towards the left side of the park but is the one player who is always available to take the ball no matter the pressure he could be under. Brilliant at picking up a loose ball anywhere in front of his back four and immediately drawing the opposition.' Archie also observed that Breitner was 'very quick; quick at beating an opponent straight on or turning away from them. He will challenge if the ball is in his vicinity but does not pick up a man or worry about defensive responsibilities.' Archie finished off his observations on Breitner by noting, 'Will attempt to take people on in penalty area or play one-twos or through passes. He is prepared to hit long range shots; has the experience and ability to change game if necessary.'

Archie didn't just write a player-by-player dossier; he also summarised Bayern's performance against Bielefeld, and he wrote, 'A good, well-organised team who all know the part they play. Technically they are just what you expect of a top German side – their crossing of the ball, superb switch of play to isolate opponents. In wide areas, quite good which has always been our experience against German teams and Bayern are no different, particularly if they can pull a lot of opponents to one side of the park, then they will look to hit a big one and then support the isolated areas in numbers.' To finish off, Archie noted Bayern's style of play: 'Augenthaler at the back started all attacking moves when goalkeeper had the ball in hand and can vary his use with either the short ball to Breitner or a long ball, especially from the right-hand side of the park to Hoeness with Rummenigge feeding off and midfield pushing up to support. I am sure they will vary attack in our game in effect when goalkeeper has ball; he will look for free players particularly Paul Breitner to start attacks or any free player.'

Having arrived safely in Munich, Alex Ferguson spoke to the press and called upon past experiences against German opposition to help his side gain the required result. He said, 'I don't know if we could ever have enough games against German sides to satisfy me, but the experience my players have accumulated against Fortuna Düsseldorf, Eintracht Frankfurt and SV Hamburg will certainly help them against Bayern. We know Bayern are top class in playing possession football and we must expect to be put under pressure, but the important thing is that we are positive when we get the ball and make the best use of it.' He finished off by saying, 'We've got to find out how good we really are.'

Bayern's general manager Uli Hoeness described the first leg as 'perhaps the most important in the club's history'. That is some testament to the importance of the game to the German side. German newspaper *Bild* though, wasn't as flattering, writing, 'Aberdeen will not provide Bayern with any difficulty. It's a good draw for Munich who could have been paired with far more difficult opponents.' The phrase 'assumption is the mother of all f**k-ups' springs to mind.

The information on Bayern that Archie provided was invaluable for Aberdeen's preparations ahead of the first game. Alex Ferguson quickly started his mind games, telling the German press that he would be happy to come away from the Olympiastadion with a 2-0 defeat; nothing could be further from the truth. At a training session on the park the night before, Fergie strolled on to the pitch moments before Archie Knox was due to begin training and told him to stand by the sidelines. Archie in turn stomped off in a well-rehearsed huff. Fergie then instructed a group of players to stand in the centre circle with other groups to take their place at each corner flag. The players at the corner flags had to ping balls to the lads in the middle and then sprint to the centre, the lads in the centre then had to ping the ball back and sprint but this time to the opposite corner flag. During this session chaos ensued, with balls flying about everywhere and with some of the lads getting hit in the face by stray balls. For the onlooking Bayern party they must have wondered what was going on. Fergie, quite brilliantly, lulled them all into a false sense of security.

On the day of the game the lads held a light training session on the pitch directly adjacent to the splendid Olympiastadion, which hosted the 1972 Olympics and the 1974 FIFA World Cup final as well as the 1979 European Cup final. The lads went through a light stretching session and practised their set pieces one last time, before heading back to the team hotel for an afternoon nap and their pre-match meeting. Hundreds of Aberdeen fans made the trip to Bavaria, each paying DM 45 (£19.50) for a match ticket. Ahead of kick-off, as the lads waited for the buzzer to sound from the referee to leave the dressing room, Alex Ferguson reminded the lads one final time of their tasks; they included 'getting early balls into the box, keep Paul Breitner quiet and show Bayern Munich how good you are'. Those tactics certainly worked on the night. Midfielder Dougie Bell, who came into the side for Gordon Strachan, wanted to be recognised for playing against the best in the business. For Dougie, the excitement of testing his skills against the German aristocrats in the shape of Paul Breitner, Dieter Hoeness and Karl-Heinz Rummenigge was as good as it gets. He wanted to be tested against the best. 'The midfield for that game was me, Simmy, Neale Cooper and Peter Weir out left. We worked so hard that night, and it was a good performance. You get a feel for it and we knew right away it would be a good night. It was a great occasion; I played very well that night where I was able to make a couple of telling runs which gives you a lot of confidence. It makes you think if I can take these guys on, then all will be OK; it helps boost your confidence.'

On that cold night in Munich, where Aberdeen were contesting their 45th European tie, temperatures touched freezing. John Hewitt huddled up beside his fellow substitutes Bryan Gunn, Gordon Strachan, Andy Watson and Derek Hamilton. On the pitch the starting eleven were holding their own and on occasions created two if not three good goalscoring opportunities. John Hewitt recalls, 'The guys did so well across there. The boys were sticking to their task and playing exceptionally well. It was a very tough place to go and try and get something out of the game. You could argue we were playing against a German international team. We did really well in Munich, but it was still going to be very tough to get through the tie.' Alex Ferguson and Archie Knox are renowned for their immaculate preparation, leaving no stone unturned when it came to briefing the lads for the task ahead. Both paid visits to the Olympiastadion to cast their own expert eyes over the Germans. Fergie even went as far as getting a friend of his who lived in Germany to VHS record several Munich games and post him the tapes, so he could cast his eyes over his opponents time and time again. No matter the name, the history or the stage, at no point did Fergie deploy tactics to stop Bayern; it was, in fact, the complete opposite. John continues, 'Fergie and Archie had the opposition watched thoroughly. They had gone across themselves to watch Bayern prior to both games. We would sit down with a dossier of the team and each individual player. Archie would give us the low-down on each player, focusing on their strengths and weaknesses. Fergie and Archie would then speak about how we would play against them, how we could set up and how we could provide problems for them. At no point did we concern ourselves about how they would set up to play against us, as we could handle that. It was all about us giving them problems.'

Many experts and observers of the game at close quarters have suggested that performance in the Olympiastadion was Aberdeen's finest away European showing. Let us not forget that only ten months previously Bayern had contested the European Cup final, losing narrowly to English league champions Aston Villa. Their average home crowd was more than 43,000 fans and it was reported that the Munich players were on general bonuses of £750 for a home win and £1,000 for an away win. It was more commonly known that if the crowd for the game exceeded 40,000 fans, each Bayern player would have received a bonus of £271 and if they made the semi-finals, they would have received a bonus of £1,357 per man. The attendance that night was 35,000.

The Dons had just held one of the powerhouses of European football on their own patch – but was that enough for Alex Ferguson? John Hewitt explains the mood of the boss after the game: 'He was pretty low-key. Fergie and Archie came in and started praising the guys and applauding them for a magnificent performance but reminded us all that the hard work was about to start once we got back to Aberdeen. Fergie and Archie had Bayern watched several times, so they knew the quality that they had. Bayern could go anywhere in the world and beat the opposition so, to come across to Scotland and play a provincial club like Aberdeen, would not exactly be an issue for them. We knew it was going to be difficult, but the one thing about us was that we really believed in ourselves as a group. We knew we could go anywhere and compete against the best. We were very much looking forward to the challenge.'

Aberdeen assistant manager Archie Knox was another who was full of praise for the performance shown in the Olympiastadion. He said, 'That was one of the best games that Aberdeen had ever played. There was no doubt we gained a new-found respect after that game – just think of the team that Bayern had. Dougie Bell was phenomenal that night for us. He was brilliant for us in Europe because the opposition were not used to that type of player who was able to run at them and dribble past them. He was that powerful he could nick the ball off an opponent and then dribble past them. Dougie was fantastic throughout our entire European campaign that season.'

Having drawn the game 0-0, Aberdeen showed a level of maturity that had not been seen before with Willie Miller having a marvellous game against the brilliant Karl-Heinz Rummenigge. Respect had been earned. After the game, a 42-year-old Alex Ferguson spoke to the waiting press and expressed his delight: 'It was a performance that made us very proud. They are one of the biggest clubs in the world with a great tradition. This result will hurt them, and they may come out snarling at our ground. We will be ready for them though.' Fergie went on to tell the German press that 'this was one of Aberdeen's most disciplined performances, and it was a great result. Although it's only half-time in the tie, we keep hitting new peaks and this was one of them tonight. There is an argument to suggest that Aberdeen won this game 0-0!' After 15 years of strenuous effort, a European semi-final beckoned.

It wasn't just Alex Ferguson who bestowed a seal of approval on his team's efforts. Aberdeen's performance was also recognised by the West Germany national team manager Jupp Derwall who observed, 'Aberdeen must be one of the best sides in all of the European competitions. I had heard they were good, but I had not realised they were that good. Bayern are the finest technical team in Germany, but Aberdeen matched them in every way. I cannot remember seeing a Scottish side play so well in Germany.' Bayern's general manager Uli Hoeness also sang the praises of Fergie's men saying, 'I warned everybody here that Aberdeen would be a great threat. I have said that they are better than Barcelona, Inter Milan and Real Madrid and I have been proved right.' Praise indeed. Two-time European Footballer of the Year, Karl-Heinz Rummenigge, also lavished praise on Aberdeen by saying, 'Rarely in my whole career have I played against a team as aggressive yet still perfectly fair, and who concentrated so intently on their objective.'

It wasn't just the performance on the pitch that was recognised. Aberdeen's 1,500 travelling support also came in for much praise from the Munich Chief of Police for their behaviour. He noted in the German press, 'They proved to be excellent ambassadors for Scotland. We had absolutely no problems with them.' The West German sports press though were quick to jump on the back of Bayern by openly stating that their pride had been wounded after the first leg and reminded the Munich faithful that the

Dons had failed against four of Bayern's rivals in recent years: Borussia Mönchengladbach, Fortuna Düsseldorf, Eintracht Frankfurt and more recently SV Hamburg. Nothing but a result was expected by the West Germans.

Second leg

Two weeks later Bayern visited Pittodrie for the first time. During that time Aberdeen comfortably beat Kilmarnock 2-0 at Rugby Park and reached the semi-final of the Scottish Cup after coming through a tough encounter with Partick Thistle at Firhill. There was much optimism ahead of kick-off. The date 16 March 1983 will go down as the 'greatest night ever at Pittodrie', but it could have been so different if it were not for the brilliant thinking of Alex Ferguson when the Dons went behind 2-1 on the night, which I will elaborate on shortly. For the game Ferguson made just one change from the team that beat Partick Thistle 2-1 in the Scottish Cup quarter-final the previous Saturday, with Eric Black coming in for Dougie Bell.

In his programme notes Ferguson called upon the fans to help the team get over the line. It was a rallying call, and he said, 'If there is ever a time when the players will value support from the terraces – this is it. I can promise that the team will be giving it everything they have on behalf of the club and if a packed Pittodrie reciprocates in the best kind of way, I am sure it can give the players that extra lift which may just make that crucial little difference at the end of the night.' Fergie was also under no illusions that this was the biggest test of his managerial career as he looked forward to the return leg, 'We are looking for a victory of any kind and that is what will dictate our approach. It is, of course, still a European tie and we must play with patience, but it would be nice to introduce a flavour of Scottish football as well. The younger members of the team reacted magnificently in conquering tension in the first leg and now they can go out and play their own game, while remembering it is a European tie. I have told them that there is no need for them to be afraid of the occasion.'

For Bayern, the Germans arrived in Aberdeen in confident mood. Skipper Paul Breitner was already thinking ahead to the game when he spoke to the press outside Aberdeen Airport: 'I think we will have more room to play tomorrow because Aberdeen's marking will not be so tight this time. I was well short of match fitness in the first game – but now I feel much better.' West Germany international coach Jupp Derwall also believed that Bayern would cause major issues for the Dons at Pittodrie, and he said, 'The Scots will not be able to mark Breitner and Rummenigge as well as they did in Munich. Because they have to win, Aberdeen must go forward and this will certainly give Munich chances to counter.'

Bayern trained at Pittodrie the night before the game, and assistant manager Archie Knox decided to go along for the experience, a decision he didn't regret: 'For the return leg I went to watch their training session at Pittodrie the night before the game and it was one of the best training sessions I had ever seen. It was so competitive. They really thought we were going to bombard them with crosses because all they did was throw crosses into the box during the session and they worked on keeping their line in the box, far enough away from their goal. There were clashes of heads and all sorts going on in that session; they were properly going at it.'

Pittodrie that night was packed and the atmosphere was electric. Very much like the first leg, John Hewitt had to be content with a place on the bench. Up to that point he had only started five games that season and continued to work hard in training to get up to speed. In the days leading up to the second leg he had a sixth sense that his tracksuit would be needed once again. It came as no surprise when Fergie named his team. 'As I mentioned earlier, due to my troubling injury, I was really fighting to get fit just to get a place on the bench as match fitness was an issue for me. I was desperately trying to get myself up to speed, and I needed game time more than anything else, be that with the reserves or getting games for the first team. I had only just come back, so I knew making the bench was the best chance for me to be involved and I was happy enough with that.'

Aberdeen made the worst possible start when Klaus Augenthaler smashed one in from 25 yards. Thankfully, before half-time, Neil Simpson grabbed an equaliser. Pittodrie came alive with a rendition of 'Here We Go' booming out across the night sky. The teams went in level at half-time with Bayern in the ascendancy thanks to the away goal. At half-time John Hewitt sat quietly in the dressing room with the game in the balance. 'We knew it was going to be a difficult game, and we managed to get back into it, but it was a concentration thing with Fergie. He always used to say that especially in Europe you must concentrate fully for 90 minutes. He would say that because we could be doing well for 85 minutes and suddenly, we have lost two or three goals and go out of the competition. The second half was just about our concentration levels being at their absolute best and if the opportunities came along to try our best to take them. We always knew with the boys that we had, especially the creative guys, that they would make openings for us. It was just a case of making sure we made the best of it.'

The level of noise at the start of the second half was deafening, but within 15 minutes of the restart the unthinkable happened – Bayern scored again, and the stadium fell quiet. Alex McLeish attempted to clear a diagonal ball but only managed to divert it towards Hans Pflügler, who somehow managed to volley home from 20 yards. There was a collective groan from inside the stadium and the home dugout. John Hewitt recalls: 'Obviously, we are playing against a top-quality side and at 2-1 all I'm thinking is we need two more goals. We were getting into the last 20 minutes and I knew we had to score quickly. Before I knew it, I received a shout to prepare myself to come on. Prior to the game my wife said to me, "You're going to come on and score the winning goal." I replied with an "aye OK". I almost laughed it off, because not for one minute did I ever believe that is the way the game would pan out. I was delighted to get on the park and try to contribute in any way. Fergie instructed me to make sure I stayed forward, to try and get on the end of things; to follow things in like we had been taught to do in training. That was it really. He told me to go out and enjoy it and, if an opportunity came along, to do my best to try and take it.'

It was in the moments after Bayern's second goal that Alex Ferguson made a decision which changed the pattern of the game, but it didn't come without much thought. In the heat of battle some moments may not feel significant at the time; it's only with the benefit of hindsight that one is able to recall the importance of such a moment. Fergie decided to gamble. One of the changes made was to substitute John McMaster for right-back Stuart Kennedy. This in turn was met by groans from the home crowd, but John explains in detail why that substitution was so important to the cause. 'The manager made a genius substitution; he takes off Stuart Kennedy despite Stuart having a great game. Stuart, though, refuses to come off. During an injury break the boss and Stuart are having a heated debate on the touchline. The boss says to Stuart, "Come on, get off the park." But Stuart replies with, "I'm not coming off, take big Doug Rougvie off; he's having a nightmare." Eventually I could see the boss losing his temper and, in front of a full house at Pittodrie, he says to Stuart, "Get aff the f**king park!"

Eventually, I get on the park, Doug Rougvie goes to right-back and Neale Cooper goes to left-back and I go into central midfield.'

John Hewitt explains further. 'The one thing about Fergie is he had a knack of being able to see quite clearly how games were developing, and he knew how to change things around for the better to try and get a result. It didn't work all the time, but he knew how to change things for the better most of the time. He knew who to put on and help turn the game for him.'

Archie Knox remembers vividly the moments leading up to that decision and I asked him recently who came up with the idea to replace Stuart Kennedy with John McMaster, 'Alex made that decision 100 per cent because I was unsure about taking Stuart Kennedy off because of his pace and he could defend well, but he convinced me that the best course of action was to get John McMaster on so he can supply a telling pass or get a shot away. At the end of the day, he and Gordon Strachan did just that with their free kick. Alex had worked with the lads on that routine the day before. To keep going at Bayern after we went 2-1 down was amazing.'

Eleven minutes after Aberdeen's double substitution the pattern of the game altered, and the history of the club changed forever. For those of us lucky enough to be there that night it's two minutes of football that will never be forgotten. Pittodrie went berserk. First came the infamous free-kick routine which led to Aberdeen's equaliser. If you watch the game back, and listen carefully to the crowd, just as Gordon Strachan and John McMaster run past the ball in a well-rehearsed act, there are clearly audible groans and moans from the Pittodrie crowd – everybody was fooled – apart from those involved. Gordon Strachan takes up the story. 'It was just one of those things that evolved from training. I think there was one routine where I had my hand on the ball and attempted a cross from a bending position, almost like a squat position, so the idea just came from one of those many different routines. I have always said that free kick created two goals. For the goal itself from the free kick, we had to get everything right. I do believe Bayern were still in shock. They were blaming the goalkeeper, they were blaming the centre-halves, complaining about where they were standing. They were still arguing when we scored the third goal. They lost focus. I believe that free kick cost them two goals.'

John McMaster continues, 'The routine had actually been discussed the previous summer – that's when it was created, coming back from the post-season and working on some routines during pre-season training. The boss and Archie Knox had the original idea; it nearly came off in a previous game. Gordon Strachan and I were always wary of the routine and when to use it. If you remember, we were the only team that sent two players out to take corners, Gordon and myself. That all had to change, though, as two certain teams from Glasgow started complaining that two players were off the park at the same time. Gordon and I were as thick as thieves, so we knew each other's games inside out; to be fair we were all like that! I always knew if I pinged a diagonal ball across the park one of my teammates would be on hand to collect the pass. That is how much we were tuned into each other.

'The reasoning for that was to get the ball forward quicker to Eric Black, Mark McGhee and Peter Weir on the wing; there was plenty of space to get the ball in behind the Bayern defence. It was a stroke of genius from the boss! So, the free-kick routine; it happened almost as soon as I got on the park. Gordon gets the ball, places it down, takes a quick look at me and says, "We're f**king this one up, Spammer" (John's nickname). Now, we are playing in the biggest game that any of us had played in before and it couldn't have worked any better against one of the biggest teams in the world. To this day I am convinced the super-efficient Germans were floored by that equaliser. Pittodrie erupted; it's by far the best atmosphere I have ever experienced in my life at Pittodrie.'

The grateful recipient of that move was central defender Alex McLeish, whose header had too much for Bayern keeper Manfred Müller. 'We practised the move on the training ground but, sometimes, players have a bit of a laugh about it and don't actually believe they can pull it off. The trigger was quite a simple one. It was the only opportunity to do it in the game as we had not received any free kicks in and around that part of the pitch beforehand, and we just knew in that moment we were going to do it! That moment when John and Gordon appear to mess up and then chastise each other, that is when I knew, in that precise moment, I had to reset myself quickly as I knew Gordon was going to deliver the ball in within the next millisecond. Gordon makes a slight movement with his right hand towards John, so we knew, in the middle, that this was going to be the dummy routine. The instruction must have come from the boss and Archie Knox on the bench to go ahead and attempt the free kick.'

John Hewitt also recalls that moment vividly. 'Alex's goal was something we had worked on in training beforehand. If you look back at the TV footage you will see that I am right underneath him; he gave me a shout so, in turn, I ducked a little bit to give him the room to attack it and get his head on the delivery. We knew as soon as Gordon and John went through that free-kick routine it was time to react. Gordon just turns around and whips in a great ball and big Alex gets up, heads it in and now it's two-each; game on!'

Most of us had not even taken our seats when Pittodrie erupted again. It took less than a minute for arguably the greatest moment the stadium has ever seen – John Hewitt's winning goal v Bayern Munich. He recalls vividly, 'The ball ended up with John McMaster and I clearly recall the flight of the ball heading towards Eric, and Eric getting a header towards goal. I was looking at John and I watched him ping a diagonal ball into the 18-yard box. My first reaction was to turn and head towards Eric looking for any knock-down or any scraps; anything really. As it happened, Eric got up so well and managed to get a great header in. I must be honest; I thought the goalkeeper was going to tip it over the bar. It looked comfortable enough for the keeper to save it. He should have flipped it over the bar, but he got it all wrong and palmed it downwards. Looking back, I came in a touch too early as my standing leg went from underneath me and I slipped, but thankfully I have managed to get my left leg round enough to make contact and luckily for me it has gone straight through the keeper's legs and into the back of the net.'

Everybody went mental; wild celebrations shook the very foundations of the stadium – what a moment. If the feelings were one of jubilation in the stands, it was just as exciting on the pitch. It's a memory that has never slipped from John's mind. 'I really can't remember what I was thinking but I do recall the chaos; Gordon was running about jumping all over the place. I recall running back to the centre circle and looking up at the main stand and blowing my wife a kiss and thinking to myself, "Please, let this be the winner." It was then a case of really concentrating and keeping our focus for the remainder of the game. It felt like an age until full time because we knew Bayern would throw the kitchen sink at us and really have a go in the closing stages. But in that final spell, we kept the ball well. Coming on as a sub I had fresh legs, so I was able to collect the ball and run at them, get by them and maybe gain a foul here and there which would slow the play right down. That last-minute challenge at the end of the game; I knew it was coming so I decided to stay down and waste some time.'

The closing minutes felt like an age, and nerves were torn to shreds. Grown men and women held their hands to their faces, some looking away, most standing in awe of what was about to happen. Folk were screaming at the ref to blow the whistle; then the full-time whistle pierced the night sky. What a beautiful sound. It took a moment to sink in, then bedlam. Please indulge me just for a moment while I cast my own mind back. My mum grabbed me and hugged me tight; I could feel my dad hugging both of us. I can still hear him saying to my mum, 'We did it, we did it!' I do not think that will ever leave me. I wish I could explain the emotions to you, but it's nigh on impossible. I cannot find the words. John Hewitt attempts to sum up those moments just after the referee blew his whistle: 'Full time was just unbelievable. I was fortunate to watch Aberdeen growing up as a kid; I used to go and stand and watch them in the old Beach End, and I have been fortunate enough to play for the club, and there is absolutely no comparison to that day. I genuinely believe there has not been an atmosphere like it at Pittodrie since that night against Bayern. Right from the word go the fans got right behind the team. From start to finish they were absolutely magnificent, and the place was heaving; fans jumping on the track, coming on to the pitch – it was an unforgettable night!'

Not long after the final whistle Alex Ferguson and his men discovered that Aberdeen were the only British team to make it through to the final stages of a European competition that season after Liverpool and Aston Villa went out of the European Cup and Dundee United slid out of the UEFA Cup. Once all the excitement had died down and the fans had long since left, Alex Ferguson met the gathered media to offer his thoughts on the game and Aberdeen's marvellous victory. He confessed once 2-1 down that he believed Aberdeen would 'go out'. He went on to say, 'We've played better than this. But it was marvellous the way we fought back twice to level the score and then win.' Fergie's substitutions that night proved to be nothing short of a tactical masterstroke which was a topic also discussed during his post-match press conference. 'Substitutions are a manager's nightmare,' Fergie said. 'Sometimes they come off and on other occasions they do not. The changes I made, bringing on John McMaster for Stuart Kennedy and John Hewitt for Neil Simpson worked. I then had all my positive players on the field, but when we went 3-2 ahead, I wished we could get Kennedy and Simpson back on. Grit and determination won the game for us and what we have got to get right now is the balance of skill.'

Bayern Munich skipper Paul Breitner was full of praise for Aberdeen after the game and admitted he believed the Dons could now go on to win the trophy. He was quoted as saying, 'The Cup Winners' Cup was the trophy I wanted most this season now that I have decided to retire. We played as well as we could, and we thought the game was over when we were 2-1 up with less than quarter of an hour to go. But Aberdeen still had some strength in reserve. In my opinion they are good enough to win this cup, and I hope they do.' Bayern's president Willi O. Hoffmann also heaped praise on Alex Ferguson's men. He said, 'I've been associated with the club for many years now, but I don't think we have had a harder game against any club. Aberdeen must be the best side in Europe at the moment and they have the ability and fight needed to lift the cup.'

There was another, less thought-of, incentive for the club to reach the semi-finals – the financial consideration. For the club to reportedly show any sort of profit from the campaign a semi-final berth was a must. It was reported nearer the time that the club made a loss of £10,000 when the squad flew to Switzerland for the Sion game and even more so when the team faced the long trips to Albania and Poland. It was also reported at the time that the cost of a charter flight out of Dyce Airport would cost the club around £20,000, but the club had no issues when budgeting for this type of luxury because the well-being and comfort of the players was at the forefront of the thinking when it came to a successful campaign. I think it is safe to say, this was money very well spent.

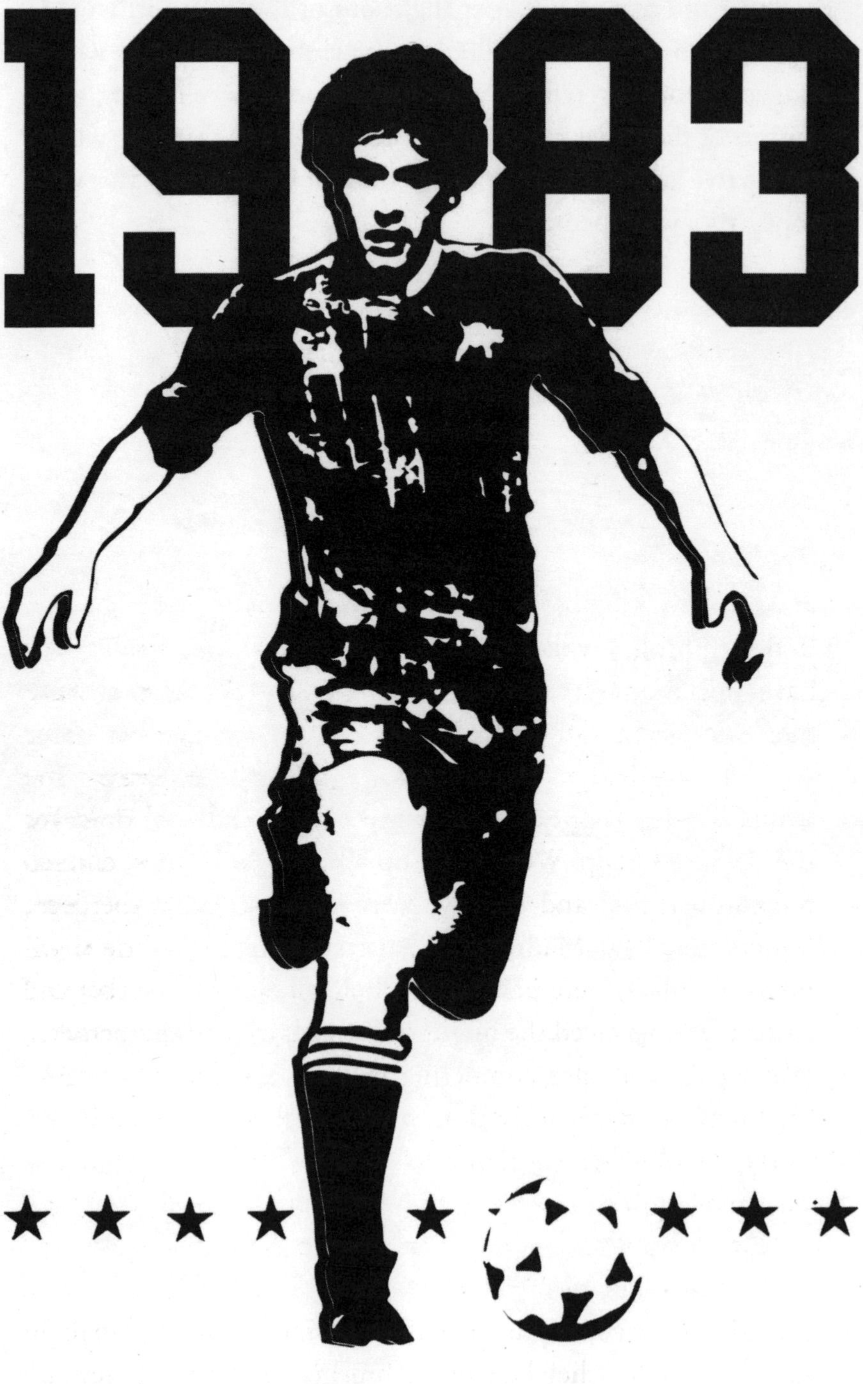
1983

SEVEN

WATERSCHEI

'I don't think I will thank you for Waterschei. Anderlecht have not beaten them for four years and Waterschei have put Anderlecht out of the Belgian Cup for the last three years. I have had reports they are unbeatable at home.' The words of Alex Ferguson on the eve of the semi-final draw for the 1982/83 Cup Winners' Cup. Thirty-four clubs entered the competition, and now we were down to four: Aberdeen, Waterschei, Real Madrid and Austria Vienna. For the semi-finals Aberdeen were paired with Belgian club Waterschei and Austria Vienna faced the might of Real Madrid. Like Aberdeen, Waterschei were also competing in their first European semi-final having impressively disposed of Paris Saint-Germain 3-2 in the quarter-finals despite being 2-0 down from the first leg. The small club from Genk, with a population of 63,000, had only in recent years progressed to the top flight in Belgium and entered the Cup Winners' Cup having beaten Beveren 2-1 in their domestic cup final. Since their promotion to the top flight in 1978, Waterschei had never finished higher than seventh place in the league. This though didn't stop Alex Ferguson and Archie Knox from doing their due diligence.

Both travelled to Genk to have their Belgian opponents watched and assessed. Archie mentioned in the match-day programme that they both paid particular attention to Waterschei's set pieces as well as the Belgians' way of defending, system and general style of play. Archie also believed that for Aberdeen to triumph they had to play the game 'the Scottish way'. He observed: 'The mistake Scottish sides have made is trying to adapt their game too much when they were involved in Europe. You can't have a set of players who play one way every week of the season and then expect them to be able to turn it on at the drop of a hat in another sort of way.' Alex Ferguson drilled home the message that their opponents must not be underestimated and that they deserved the 'utmost respect'. He said in his programme notes ahead of the game, 'I have been over to watch them carefully and I have been left with the impression they will be difficult to master because their manager is a clever guiding hand behind them. Our visitors may not be among the best-known teams in Europe's soccer scene, but supporters can rest assured that they are a very comprehensive squad who are technically sound and have an admirable attitude towards their responsibilities.'

With both Archie Knox and Alex Ferguson having observed Waterschei up close and personal on two separate occasions, a dossier was drawn up for the players to study outside of training. The first dossier documented Waterschei's 'general system and style of play'. It read: 'Their normal system is three markers with a sweeper, four midfield players and two strikers. The midfield varied slightly in the two games we have seen them play. In the game away at Brugge they played with the four across the middle. In the home game against Tongeren, Pierre Plessers played slightly further forward of left midfield.

The strength of this team is most definitely in their teamwork as opposed to any outstanding individual play. They look to keep possession with the minimum of chasing about. Every player shows a willingness to be involved in possession and this stems from the confidence that this team are displaying at the moment.

'They took chances with their possession against Tongeren and this looked to be over-confidence. In both games when defending they certainly challenged in the middle of the park, preferring to shut up shop in those areas rather than let the opposition into the penalty area. Their markers are prepared to move positions in order to keep tight against their opponents; attacking midfield player will cover back area if two of the markers get caught in the same position. In midfield all the players are very aware when changing positions; they hardly ever got caught having two players in the one area. The front two move well to get themselves on the ball but they need players to support them as neither player is very strong.'

Just as a point of interest, former world number 1 tennis player Kim Clijsters' father Lei played for Waterschei against Aberdeen in both games. Alex Ferguson and Archie Knox noted this about his style of play. 'Played sweeper in both games and played this role really well. Has the ability to sense when he should be giving cover to the other back players and when to come out against a player breaking through. Does not swap over with the other back players when an opponent is breaking through but comes right out against that player. He never allowed a situation to develop where an opponent came close to the penalty area before he came out. He was always out at the first sign of the opposition having an extra player in midfield. He did this more confidently in the home game. In both games was prepared to either drive forward when he was on the ball or go into midfield to receive a pass from the markers or come forward as an extra player when the ball was in front of him. Aggressive player who has the ability to influence others.'

That night of the game, 6 April 1983, Aberdeen played the Scottish way with power, pace and penetration aplenty. The Belgians simply couldn't cope. The tone for the game was set before kick-off. There is fantastic footage on YouTube as the teams enter the tunnel area from the dressing room. Just watch the sheer determination on Willie Miller's face as he and his colleagues wait to enter the field of play. There is a fortitude to his body language which suggests Aberdeen were never in any danger that night. Alex Ferguson's men got off to the perfect start despite the weight of expectation on their shoulders that spring evening. Striker Eric Black explains more: 'From a provincial club point of view, we had become favourites to get through that tie as everybody was now sitting up and taking notice of us after we had put Bayern Munich out of the competition. To score the early goal, and then another not long after, was more of a relief personally speaking. To win a semi-final of a European competition 5-1 is almost ridiculous. We had put ourselves in such a strong position and it was a phenomenal achievement – I think that spoke for the mentality of the players. Even though we overran Waterschei that night, it wasn't something I got overly carried away with. I was still a young man, living the dream if you like. I was always of the opinion that we played, we won a cup, I would go on holiday, I would come back and play, and we would win a cup again, or the league. I thought that's how it worked up until I left!'

Midfielder Neil Simpson, who had been a rock in midfield all campaign, recalls the mood in the Aberdeen camp in the days leading up to the game: 'We were feeling fairly positive even though we had lost our previous league game against St Mirren at Pittodrie on the Saturday. The attitude was almost like, well, that game has gone, we now have a European semi-final to concentrate on and it was rare for us to lose two games in a row. My main recollection of the days leading up to the game was just thinking what a fantastic opportunity we had to get to a major European final. The afternoon of the game Fergie had phoned the fire brigade and asked them to come down and water the pitch because that time of the year the pitch was bobbly and hard so the fire brigade spent a good while watering the pitch, leaving it nice and skiddy, which meant we could knock the ball about and get the ball moving quicker across the surface. The mood was positive despite the fact that we had lost the previous Saturday, which in effect cost us the league title that season.'

Eric Black had put the Dons ahead exactly one minute 22 seconds into the game, but then just two minutes and six seconds after Waterschei kicked off again, Aberdeen scored a second. Neil Simpson takes up the story of his magnificent solo goal: 'It was just my momentum taking me forward to be honest. I didn't think that I had a chance of scoring here; my first thought was that I could intercept the ball. I was watching how that move was developing and when the Waterschei player won the ball I could read that he was away to pass the ball, so my instinct was to try and intercept the pass. My first touch took me to an area where the same player who I had intercepted the pass from was coming in from my left, so I was able to control the ball and move inside him which then in turn meant I gave myself enough distance between myself and the next defender to be able to move the ball to my right and skip past him. Then I realised that the goal was right there in front of me and I was inside the 18-yard box ready to get my shot off. My effort at goal wasn't a trundler but I had given it enough that the power of the shot had too much for their goalkeeper, and when it hit the back of the net that's when I set off on my celebration run – that was a great moment.'

Aberdeen went into half-time two goals to the good and in complete control of the game. Neil recalls the instructions from Alex Ferguson and Archie Knox during the 15-minute break. 'It was just about more of the same. The only word he kept using was "intensity": they will not be used to it, get at them, quick throw-ins, quick free kicks and keep the game high impact. It was all about keeping that element to our game going in the second period. Thankfully, that's exactly what we did because we added a third and then a fourth 20 minutes after the start of the second half.'

Aberdeen even had time to add a fifth when Mark McGhee scrambled home his effort after a good old-fashioned 'stramash' inside the Belgians' six-yard box with just seven minutes left on the clock. Waterschei had no answer for Aberdeen that night as the Dons ran out 5-1 winners. Nobody expected that type of result in a European semi-final; Aberdeen were the talk of the town. Not surprisingly a delighted Alex Ferguson said after the game, 'I stated beforehand I'd be happy to take a one-goal lead to Belgium. We produced superb form to give us the advantage we wanted. While nothing will be taken for granted, we obviously travel there confident of reaching our first ever European final. I couldn't have asked for more from my players. Doug Bell was magnificent and proved me right by his attitude throughout the game. He was tiring badly when I took him off and it was important then for us to consolidate our position. In the second leg we must play to the Bayern plan that has proved so successful for us in the past.'

Meanwhile Fergie's counterpart in the dugout, Waterschei manager Ernst Künnecke, dismissed his side's chances of reaching the final by saying, 'We have no chance whatsoever. We can make a game of it in Genk, but I cannot see any team scoring four goals against Aberdeen. They simply swept us aside. In fact, I feel it will be two or three years before I can have my team able to play in that type of fashion. The scoreline tonight was a clear indication of the difference in standards between the two sides. As far as I can see the second leg will be a formality.' There were many football dignitaries in attendance at Pittodrie that night to watch Aberdeen sweep Waterschei aside, including former England manager Alf Ramsey, current Scotland manager Jock Stein and, more interestingly, Real Madrid coach Luis Molowny, who said this of Aberdeen after the game: 'I was very impressed by the power, strength and ability of Aberdeen of whom we do not know that much in Spain. If it turns out to be a Real v Aberdeen final, I expect it to be very difficult for us judging by the Aberdeen performance tonight.' Like the Bayern victory, the Aberdeen fans stayed behind long after the full-time whistle in the hope of seeing their heroes take another lap of honour, but this time Alex Ferguson was resolute; the players will not take to the field, despite winning 5-1; it was only half-time after all.

Waterschei's Icelandic striker Larus Gudmundsson was only 21 years old when he prepared himself for the biggest game of his club career to date. Larus had already been capped seven times by his country and was Waterschei's top goalscorer in the competition with five goals. He was a player Alex Ferguson and Archie Knox respected, and this was evident by the words used to describe his style of play in the dossier drawn up to describe each and every Waterschei player. It read, 'Excellent player, good touch and well balanced with fair pace, good skills and definitely a danger, must be watched. Just coming back from a cartilage operation.'

It was a tie that Larus and his teammates were very much looking forward to but Larus admitted, when he spoke to me for this chapter, that when the draw was made, the Belgians were hoping for a more favourable outcome. He explains, 'We were hoping for Austria Vienna; we knew Vienna well as

Austria is close to the Belgium border and we knew they didn't have the right quality to go on and win the Cup Winners' Cup. In Iceland we always followed the game in the UK; I knew how the game worked there and how tactically the game was played. We were familiar with what to expect that night at Pittodrie.'

Once the draw was made, Waterschei manager Ernst Künnecke sent his spies to watch Aberdeen and started gathering their intelligence on Alex Ferguson's side. Waterschei were just as meticulous in their preparation for the semi-final, as Larus recalls: 'Our coach had watched Aberdeen before and made us familiar with their players, telling us how strong Aberdeen were; he knew about Aberdeen's mental strength; he knew they wanted to win every game. He told us we needed to be aware of a few players including Gordon Strachan and Mark McGhee. We also knew Aberdeen had a strong defence with Alex McLeish and Willie Miller. I knew what was expected but I am not sure all the Belgian players knew what was coming that night. I knew Alex McLeish and Willie Miller were both Scotland international players and that they were physically strong and very well organised. I was expecting a difficult and hard game against both. I had a cartilage operation only six weeks before the Aberdeen game. I knew I wanted to play but I wasn't 100 per cent fit; I wasn't in my best shape. It most certainly affected my performance that night.'

Coming into this game, Waterschei recorded what could be argued as their finest result after coming from 2-0 down to beat Paris Saint-Germain 3-2 over two legs in the quarter-finals. It was a huge result for the club from Genk. Larus explains the mood in the Belgian camp as they prepared for the first game at Pittodrie. 'We had played so well against Paris Saint-Germain, especially in the second game. We had a lot of confidence coming into the Aberdeen game, and we really believed we could win the game at Pittodrie. The start of the game was so disappointing because we had prepared very well for the game and we honestly believed we were going to have a great night, but instead we go a goal down in the first minute. We were strong defensively and hit teams on the counter-attack. We were surprised to go a goal down so quickly in the game. When Aberdeen scored their second goal, I already thought the game was over. It was quite common for us to only concede one or two goals if we lost a game. Aberdeen were so motivated that night and they were so physically aggressive. I just felt, right from the beginning of the game, that we had no chance. That was my professional feeling; I knew it was going to be a difficult night. Our coach was very experienced; he was a great coach. At half-time all he did was attempt to motivate us to try and score a goal in the second half and not to lose our spirit. He did and said all the right things during the break, but as I said Aberdeen were so motivated and their fans were so passionate that it made the atmosphere difficult for us.'

It was to get worse for the Belgians when Aberdeen went 3-0 up on 68 minutes thanks to Mark McGhee's deft flick at the front post and only two minutes after that the Dons added a fourth when Mark McGhee this time played provider and crossed for Peter Weir to head home. The Belgians looked dead on their feet and broken with 20 minutes still left to play. Larus though did pull one back for Waterschei on 75 minutes after he headed home from a tight angle. If you watch back at the footage, Larus does not celebrate his goal, and there is a sense of resignation in his body language. He explains, 'I think I was still in shock; after we went 3-0 down, we really felt the strength of Aberdeen. In my mind I knew that this goal would help us, but I was still afraid that we could concede one or two further goals. I really didn't get the feeling when you know you have a chance after I scored; the spirit wasn't there which was unusual for Waterschei, because we normally had such great spirit. On the night we were missing one of our key defenders, Pierre Plessers, so we had to move our holding midfielder, Lei Clijsters into central defence but he wasn't used to playing that position, so we were a little out of shape.'

In between the first leg and return leg in Belgium, Aberdeen faced both sides of the Old Firm. Rangers won 2-1 at Ibrox, but the Dons came through a brutal Scottish Cup semi-final against Celtic, having won the game 1-0 thanks to a 65th-minute Peter Weir header. Aberdeen travelled to Brussels and then made the 93-kilometre trip east to Genk on the Tuesday ahead of the game without Neale Cooper, Eric Black, Dougie Bell and Gordon Strachan, who all suffered injuries at Hampden. The travelling party stayed in the Dutch city of Maastricht and then travelled the half an hour journey by bus to the game. With the Dons protecting a 5-1 advantage, most believed the tie was already over; there was a formality to the game as Larus recalls: 'That game was more like a friendly game. We all knew after the first game that it was almost impossible to turn the result around. The game wasn't aggressive at all. We were so disappointed after the first game that we decided to try and play to our absolute best for our fantastic fans and go out of the competition with some respect. One-nil was a good result for us on our home ground. After we played Aberdeen, we saw how strong they were, and Gordon Strachan went on to become one of my all-time favourite players; I loved him as a player. We knew Aberdeen had some skilful players and even though Real Madrid were a great team, they were not as physically strong as Aberdeen. I expected Real Madrid to win the game but have a very tough 90 minutes against Aberdeen, but in my heart, I was supporting Aberdeen. I honestly thought they could win the game. We knew how brilliant Alex Ferguson was as a coach, and we just had to look at him to see that star quality in him. He was on a different level and we could really see that in those early days at Aberdeen.' Larus finished the Cup Winners' Cup campaign with six goals to his name, joint second with Mark McGhee. He played for Waterschei for one more season before heading to the German Bundesliga for a number of years with Bayer Uerdingen and 1. FC Kaiserslautern before heading back home to Iceland where he played out his career. Larus gained 17 international caps for Iceland, scoring three goals between 1980 and 1987.

Recently a friend of mine, Ally Stuart, reminded me of a story he once told when working as a taxi driver in Aberdeen. During the 2004 UEFA European Championships, Ally picked up a gentleman from the airport who had travelled to the city for work. This gentleman so happened to have played against Aberdeen for Waterschei and proceeded to tell Ally his story. After the draw was made, Ernst Künnecke made the Waterschei players watch hours of video footage and told them all to concentrate their efforts mainly on Gordon Strachan. 'There was never any mention of Dougie Bell,' the gentleman told Ally. 'Mr Künnecke had no idea who Dougie Bell was,' he continued. As he paid his fare to Ally, having arrived safely at his destination, he left Ally with these words: 'Dougie f**king Bell – we all knew who he was by half-time.'

After the game, Alex Ferguson reflected: 'Losing our undefeated record was a disappointment but we are delighted to be in a European final. We had our chances to win the game in the early stages of the second half, but we didn't take them and paid the penalty.' He went on to say, 'The result was disappointing on the night as we should have won convincingly. That was our first defeat in the cup and the boys were all dejected – changed days from when we used to do somersaults after a draw at Ibrox or Celtic Park. At the meal afterwards, I toasted the players with champagne and congratulated them on a magnificent achievement in reaching the final. We were all very proud of them.' Waterschei coach Ernst Künnecke commented, 'We knew that we couldn't beat Aberdeen after the first leg, but we were determined to at least win the return game, and I'm glad that we gave our own supporters something to cheer about.' He finished off by saying, 'I wish Aberdeen all the best in the final because they certainly deserve to be there.' Neil Simpson also recalls the immediate post-match period. 'It was like a morgue in the dressing room after the game; we were all very disappointed we had lost our unbeaten record in the competition. There were a few "well dones" going around and a few pats on the back, but by and large the feeling was one of disappointment. From a personal point of view, I had not said anything before the game, but I felt like I had a touch of the flu. I could feel the shivers coming on, but I wanted to play because I had played in every game before that – that's the things you do to make sure you play in these big games. I played the entire game but went straight to my bed as soon as we got back to the hotel; I really didn't feel well.' Despite the obvious disappointment of losing their unbeaten record, Aberdeen had reached their first ever major European final. Just as a point of interest, to finish this chapter off, Neil travelled back to Genk and visited the site of the old stadium to complete his UEFA pro licence qualification in 2018. The stadium is now the home of KRC Genk after Waterschei and KFC Winterslag merged in 1988.

Next up, the 1983 Cup Winners' Cup final v Real Madrid and a date with destiny.

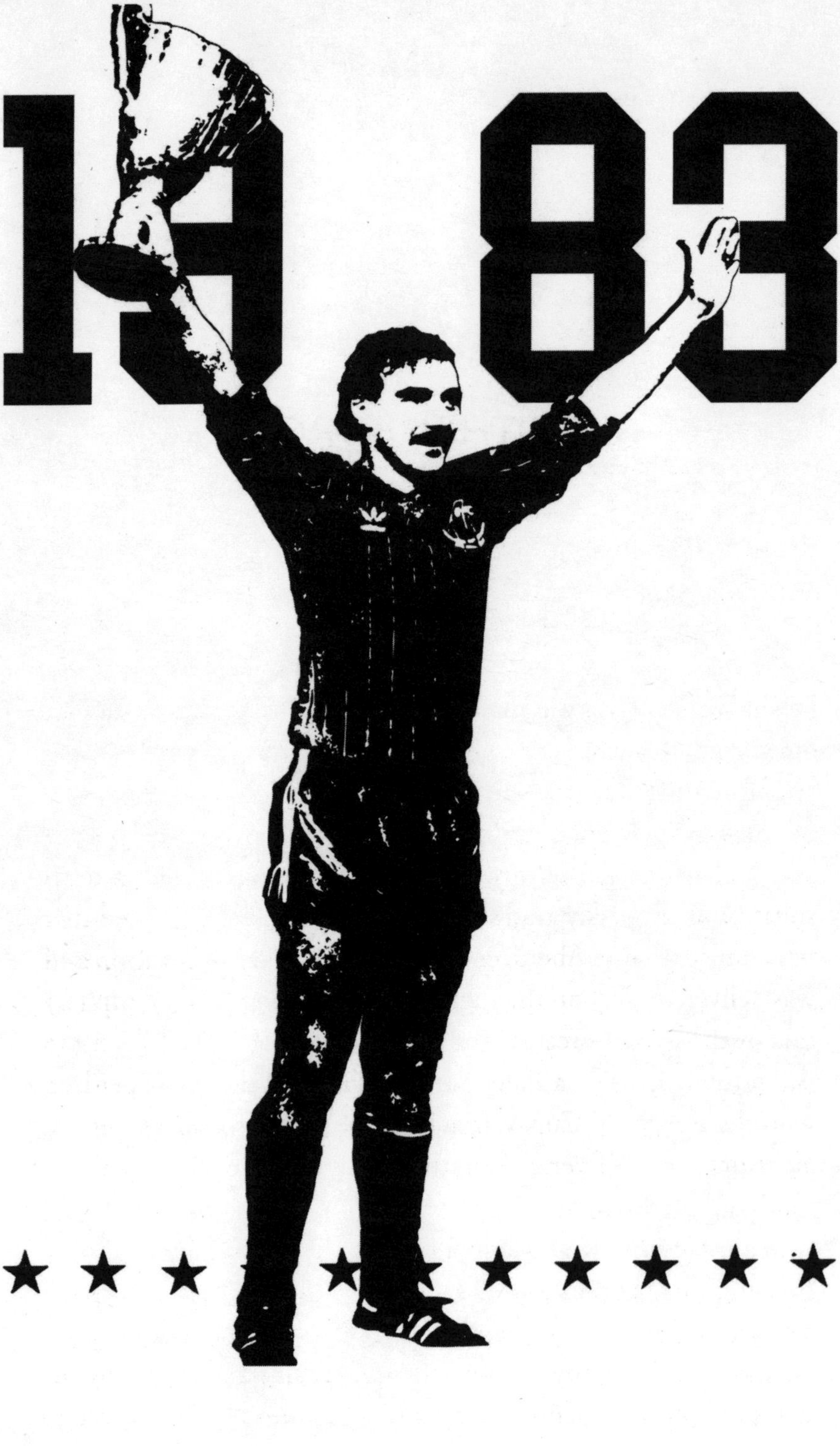
1983

EIGHT

GOTHENBURG

Legendary Real Madrid manager, the late Alfredo Di Stefano, sat quietly, and his words and tone were one of disappointment. He attempted to offer the waiting press more, but his delivery was one of struggle. Then, with head almost bowed, he looked up and said, 'Aberdeen have what money can't buy: a soul, a team spirit built in family tradition.' He then left. It is a quote that has come to define Aberdeen Football Club as an institution and was delivered aptly on the night of the club's greatest triumph by one of the game's greatest ambassadors. The date 11 May 1983 is, and will remain, a date like no other; it's the day Aberdeen won the European Cup Winners' Cup, the most magnificent of all triumphs. The venue was the wonderful Ullevi Stadium in Gothenburg, Sweden.

Spanish giants Real Madrid had not won a European trophy for 17 years, but in Alfredo Di Stefano they had a manager who was hoping to stir emotions that had been lost on Real Madrid fans for many years on the European stage. Knowing the competition well, Señor Di Stefano was gunning for his second

Cup Winners' Cup triumph in the space of three years having won the trophy with Valencia in 1980. En route to the final, Real Madrid had beaten Romanian side Baia Mare 5-2, Ujpest Dozsa 4-1, Inter Milan 3-2 and Austria Vienna in the semi-finals 5-3 on aggregate. They came into the final as firm favourites. Despite this tag Señor Di Stefano was full of respect for Aberdeen, and in particular one flame-haired midfielder. 'Everybody's telling me about Gordon Strachan, and he had a good World Cup in a very difficult group, but if you start worrying about Strachan, you'll find that a man you know nothing about will score three goals against you. Football teams aren't just about one man. The good teams are the ones that rely on all 11 men – not just one. Aberdeen are one of those teams. They're going to give us a good game. You reckon it might be important that I've got more experience of European finals than Alex Ferguson? That's rubbish! You won't see Di Stefano or Ferguson on the scoresheet in Gothenburg. The players are the ones who are going to win or lose that game, just the same way as any other. I was very cautious about Waterschei. I'd sized them up as a very good, solid outfit that would give us a lot of problems. That 5-1 win by Aberdeen at Pittodrie was a big surprise to me.' Di Stefano finished off his pre-match thoughts by saying this when asked about Real Madrid's chances in the game. 'Confident of winning? If we weren't, we'd stay in Madrid and save the air fares!'

From the Spanish press there were mixed reports, but most believed the trophy would be heading back to the Spanish capital and the Bernabeu Stadium. One newspaper, for example, reported that Real Madrid 'will take the trophy back to Madrid at the expense of the brave Scots'. Another newspaper called upon Real's former glories in Europe to help get them across the line against Aberdeen: 'Real are past masters in European fields. They have been over such big games like this so many times. In Sweden they will be expected to draw on their previous experience which should be enough to see off Aberdeen, who are making their first appearance in a European final.' But some members of the Spanish press were not so dismissive of Aberdeen's chances in the game, and one paper commented: 'The Scots should not be underestimated. They show great passion and spirit, typical of the British style. Madrid should have enough class to counter the Scots' determination and battling character. Aberdeen did beat Munich on the way to the final so any side that can master the Germans will have to be shown respect.'

Aberdeen manager Alex Ferguson left no stone unturned when it came to the detailed preparation for what was the biggest test of his football life. As commander-in-chief he was ready and fully prepared to face battle, a very modern David v Goliath encounter. The preparations for the game began as soon as Aberdeen secured their place in the final. Aberdeen's second leg encounter against Waterschei was unusually scheduled for a Tuesday night, which meant the very next morning Alex Ferguson was able to fly directly to Madrid from Brussels to watch Real Madrid host Austria Vienna in the semi-final second leg. After observing Real Madrid comfortably beat Vienna 3-1, Ferguson phoned Archie Knox and said, 'We've a hell of a chance, I'm telling you. What a chance we've got.' From that point forward Ferguson and Knox never wavered in their belief that Aberdeen had every chance of beating Real Madrid on their day. But the preparation didn't come without its difficulties as assistant manager Archie Knox now explains when attempting to watch Real play against Valencia the weekend ahead of the final. 'I went on the day of the game. I flew from Aberdeen to London and from London to Alicante and hired a car to drive up to Valencia. While I was driving, I noticed there wasn't a single soul passing me in other cars and I started to wonder if I had got lost. Not long after I discovered I was on a new toll road and none of the locals used it as they didn't want to pay.

On the way up my car broke down and these are the days before mobile phones remember, so I had to wait until the car would restart which thankfully it did. By the time I got to Valencia I was running late; I needed to get to the hotel, shower and change and then meet the Real Madrid representatives and travel with them on the team bus to the game. When I got to the hotel some Real Madrid directors, a couple of players and some of the coaching staff were already waiting in the hotel foyer. I checked in and asked for my tickets for the game, but the receptionist told me there were no tickets for me. I decided I would just head to the stadium to see if my ticket had been left there. I quickly went to my room, got changed into my Aberdeen suit and tie, came back down and the bus had already left. I arranged with a taxi driver to get me as close as he could to the stadium, but we hit traffic about a mile and a half away from the stadium and kick-off was only a few minutes away, so I decided to jump out of the taxi and run to the stadium.

'I got to the stadium five minutes after kick-off, and I am looking for the directors' entrance which I eventually found. I explained who I was and why I was there but once again, no tickets. By this point 15 minutes had already been played in the game and I am walking around the stadium trying to find my tickets. I knew I had to get into the stadium, so I managed to get past the stewards and ran up the stairs. Those same stewards came running after me, grabbed me, put my arms around my back and frogmarched me out of the ground. I saw some local policemen outside and I went over and asked for help. I explained who I was and what I was doing and one of them took pity on me as he was a big football fan. He told me to follow him and while he was talking to and distracting the stewards, I had to run back up the same stairs as quickly as I could. That's exactly what I did! I managed to get myself to a position near a barrier where I was able to watch the game through some guy's legs as he was standing a level above me and take my notes on the game! When the full-time whistle blew, all I wanted to do was get out and get to the nearest pub, have a couple of pints and then make my way back to the hotel. When I got back to the hotel there was a knock on the door from one of the receptionists who handed me an envelope, and on the envelope were the words, "Billy McNeill, Celtic Football Club". The clubs had obviously completely confused the situation and who was supposed to come to the game and must have believed Billy was coming and not me, hence why I never received my own ticket for the game!'

Alex Ferguson and Archie also had to deal with issues closer to home. Before flying out to Sweden, Ferguson had one huge decision to make. He once said of full-back Stuart Kennedy: 'He epitomised everything that Aberdeen was all about back then. He was as dedicated a professional as I had come across.' The Gothenburg story, as wonderful as it is, does not come without its tale of woe. Since signing for the Dons back in June 1976, Stuart was a regular in the side and a hugely popular figure in the dressing room. He was a fitness fanatic. Against Waterschei in the Cup Winners' Cup semi-final second leg, Stuart caught his studs in the running track which ran around the pitch and damaged his knee. Something which, although it looked so innocuous at the time, sadly ended his career. That, though, didn't stop Ferguson naming Stuart as a non-playing substitute for the final. Full-back John McMaster remembers that time well and openly confessed that if Stuart had been fit to play, John would have missed out against Real Madrid, as he explains: 'Stuart would have played and I would have been on the bench! As players we all knew our place. The boss wanted the aerial threat from big Doug Rougvie at left-back which would have been balanced by Stuart's fitness levels at right-back. Two weeks before the final, Stuart needed to go for some minor surgery due to some problems he was having with his knee. Unfortunately for him, he couldn't get back to doing what he normally did, which was making those bursting runs up and down the right touchline. The problem was he was attempting to kid the boss while doing all these runs here and there. It was an attempt to let the boss think he was fine, but the boss knew! Sir Alex took a hold of him one day and asked him to join him out on the park at Pittodrie, and he asked Stuart to do two sprints up to the halfway line and back. After the sprints, the boss grabbed a hold of him and pulled him in really close and said to him, "Gonna stop all this f**king nonsense. I'm going to put you on the bench, so stop trying to impress me because I know that your knee is f**ked. You are going on the bench because of everything that you have done for us." Stuart came into the dressing room and told us what the boss had just said to him, and we were all stunned, but in a good way may I add. That was a fantastic move by the boss to do that; for me, that was a work of art. By doing that, the boss relieved that tension regarding Stuart playing in the game because we did wonder. The boss put a stop to that which gave us all a lift because we knew Stuart was going to be a part of the squad.'

It wasn't just Stuart Kennedy who gave the boss cause for concern. For midfielder Dougie Bell his dreams all came crashing down after the Dons played Celtic in the Scottish Cup semi-final at Hampden Park. It was a game not for the faint-hearted, and players were going down like skittles, which forced the already injured midfielder to soldier on for 90 minutes. On the bus on the way home, Dougie's ankle started to swell to the point where it was becoming a serious concern. The next day, Ferguson and Knox arrived at his house in the Bridge of Don to take him to the hospital where a very badly sprained ankle was diagnosed. For the next ten days Dougie had to endure a plaster which at the time appeared to have the desired effect until the Sunday before the final. Fergie had organised a bounce game at

Easter Road to check in on Dougie's fitness as well as that of Eric Black. At half-time Archie told him that Fergie was thinking about starting him against Real Madrid, so he needed to do a bit more in the second half. With Archie's words ringing in his ears, Dougie upped his game and began those marauding runs for which he was starting to make a name for himself. Then disaster struck. Dougie was caught by Paul Kane and the ankle which had caused him so much grief went again. He was devastated and out of the side. Eric Black though came through the test and was available for selection.

Twenty-four hours later and with the team now camped up at their base in Kungälv, a small town just outside Gothenburg, the lads trained without Dougie who desperately wanted to be part of it all. He was that desperate he even considered a request to the medical staff for a painkilling injection. That request fell on deaf ears and then came the moment he knew he wasn't going to make it. 'Fergie took me to one side and said, "Look, I'm really sorry but you'll miss the final." I asked him if I could get an injection so he could at least put me on the bench, and I could maybe come on for half an hour or so, but he said no as he wanted to put Stuart Kennedy on the bench. He did say that my chance will come again as he believed in me and my game. I was extremely disappointed but that is just the way it is.' For Dougie, his solace came in the shape of the legendary figure of Jock Stein who had travelled with the team to Sweden after an invitation from the boss. 'When I first found out about Stuart, I must be honest, I was a bit sick, but Mr Stein was great. When we were travelling on the team bus to the stadium, he sat beside me and he said I had done a lot to get the team here, which meant a lot to me as this was the Scotland manager telling me I had played my part getting the team to the final, so it really meant a great deal.'

Those were two injuries that Alex Ferguson was fully aware of, but behind the scenes two further players were having their own issues. Central defender Alex McLeish takes up the story of how he nearly missed the biggest game in the club's history. 'At the time I lived up in Westhill and we had paving stones delivered to the front of the house. I made the mistake of lifting the paving stones and carrying them, on my own, to the back of the house. I had convinced myself by then that I was a big, strong guy having done a good deal of weight training in the gym. I took about six of them through and my next-door neighbour, who was a painter and decorator by trade, said to me: "Alex, you will do your back in doing that; you are supposed to roll them." Next day my back was in bits. Roland Arnott [Aberdeen's former physio] got battered right into it. I had missed the Kilmarnock game, which was our last game before the final, so Roland had a good week working away trying to make sure I would be fine for the Real Madrid game. Even when we got to the "Fars Hatt" Hotel just outside Gothenburg I couldn't sleep on the bed. I had to take the mattress off the bed and place it on the floor because the feeling was so irritable. I had a deep, dull ache in my back and, after placing the mattress on the floor, I was able to get comfortable and get some sleep but, trust me, there was no way I was missing that final for love nor money.' Whispers of big Eck's back problem had started to circulate among the support and when quizzed about this by *North Tonight* presenter Frank Gilfeather as the team arrived at the stadium for the game, Alex Ferguson was quick to dismiss such rumours. He said quite sternly, 'A load of rubbish, rubbish!'

Like Alex McLeish, Aberdeen defender Doug Rougvie was another who almost missed the game due to a rather unfortunate incident – he fell off his bike. He takes up the story. 'It happened on the Saturday afternoon ahead of the final on the Wednesday. We didn't have a game that day due to playing against Kilmarnock the Thursday before. The reason I bought a bike was because I had missed a whole pre-season beforehand due to an Achilles injury, so I used to bike back and forward to Pittodrie to help in the recuperation of my Achilles. I was at the top of Kingsgate and skidded as I went around a corner. I came off the bike and fell heavily on to my hip and I immediately thought, "Oh no, I can't miss the Real Madrid game because I fell off my bloody bike!" A couple of guys in a car, which had been right beside me as I fell, stopped, picked me up, dusted me down and sent me on my way! We trained on the Sunday morning and I felt stiff due to the bruising in and around my hip. Obviously, I kept it nice and quiet and thankfully it went away – thank f**k.' Thankfully, with no lasting damage, Doug was free for selection.

The team travelled to Gothenburg on the Monday morning ahead of the final. With the lads out in the sticks, the wives meanwhile stayed in a plush hotel in the centre of town after Alex Ferguson initially joked with them all that they had to stay in an old army barracks as all the hotels were fully booked. For the lads it was a case of settling into their new surroundings and preparing for the game.

On the Tuesday Aberdeen trained on the pitch at the Ullevi Stadium. Four members of the press who had gathered at the stadium to watch the training observed that Real Madrid were only there to practise penalties – was this a statement of their intent for the night? Having arrived back at the team base, Ferguson sat with the travelling press pack to offer his thoughts ahead of the game. With Scotland manager Jock Stein in close proximity, Ferguson called upon Celtic's European Cup triumph of 1967 as a means of inspiration. He said, 'Celtic's victory was as much down to bravery as skill. They went out and had a go and I want my players to do the same. Sure, we respect Real Madrid, but we don't fear them. I don't want any of my lads to be overawed by the occasion or we might be beaten before we get started. The players have grown in confidence as we have progressed in Europe this season and I know they have tremendous belief in themselves. I want them to be positive and not sit back. Their attitude must be right.' Alex Ferguson was also quick to apply his gratitude to his assistant manager Archie Knox, who worked tirelessly behind the scenes to prepare the team. 'Archie has done a super job this season. His reports on our European opponents have been first class. We like to do our homework as thoroughly as possible and leave nothing to chance. Real had several players missing through injury the first time I saw them, and conditions were deplorable. From what I saw they have a better midfield than Bayern Munich, who are the best side we've played in Europe so far. We have a great chance. After all, we're in the final. We'll never have a better chance. We know we have no divine right to win but I feel the players will respond to the occasion and give us a really good chance. We will have five international players on the field, and they are showing no trace of nerves which will reassure the younger ones that Aberdeen can beat Real Madrid.'

Close to 15,000 hearty Aberdeen fans made the trip to Gothenburg by air, land and sea. The St Clair ferry with 500 souls departed Aberdeen harbour at 1 p.m. on Monday 9 May for the 27-hour-long trip across the North Sea, arriving safely in Gothenburg the next day. It was already proving to be the trip of a lifetime. A match ticket, depending on the location within the Ullevi Stadium, cost between £8 and £12; the cost of the entire trip averaged £200 per fan. Twenty-four extra flights, all full of Aberdeen fans, left Aberdeen Airport on the morning of the game to fly direct to Gothenburg. Some fans travelled all the way from Aberdeen to Gothenburg by coach. One group travelled 604 miles from Aberdeen to Dover, then took a 90-minute ferry crossing from Dover to Calais and from there drove another 522 miles up to Kiel in Germany with one final 14-hour, overnight ferry crossing from Kiel to Gothenburg – the trip took three days. Aberdeen fan Graham Rhind recalls his coach being fitted with bunk beds to the interior of their bus which made the long road trip to Gothenburg that little bit more comfortable, albeit they had to share with other fans. They also drove from Aberdeen to Calais and from there drove all the way to Hamburg where they nearly missed the connecting ferry to Gothenburg. Thankfully, they all made it in time for the big match. All the preparations had been done, and there was nothing left to do now but play the game.

Ferguson named his team the day before the game. While sitting in a plush banqueting hall at the team's base, he explained the reasons behind the team selection. He said, 'Eric Black has had a great season and he can score goals that no one else can score in the air. Although John Hewitt has done well for me, Black deserves his place, and he is in there on merit. I'll play Neale Cooper in the middle of the park because that's where he is at his best and not at right-back. I'm not worried at all about the full-back partnership. John McMaster can play really well in defence and big Doug Rougvie is in a position where he will feel really comfortable.' Archie Knox fully backed the team selection. 'When you are an assistant manager, you can have arguments with the manager and stuff like that but whenever the manager has made a decision which is different to your own, you have to back the manager all the way. Never in my career did I go and speak to anybody about team selection and question the manager's selection, never. It was my job to back the manager. Alex picked the team that he believed was the best team and the team that had the best chance of beating Real Madrid.'

The players were left to their own devices to prepare in their own way. The mood was one of quiet confidence. Full-back John McMaster explains whether he did anything different to the norm when it came to the final against Real Madrid. 'No, absolutely nothing at all. That is why we were so relaxed about the whole occasion. The boss organised everything – from the area where the hotel was situated to the wives joining us for the actual game. The name of the hotel was "Fars Hatt" which is Aberdonian slang for "where's that". I thought that was genius from the boss as it made the local lads feel right at home. The boss invited Jock Stein which made us all sit up and take note. We were training in the Ullevi Stadium on the Tuesday with Real Madrid on one side of the park and us on the other. The boss was worried about how we would react to Di Stefano; he was worried that we may freeze, so we are all out on the park and the boss comes walking over with Jock and we could see all the Real Madrid players looking and pointing towards Jock Stein. The boss completely turned that mindset on a sixpence; the whole mentality changed. That made us all more relaxed because the whole routine was just like any other normal game, the only difference being that we were in Sweden. The boss organised all of this, because he never wanted at any point the boys over-thinking things.'

Striker Eric Black was just 19 years old when he played against Real Madrid; he explains his emotions and feelings as the game edged closer. 'I do recall feeling nervous. We were waiting to find out from Fergie who would be starting the game. There wasn't much talk about Real Madrid from either Fergie or Archie Knox once we reached Gothenburg which, I believe, was a planned move on their part; it was to remove any fear that we may have had about their jersey or their history. I remember walking out of the tunnel and the referee shouting at us to get a move on. I recall standing ahead of kick-off looking very smart in our tracksuit tops and thinking what a fantastic occasion this was to be involved in. Once the whistle went and I got my first touch, any nerves that I may have had disappeared almost immediately. That's when I knew I was in the game and there was no time to worry about nerves as I knew there was a job to be done.'

Midfielder Gordon Strachan, as you would expect, took it all in his stride. 'Absolutely no feelings, no fear whatsoever. We had nothing to lose. We were on a journey that was going upwards. Winning was part of our mentality. We had won the Scottish Cup in '82, '83 and '84. I then went to Manchester United and won the FA Cup in '85. I used to think that this was meant to happen every season. I think semi-finals are more nerve-racking than finals. Finals are great. The final against Real Madrid was just a thrill, which is what you did as a kid, when we were playing on the streets. You either wanted to be Real Madrid, or in my case Hibs versus Real Madrid. Real Madrid were always in your dreams somewhere along the line, or your fantasy, and there I was, living out my fantasy for real.'

Captain Willie Miller was now in his 11th season with the Dons. In Gothenburg he was 28 years old but by then a seasoned campaigner with nearly 500 club appearances to his name. He had been there and done it, so how did he personally prepare his troops to face one of Europe's greatest ever club sides? 'All I can remember is the usual stuff before going out. I wasn't particularly vocal in the dressing room. I preferred to lead by example rather than too many words – you do not need many words. You just need the rallying call before you go out because you have spoken before to Alex [McLeish] or Jim [Leighton] or your full-backs. The manager by that point has already said everything he has to say. The team by then should know what they are supposed to do. I think you can overdo it at times; it should just be a rallying call as all the hard work has already been done prior to the game.'

For winger Peter Weir, he recalls vividly the astonishing number of man-hours spent by the management team to ensure the players were all fully prepared for what lay in wait in Gothenburg. 'Fergie and Archie both went over to Spain to watch Real, and after the first game Fergie called the chairman and told him what a great chance we had. Not long after, Archie went over again to watch them ahead of their game against Valencia, but when he arrived the tickets were missing but, thankfully, he was able to get into the game to watch them. He was also able to get enough information on Real Madrid by watching them on Spanish TV and speaking to plenty of people in the Spanish game. He was able to put together a dossier on all the players, their strengths, their weaknesses, the systems that they were used to playing. Again, we were underdogs, nobody in the build-up to the game talked about us, and everybody expected us to lose and for Real Madrid to lift another European trophy. That didn't bother us as we quietly stayed out at the hotel and relaxed, but we did believe in our own ability. I'm not saying we were confident of winning the cup, but we knew we would go out and give it absolutely 100 per cent.'

Then came the day itself, as John Hewitt recalls: 'In Gothenburg we had a light training session in the morning and then a pre-match meal about lunchtime; then we would have a chat. We then went off to bed for a sleep and one final briefing from Fergie and Archie late afternoon before setting off on the bus. Everybody was clear in their minds what was expected of Real. It was a lovely summer evening when we trained the night before but, later that night, it absolutely chucked it down with rain. The rain was that torrential that by the time we reached the stadium there were discussions going on about moving the game to the following day because there was so much water lying on the park. We knew the game would go ahead though, so it was a case of knuckling down and simply getting on with it.'

Alex Ferguson had choices to make when it came to his team selection against Real Madrid after Stuart Kennedy's confirmed absence. He decided to play Doug Rougvie at right-back with John McMaster occupying the left-back berth. Did this slight change of role ever affect Doug's own preparation for the game? 'That wasn't a problem for me at all as I could play right-back, I could play left-back, and I was never fazed by that. It was

Frank Munro scores Aberdeen's first ever goal in a European game against Reykjavik at Pittodrie. Frank would grab a hat-trick that night in a 10-0 win. September 1967. *Aberdeen Journals*

Jens Petersen scores Aberdeen's ninth goal v Reykjavik in 1967. *Aberdeen Journals*

Aberdeen prepare to board the flight to Vienna for their first ever away game in the European Cup. September 1980.

Aberdeen fans queue around the stadium in hope of securing tickets for the game against Liverpool in the European Cup – many faithful fans would be left disappointed which in turn made the club rethink their ticketing process. October 1980

Aberdeen suffer a heavy 4-0 defeat against eventual European Cup winners Liverpool at Anfield but the lesson learned on the night proved to be invaluable for Sir Alex Ferguson and the team. *Getty Images*

Stadion 1st May, Pitesti, Romania gets ready for the visit of Aberdeen for a UEFA Cup tie, November 1981. *Kevin Stirling*

The coin is tossed and the teams are ready for kick-off. With Aberdeen trailing 2-0 at half-time, this prompted the now infamous tea-urn incident with Sir Alex Ferguson in the Aberdeen dressing-room. Whatever he said it worked as the Dons forced a 2-2 draw to progress to the next round. *Kevin Stirling*

Peter Weir celebrates Aberdeen's third goal against UEFA Cup holders Ipswich Town. September 1981. *SNS Pix*

The team celebrate in the dressing room after beating Ipswich Town 4-2 on aggregate. *SNS Pix*

Neil Simpson scores Aberdeen's equaliser v Bayern Munich. March 1983. *Getty Images*

Alex McLeish heads home against Bayern Munich after John McMaster and Gordon Strachan's brilliant free-kick routine to make it 2-2 on the night. *SNS Pix*

Pittodrie goes berserk as super-sub John Hewitt nets the winner. *SNS Pix (left) and Aberdeen Journals (right)*

After a good old-fashioned stramash in the six-yard-box, Mark McGhee
slots home Aberdeen's fifth goal v Waterschei. April 1983. *SNS Pix*

Eric Black opens the scoring against Real Madrid in Gothenburg. May 1983. *Getty Images*

John Hewitt celebrates as he beats Real Madrid's goalkeeper Agustin to score the winning goal in extra-time.. *Getty Images*

Aberdeen's greatest moment: captain Willie Miller holds aloft the Cup Winners' Cup. *Getty Images*

Neil Simpson opens the scoring against European Cup holders, SV Hamburg, in the Super Cup final 2nd leg at Pittodrie. December 1983. *SNS Pix*

Mark McGhee seals Aberdeen's victory against SV Hamburg in the Super Cup Final. *Aberdeen Journals*

Aberdeen officially become Europe's No.1 team after beating SV Hamburg 2-0 in the Super Cup final. *Getty Images*

Mark McGhee scores his hat-trick against Ujpest Dozsa in The 1984 Cup Winners' Cup quarter-final at Pittodrie. March 1984. *Aberdeen Journals*

Darren Mackie heads home a superb opening goal v Dnipro, that goal was soon nicknamed the £1 million goal. October 2007. *Newsline Scotland Press Agency*

Jamie Smith celebrates his and Aberdeen's second goal v FC Copenhagen on another memorable night under the lights at Pittodrie. December 2007. *Getty Images*

The victorious team celebrate qualifying for the knock-out stage of the UEFA Cup after defeating FC Copenhagen 4-0 at Pittodrie. *Derek Ironside*

Bayern Munich captain Luca Toni leads out his side, 25-years after the two sides first met in a European competition – could history repeat itself? February 2008. *Getty Images*

On-loan midfielder Josh Walker opens the scoring for Aberdeen against Bayern Munich. *Getty Images*

Sone Aluko smashes home Aberdeen's second goal against Bayern Munich but the Germans would have the last laugh. *Getty Images*

Niall McGinn fires Aberdeen into a two-goal lead against Groningen. *SNS Pix*

Adam Rooney buries his penalty to give Aberdeen the lead against
Groningen in the Netherlands in a Europa League qualifier. July 2014. *SNS Pix*

Aberdeen midfielder Peter Pawlett heads home Aberdeen's second goal against Rijeka in a Europa League qualifier. This was Rijeka's first defeat at home in thirteen European games. July 2015. *SNS Pix*

quite simple back then. All we needed to do was give it to wee Gordon or Peter Weir and our opponents would immediately be on the back foot; all we had to do was push up and get ourselves organised. If we had the chance to get up the park and join in the fun that is exactly what we did. We had so many match-winners in that team it was untrue.

Ahead of kick-off, while still in the confines of their dressing room, the management team did their best to remain level-headed and calm. That behaviour had the desired effect as Doug explains. 'Fergie tried his best to keep it under wraps but, between the boys, we had a feeling that we were going to win the cup that night. Real Madrid were a fantastic team at the time, but they were beatable and that was proved correct on that night.' To suggest this was the biggest game any of the staff had been involved in is an understatement. The planning had been meticulous – you could argue it almost bordered on the obsessive – but without the attention to detail, the course of history could have been so different. Alex Ferguson had spent days scheming a game plan so, with so much at stake, did at any point nerves, tension or anxiety present itself through the boss? John Hewitt recalls, 'They were fairly jovial, very calm in fact. They both went around us all in the dressing room and had a quiet chat as naturally there were some nerves and tension among the lads. I think due to the importance of the game, if you do not suffer from nerves, there has to be something wrong with you. Fergie was brilliant at making you feel like you were the best player in his team no matter what position you played. He would remind us all that this was a showcase event and we all deserved to be there. He always knew how to deal with us individually and as a team. They looked totally relaxed as we headed out. It was a horrible night; the conditions were awful, but I thought we adapted really well, and we should have won the game in the 90 minutes.'

For those that were lucky enough to be in Gothenburg there are so many fond memories of that trip, but I defy anybody at any point during a conversation not to mention the rain. The heavens opened early afternoon and continued for the best part of the day. Camped inside a shopping mall for shelter, many of the travelling fans quietly started to display signs of nervousness – could the game be in doubt?

Peter Weir remembers well the hours ahead of kick-off. 'We went for a sleep in the afternoon after having a light training session in the morning. Most of the boys after lunch liked to get their heads down or listen to music or play cards before setting off for the match. I woke up about 5 p.m. and looked out of the window and saw the rain lashing down which didn't overly bother me at the time. On the bus on the way to the stadium you could see the amount of rain that had caused water to sit on the roads and surrounding areas. It was only then that it crossed my mind that maybe the game could be in jeopardy. Where I did take solace is the fact that unless the whole park was covered in water, there was no way a big European final was going to get cancelled with the crowds making their way to Sweden from Scotland and Spain. I recall the referee going out to inspect the pitch where water was lying on the park, especially in the goalmouths. If this had been an ordinary league game the officials may possibly have called it off. I personally love playing in heavy weather. I loved to attack players who enjoyed diving in and attempting to kick you up in the air. It suited us more as the Spanish players were only used to playing on dry surfaces back home due to the climate. To be honest when I saw the state of the pitch it gave me a boost more than anything else knowing how damp the surface was.'

Thankfully, and much to the relief of everybody involved, the game went ahead. Aberdeen were competing in their first ever European final; Real Madrid their 11th. The weather was atrocious but that played right into the hands of the Aberdeen players. Alex Ferguson gave one more television interview to match commentator Brian Moore before making his way back to the dressing room, and his exterior was as calm as it had ever been. He said, 'Strangely enough I am calmer than I normally am. I stay out of the road of the players because I do not show my nerves to them if I have any, so I let them get on with it. In this moment in time there's not a lot Alex Ferguson can do.' When quizzed by Brian Moore on the individuals who may help swing the game in Aberdeen's favour, Ferguson responded by saying, 'The back four is our most experienced part of the side so we normally just expect them to be solid and not do anything daft; the midfield and the front players, particularly the front players who will be the important ones who are the front two of McGhee and Black who are quick and have good movement; they are used to playing against man-markers; they are used to challenges from behind which we expect from Spanish sides, so I am quite confident they can handle that. Where we play Strachan and Weir depends tactically what they are going to do with Strachan and Weir. Sometimes we play Weir forward in the left-wing position or we withdraw him. Strachan could be the other way about; these things are important.' He finished off his interview by saying, 'They are a young side but they are a brave side.'

That bravery was in evidence when the teams walked out of the tunnel side by side; there was an air of determination on the faces of the men in red. For us fans, there was a lump in the throat. The game started brightly with both sides having their fair share of possession in the opening stages. Eric Black's first touch after a few minutes was to bring Mark McGhee into play; his second touch was simply jaw-dropping. The game was barely five minutes old when Gordon Strachan delivered a driven cross into the 18-yard box at shoulder height after a poor kick-out by Real Madrid defender Johnny Metgod. Out of nowhere Eric attempted the most audacious scissor-kick from the edge of the box which cannoned off the bar. It was an astonishing effort and if you look at it closely you will see that Real Madrid goalkeeper Agustin gets the slightest of touches to tip Eric's effort on to the bar. Was that effort a statement of intent on his part? 'No, I don't think so. I wish it had gone in because I would have been remembered more for that than the wee tap-in from three yards!' Eric laughs. 'It was just something that happened in the game. As the ball came in the technique was all about me thinking this is the best way to connect with the ball and attempt a shot on goal. I had a quick look and could see I was about 20 yards out so, with the angle of the delivery and height of the ball, it was just an instinct to try the scissor-kick. There was nothing premeditated about that effort; it was all about the game getting under way, the ball coming at me from a certain direction, and trying to score.'

Just two minutes later, and with the travelling Red Army now very much in fine fettle, Eric won a corner for the Dons. As Gordon Strachan jogged over to the corner flag, Eric nonchalantly walked to the six-yard line placing himself between Agustin and central defender Paco Bonet. Eric takes up the story of Aberdeen's opening goal. 'We worked in training on drilling the ball into the box and big Eck [Alex McLeish] making a late dash into the box and trying to make some sort of positive connection. At that point, my thinking was to try and get around the goalkeeper and try and position myself anywhere near the goal itself where, maybe, I could block the goalkeeper's view, or just make a nuisance of myself. I was hoping Eck's header would fall to me and I could get some sort of touch on it, or deflect it towards goal, or even if Eck's header were on target and the keeper spilled it, I wanted to be able to capitalise on that or ready to pounce. All I was thinking was to try and get in and around the line of the ball, be alert in that moment to the second ball and, thankfully for me, that's exactly what happened, and I was able to squeeze the ball home.'

All pre-match nerves soon settled, not just from the fans in the stands but more importantly down on the bench. Substitute John Hewitt was just as impressed. 'We started the game so well, straight out of the traps; Eric scoring the opening goal really helped settle us, and then I felt we dominated the game in the first half. I honestly believed if we could have scored a second the game was finished but, as it turned out, they got their penalty due to the wet weather and the ball sticking on the surface; it was game on then. After that it was a case of regrouping and remaining positive; keep doing what we had been doing because we were certainly creating good opportunities, so it was just a case of trying to put one away.'

Aberdeen had made the perfect start but, in a flash, Real Madrid were back in the game. Fifteen minutes after Eric Black's opener, in what was their first flurry into Aberdeen's final third, Alex McLeish collected a loose ball and attempted a routine back pass to goalkeeper Jim Leighton but, on the sodden pitch, the ball held up and Real forward Santillana nipped in and Jim took him down inside the penalty box. The ref pointed to the spot. In that exact moment Alex recalls what went through his mind. 'I wish I hadn't bloody well done that! I just wanted the ground to open and swallow me up. It was an awful moment. I had said to the players in the dressing room after the warm-up to be mindful of their back passes. I told them they would probably have to chip the ball back otherwise it would drag in the water. I think because Willie, Jim and I were so instinctive back then, we had a sense of telepathy. We could do it almost without looking because we knew it would be a safe pass, and when it came to me, I didn't think to myself: "Alex, remember to lift the ball back because there's loads of water on this pitch." It was just an instinctive pass. That is probably an example of the repetition training I mentioned earlier because, if we had practised that in training, I could guarantee 99 times out of 100 that would have been a safe pass but, because of the water, it slowed up and big Jim had to bring the guy down. But my mind is at peace because I had an assist in the first two goals that night!'

A captain and a leader has many roles to play on the pitch, but one which he, or she, must be aware of is the need to encourage and, at times, reassure if things are not quite going to plan. On that rain-soaked night, skipper Willie Miller had the clarity to recognise that his good pal Alex McLeish needed a quiet word of comfort after he gave away the penalty which led to Real Madrid equalising. It was a body blow after the Dons had started the game on the front foot. Willie explains: 'We said before the game to watch the back passes because it's so wet; don't attempt a back pass! In those days to play a back pass, it was a big part of the game, and big Alex obviously thought it would make it. All I said to him was, "Come on, big man, just get on with it, just put it behind you and put it out of your mind." That's exactly what he did as his performance after that was brilliant.'

Brilliant his performance was. In his own humble words Alex McLeish quietly reflects that the final against Real Madrid was probably his finest performance in an Aberdeen shirt. 'Maybe it was, yeah! I remember not long after the penalty incident I almost got myself into a spot of bother, but I had to dribble my way out of it. Maybe the gaffer thought to himself that I had gone to pieces as I was now trying to dribble past two or three players. Somehow, I was able to weave my way through these players. Sir Alex had a word with me about the back pass, but that was quickly resolved. I didn't plead innocence but the fact that I didn't meant it helped calm the situation. Archie Knox came in and said to us that we have a "bloody cup to win here", and after that everything was fine. It was still in my head as I felt I had let down my teammates, but I knew I had to get rid of those thoughts quickly as I knew the gaffer would be calculating and evaluating if I was going to crack but, thankfully, he left me on. I had to go out and make sure I was flawless and make sure that Real Madrid didn't create any more chances or near misses that were related to me at any cost. I had to be vigilant for my teammates to ensure we were getting our shutout in the second half.'

From the outset Aberdeen were thorough in their approach to the game. Real Madrid realised they had a game on their hands after Eric Black rattled the woodwork and then took the lead all within the first seven minutes of the match. With the rain playing its part in Real's equaliser the teams went into the break all-square. With the lads now camped in the dressing room sipping warm tea, the manager's first port of call was surprisingly winger Peter Weir. 'The manager had a go at me before anybody else. He wanted me to push forward more as he believed I was playing too much like a left-midfield player instead of a left-winger. To be fair he did set out not to rush the game at all, and he wasn't looking for us to go gung-ho from the off, just to bed ourselves into the game first and not lose the game in the first 20 minutes. Even though we took the lead and then lost a bad goal, not much else happened in that first half. There wasn't a great deal of action, so all Fergie reminded us to do at half-time was for me and Gordon to get more forward and attempt to get at their full-backs. When I look back there is an argument to say Fergie won the game at half-time, because tactically he wanted myself and Gordon to attack the flanks more and get more crosses into the box which we certainly achieved in the second half and extra time.'

John McMaster, who was hardly troubled down his side in the opening 45 minutes, recalls the half-time team talk well. 'So, we come in at half-time and Alex is killing himself over this back pass that he made which obviously led to Real's equaliser. The boss starts tearing into him, calling him all sorts of names, and after a few seconds of continued abuse big Alex lifts his head, looks directly in the boss's eyes and screams, "I f**king know." The veins were popping out of his neck and his forehead, his teeth were gritted and his eyes were wide open staring the boss down! It was so funny. He then says to the boss, "I know, stop f**king talking about it will ye." Do not forget, Alex played a major role in another well-worked set piece that most folk have forgotten about – our opening goal! It was a brilliant corner from Gordon, and an equally good header across the box from Alex, which gave Eric the opportunity to open the scoring for us.'

Once the second half settled, Aberdeen went on to dominate. If you take into consideration the quality of the opposition and the testing conditions, the Aberdeen players put in a hell of a shift. Peter Weir that night was outstanding. In one distinct move he danced his way past a host of Real Madrid players before attempting a cross which took a wicked deflection. With the ball heading nicely towards Eric Black it was an opportunity that you would expect him to get, at the very least, on target. Somehow, he managed to head the ball over. Once that chance had come and gone did Eric have thoughts that maybe this game was going to go all the way to extra time? 'My thoughts would not be as calculated as that during a game. I would never think ahead to the outcome of a game. If you look at that chance, and the deflection it took, and then the amount of spin on the ball, you can quite clearly see how difficult that chance was. The ball bounced off a corner of my head and went straight over. It was a good opportunity and, obviously, I was disappointed I didn't get the header right, but I always believed that more opportunities would come in the game as we always made openings as a team. We had so many chances in that game that, possibly, some thoughts of not taking them started to creep in but, ultimately, those same thoughts proved wrong in the end. If my chance had gone in the game would have been over sooner, but it certainly made for an entertaining evening.'

With just under ten minutes left in the game, Eric contested an outswinging cross from Doug Rougvie. His header was just off target, but he landed heavily and stayed down. After a quick assessment from physiotherapist Roland Arnott, Eric managed to carry on for a few more minutes before hobbling off to be replaced by John Hewitt moments before the full-time whistle. When he came off, he looked devastated – but did fate play its hand that night? 'It certainly turned out that way. Due to my recurring back injury, I was prone to going over on my ankle. It was all related because I was constantly overloading the outside of my foot. With the pitch being heavy, and then getting a crack on it while contesting a ball, I remember going right over the top of it and I knew straight away I was in trouble. I could see the swelling form almost immediately. I knew I was in trouble but, strangely, I couldn't feel it because I still had that adrenaline going through my system. I just wanted to carry on, so I was absolutely devastated I had to come off because, obviously, I wanted to contribute more to the game. However, as we all know, the man who replaced me didn't do too badly. Maybe these things are just meant to happen; maybe fate did play a role that night, and I am certainly glad it did. Can you imagine if I'd had to stay on and we'd lost!'

With the Dons in control of the game, but unable to find that decisive second goal, the game edged ever closer to extra time. In the final minutes, the instructions continued to flow from Alex Ferguson and Archie Knox on the touchline, as you would naturally expect. Did Willie Miller feel the need to increase his vocal capacity to reaffirm those instructions on the park during those closing stages? 'No, that's what I did naturally. If you go back to the Bayern Munich game, when we did take the lead and we had some minutes still to go in the game, all I can remember doing for the remainder of that game is talking, organising and focusing. Karl-Heinz Rummenigge alluded to that in one of his post-match interviews where he said that "it was all about their organisation". I just remember being so focused, and so driven, and so vocal, because they were still very much a threat. One goal from them puts us out of the competition so it was all about making sure they didn't create any more chances in the closing stages of the game.'

The game finished 1-1 despite the Dons' best efforts. The lads simply couldn't find a way through, but they had performed quite magnificently. Alex Ferguson was right. Real were there for the taking and all his pre-match studies had proved that. I defy anybody to argue that the Dons in regulation time had not been the better side. Up in the stands the fans readied themselves for another 30 minutes of football. It was wet, cold and a touch miserable but that was all about to change in one unforgettable moment. John Hewitt explains what his instructions from Fergie were as he readied himself to enter the arena. History was about to change. John takes up the story. 'He felt we needed an outlet up the park. Having fresh legs and some pace, Fergie hoped to keep the game long so if the ball were knocked up front, I could run into the channels which in turn would help the back four get further up the park. As it turned out, after I came on, it was so difficult to get a hold of the ball as it kept sticking on the surface. I got caught a couple of times with the ball between my feet and all I could hear was Fergie shouting at me, "Hewitt, get up that f**king park." It's a myth that he was going to hook me not long after I came on. He knew I was capable of taking a chance if it presented itself. I think I dropped a little too deep because I had fresh legs and I was desperate to get involved in the game.

Going into the extra period the mood was one of optimism, and the lads were champing at the bit to get going again. Peter

Weir was one such player. 'We were a very fit side; I loved the heavier pitches so when I think back and the amount of joy I got down that left-hand side being able to get good crosses in for Eric [Black] and Mark [McGhee], we were actually really unfortunate not to go ahead. I do believe we were the better team the longer the game went on; we were well and truly in the ascendancy. They looked to me to be a little tired and quite happy sitting in, soaking up the pressure and holding out for penalties. We as a team didn't want to go to penalties – that was discussed a couple of days before the game as almost not being an option – so we were confident of winning the game outright going into extra time.'

For full-back Doug Rougvie, he was fully prepared to carry on where the boys had left off in regulation time, by taking the game to the Spaniards and continuing to play on the front foot. 'Extra time held no fear for us whatsoever as many of our cup finals went to extra time back then. Fergie and Archie Knox were determined to get us fit, and they certainly managed that by making us run a lot as well as the ball work. Gordon had two unbelievable chances to win us the game that night in regulation time. He was getting dog's abuse from me for not sticking them away. I said to him at one point, "Hey, wee man. Gonna stick one of these in the back of the net? Stop f**king about."'

For the winning goal, John Hewitt's starting position is quite deep inside his own half. Peter Weir quite brilliantly makes room for himself to deliver a perfectly placed pass into Mark McGhee's path. John, by this point, is already on the move heading directly towards goal. The move takes precisely 13 seconds to execute from Peter robbing the Real player to John heading home. Not at any point did John deviate his run, but he was conscious of what Mark McGhee would do next. He takes up the story of the moment the club's narrative changed forever: 'The thing about Mark is – ask any of my former colleagues and they will tell you – that we were never sure when he was going to deliver the ball. He had a habit of doubling back, beating his opponent and then trying to beat him a second time. For the winning goal I ran directly towards goal, running in on the goalkeeper. I had no defender to beat. I could see the goal the entire time I was running. I could see Mark and the full-back so all I was focusing on was making sure I was in a position that if he were going to play it in with his left foot or come inside on to his right foot, I needed to be somewhere in a central position so I could get myself on to it whether it be my head or my foot. I was so focused on Mark; he's taken his touch and then played it in with his left foot early; I'm fully focused by now watching the ball come across. At the same time, I can see the goalkeeper, but he was rooted to his line. When he decided to come for the ball it was too late. I knew it was too late. To be honest I couldn't miss, it was just a case of keeping my focus and my concentration and then basically just let the ball hit my head and direct the ball towards the empty net.'

John explains the emotions in that precise moment and where he found the strength in his legs to celebrate in the manner that he did. 'I've scored and I've gone down. It's muddy and wet so I've picked myself up and wiped my hands all over my shirt to get the mud off. I've then moved to the side and jumped and the next thing I know I'm getting wrestled by big Doug Rougvie. He pulled me down, and to be honest, I can't really remember much after that. I used to get so much stick for my style of celebration. The lads used to say to me, "What the hell is that you're doing? Is that the Highland fling?" The celebration was just a reaction.'

In the seconds after John picks himself up from the park and wipes the dirt off his hands, the first to join him in celebration is full-back Doug Rougvie. Doug recalls where he found the energy to run the length of the pitch to join John in those now iconic celebrations. 'When the move started for John's winner, we all pushed up in support. I had nobody to mark so I just kept running up the park. By the time the ball hit the back of the net I was already in the final third which is obviously not picked up by the TV cameras as they are focused on John. I ran to him in a flash but, thankfully, it wasn't too far to run! That feeling when John scored was indescribable, but we gave Real Madrid such a doing that I honestly believed the goal was coming. I am glad it did because I didn't want to face penalties. I know for a fact Willie [Miller] would have missed and big Eck [Alex McLeish] wouldn't have fancied one, so I'm glad we finished Real off when we did.'

For John it is a moment he cherishes. 'I can take my mind back to 1983 and picture the goal as clear as a bell; it's something I don't think I will ever forget. I can still see it now, heading towards the goal. I can see Mark, I can see the goalkeeper, and when I made contact with the ball. Whenever I see a clip of the goal it brings the memory back to me so much more. I get stopped in the street by fans asking to shake my hand and wanting to thank me for that moment. That really is a great feeling to be the one that won the cup, plus being a local boy as well which I think makes it even more special. This may sound a bit strange, but I am not one for dwelling on the past and history. Obviously, it's the highlight of my career; it's the highlight of Aberdeen Football Club's career, and it will probably never ever happen again to not just Aberdeen but any Scottish club. I have seen clips of the goal and, obviously, it does give me a great feeling knowing that I scored the winning goal. The way I look at it is I was very fortunate to play with a great squad of boys, because success isn't about individuals – it's a collective group effort. Even the boys who didn't take part in the actual game on the night, they played their part throughout that season to help us win the cup. We really did have a great squad of players which Fergie was able to inherit, bar one or two, and then instil in them a belief that we were better than Celtic and Rangers, and that we could go to Celtic Park or Ibrox and win. Pre-Fergie, Aberdeen teams would be thinking if they go to Glasgow and get a draw it's a fantastic result. That was the difference with our squad; we had a different mindset, and we went down there to win, which was all because of Fergie's will to win. He used to hate going to Glasgow and losing because, in the press conference after a game, the press members would rile him and ask him questions which really annoyed him. If we won, he was the first into the press room; he couldn't wait to get in there and speak to the press.'

The build-up to the goal has never been lost on any of the lads involved that night despite the passing years. Eric Black is no different. 'One hundred per cent – I was obviously viewing the move slightly differently to my former teammates, but I can clearly recall the moment we all rose from the bench when Peter [Weir] knocked the ball into the channel for Mark [McGhee] to chase. I remember thinking there was plenty of space with only a couple of defenders in position. We all rose from the bench looking across when Mark delivered his cross. At that point we are all thinking the same: "The keeper's not getting that," and then, suddenly, the ball is in the back of the net. It was pandemonium, and what a feeling that was. I remember that moment so vividly! I have been fortunate to play in many cup finals, including two in France which were exceptional experiences but, at Aberdeen, I was with a special group of players. It comes very close to representing my country, which I was fortunate enough to do a couple of times, but the magnitude of that victory against Real Madrid, and the group of players that were involved, makes that the most special moment in my career without doubt. If you add in the euphoria when we got back to Aberdeen, and what we achieved, it was amazing. I have to say though as a young man, it didn't really sink in what we had achieved and I doubt it will be replicated by any Aberdeen team again or, probably, any Scottish team again. Now, I can take a fair bit of pride knowing I was part of something that was incredibly special.'

As Real attempted to start a move down the right flank, Alex McLeish was in his usual central role, patrolling that area with care. Upon Peter Weir nicking the ball, Alex watched on carefully at what developed next; it is a moment he has never forgotten. 'Oh yes, that moment has never escaped me. I can still see Peter [Weir] clipping the ball through to Mark [McGhee] who made one of his trademark runs down the channel and then crossed the ball for the wonderful Johnny Hewitt to head home. John did so many great things for us when we played together; scoring goals in cup finals, and the fastest ever goal in the Scottish Cup against Motherwell, and then to score those two goals in that tournament. I can remember coming off after the Bayern Munich game thinking this must be the greatest game ever at Pittodrie. I knew we had made a bit of history that night by beating the mighty Bayern. After we beat Bayern, we did start to wonder if we could go on and win the competition. All the Bayern players had said before the game how they always score away from home which prompted Sir Alex to say in his team talk: "Just score one more goal than them. I am not interested in the score, just score one more goal than them; that's it in a nutshell." We didn't really account for going behind twice in the game and then getting it back, but that was the resilience of the team and the mental strength of the group at that time. I think we had an arrogance about us ahead of the final. The Real Madrid players could hear us shouting; I think this was an exercise in trying to intimidate them somewhat, especially with big Doug Rougvie's toothless grin. One or two of us were shouting and bawling in the tunnel which some of the Real Madrid players attempted to replicate, but by mimicking us we felt that gave us more of a determination to beat them. They must have thought that we were not capable of beating them. I'm not sure whether they underestimated us or we were just streets ahead of them on the night – it might have been both!'

Willie Miller takes his own mind back to the moment the ball hit the back of the net and attempts to convey his emotions in that exact moment. 'The emotion was that we had done it; that's exactly what I thought. We battered them, we absolutely battered Real Madrid. In the second half, and extra time, there was only one team in it, so it was just a case of getting the second goal. We got it, but we all knew the game wasn't finished! I did sprint up and jump all over John. I can clearly remember doing that – eventually I got there,' Willie laughs. 'I then give away the free kick right at the death. It was never a free kick. I have no doubt I won the ball. Back then tackling was part of the game. I have gone in, made the tackle, and I have won the ball, but the ref blew up for a free kick. That was a nervous moment, but it just whizzed past the post. Jim said he had it covered, but I'm not so sure!' Willie laughs again. 'Once the ball flew past the post, that's the moment that I knew we had done it.'

Peter Weir played an instrumental role in Aberdeen's winning goal from robbing the ball inside Aberdeen's own half to picking out Mark McGhee out on the left flank; the move only took 13 seconds. 'I remember picking up the ball in our own half and making my way forward. I was able to skip past one guy then another. Suddenly, I find myself in the outside left position which is my normal position but very aware that Mark is ahead of me in space. I decided to pop a ball into his path for him to run on to. Mark never really had a great left foot, but somehow he managed to whip a great ball across the box for Johnny and we all know what happened next. That was a wonderful feeling, and everybody was jumping on top of each other. I remember big Doug Rougvie sprinting past us all to go and grab Johnny after he scored. It really was such an emotional feeling at that point in the game, but immediately your train of thought changes to "Can we go on and hold on for the remaining minutes of the game?"'

Assistant manager Archie Knox refreshed his memory for this book and confessed to me that John Hewitt's winner is one of his most treasured football memories. 'I will always remember when we came out of the tunnel for the start of the game, one of the Scottish journalists came over to me and told me he had nowhere to go and sit, and ideally he wanted to be close to the dugout, but that wasn't allowed because he wasn't part of the Aberdeen party. He asked me if I could get him a club tracksuit so he could stand near to the dugout. Teddy Scott arranged a tracksuit for him, so he was now able to watch the game from just behind the dugout. When John Hewitt scored the winner, I am running halfway down the park, punching the air and all the usual sort of celebration and just as I turned to come back this very same journalist met me and jumped on top of me and knocked me to the ground, and we both fell to the floor. At the full-time whistle when Alex went down in a heap, I do admit that I stepped on him to get over him in my eagerness to get on the pitch to join the lads. That moment was incredible and when we got home, to see all the crowds out on the streets to welcome us home really was phenomenal.'

Having taken the lead, Aberdeen had eight minutes to hang on, and it was the most agonising of waits for the full-time whistle. Just when the lads thought they were home and literally dry after the heavens had closed, Real Madrid were awarded a free kick just outside the box with only 30 seconds left. It is a moment Peter Weir and his teammates have never forgotten, notwithstanding the passing of time. 'I just said, "Please, God, don't let them score," and all the boys picked up on this that were standing in the wall. Those words just came out, and I have no idea why as I am not a religious person or a churchgoer. I have met the lads so many times since at various functions and they all say that I was praying to God,' he laughs. 'I just so desperately didn't want them to score that those words just fell from my mouth. When the ball flew past the post it was sheer relief, and I knew then that we had done it. When the referee blew his whistle, it was just elation, and utter pandemonium. It was fantastic for the fans who gave us incredible support throughout the game considering the awful conditions they had to endure for most parts of the game. I must be honest it was hard at first to take it in, and I was immediately thinking of my family up in the stands. I was able to pick them out from the crowd and go over and talk to them; that really was amazing. For five minutes after the whistle, Fergie is running about like a madman after being sent flying by Bryan Gunn from the dugout. For a small club like Aberdeen to win the Cup Winners' Cup against a fantastic Real Madrid side, it really was the stuff of dreams. I sometimes look back and think, "Wow, did that actually happen?" It was a great team that we had back then with the right manager and coaches. It's something I'll never forget.'

Once the players had received their plaudits from the Aberdeen fans, the lads slowly started to make their way back to the dressing room. There were scenes of jubilation but defender Alex McLeish, despite the significance of the win, had other things on his mind. He explains. 'At full time the boss came into the shower area where I was feeling a little sorry for myself, even though we had just won a major European final, and told me how well I had played in the second half. He told me I had stood there like a rock and didn't dig a hole and fall into a trap. I had my head bowed in the shower looking down at his shoes; all I could see was the boss's trousers and shoes getting soaked by the water. He told me how proud he was of me and praised me for having the strength not to crumble after the penalty incident.' Praise indeed from the boss. This author also wondered if John McMaster could sit and analyse the game for TV, how would he describe the performance? 'I think we should have beaten Real Madrid three or four nil. We gubbed them over 90 minutes and the game should never have gone to extra time. I think I had one of my best games for Aberdeen that night. The boss said to us beforehand, "You want to come off that park knowing you gave it your all," and that is exactly what we did; in abundance. Sir Alex was brilliant at saying things at the right time and doing the right things at the right time. That wasn't an act, it was instinctive.

Gordon Strachan also concurs that on the night Aberdeen were the better team, who handled the conditions better than their Spanish counterparts. 'Oh yeah, we were the dominant force. We were a group of players who, as a team shape, were far better. As individuals, on the night, we were far better. I have got to say, at the end of the game, by looking at them, and talking to them, including their manager, Alfredo Di Stefano, they knew they had just been beaten by the better team. There was none of the histrionics that you usually get from the Spanish teams where they moan at the referee or are jumping about, pushing and shoving. It was a case of right, we have just been beaten, let us get off the pitch and let these guys enjoy themselves. I honestly didn't think it was a huge thing for Aberdeen Football Club to be beating Real Madrid because I just believed that is what we were supposed to be doing. We were beating teams like Rangers and Celtic, and they had won European trophies, so it was just part of the deal that we won European trophies. It wasn't like Leicester winning the Premier League or something ridiculous like that. People were talking about us and people were thinking what a good side we were. It wasn't like one of these fairy-tale rides as we had already grown into this. Teams didn't want to play us, so I really didn't think that winning the Cup Winners' Cup was such a big deal.'

After such an achievement, did the players and staff have a night to remember back at their hotel headquarters? John Hewitt recalls, 'No, believe it or not, most of the guys went straight to their bed after we got back to the hotel. I personally went to bed reasonably early, but I do remember waking up to a beautiful morning. The hotel had an open-air swimming pool with a small diving board and Gordon [Strachan] and Mark [McGhee] were still outside beside the pool. Mark was obviously still suffering from having one or two too many drinks after we got back, and he was giving the gaffer stick, all in good fun may I add, but I don't think the gaffer was too happy and, as a punishment, he made Mark go down to meet the fans off the *St Clair* while suffering from a bad hangover.'

The boys who played their part that night only started to appreciate the magnitude of what had been achieved in the hours after the full-time whistle. It was only upon returning to Aberdeen and stepping on the bus for the open-top parade through the city that the significance of what they had done started to sink in. Willie Miller recalls, 'Yes, that would be about right; I think all the lads will say it's something that we never envisaged happening – that amount of people turning out and filling up Union Street. There were thousands of people – probably the whole city turned up to see us come back from Sweden. I think that was the start of it. Thereafter it was recognition from abroad. Back then it was rare to get a letter from abroad before we won the Cup Winners' Cup. Then, suddenly, we are getting letters from every country in Europe asking for autographs and pictures and people wishing us well. That puts you in a place when Aberdeen becomes a recognisable name in European football, which puts you right up there with some of the greats. Barcelona, Aberdeen and then Juventus are the names on the Cup Winners' Cup in the year before and the year after we won it. When you mention those names, it's fairy-tale stuff, it really is.'

John Hewitt said, 'The achievement began to sink in for me when the open-top bus hit the top of Holborn Street. I remember looking out and thinking, "Bloody hell." There were thousands of people for as far as the eye could see. Folk hanging out of windows, climbing up street lamps, on top of office roofs, you couldn't even see the actual street. The bus came to a standstill and crawled its way down Union Street. It felt like an age before we hit Castlegate and then we hit King Street, and it was just the same. I couldn't believe it. When we eventually made it to Pittodrie I just remember seeing all the fans sitting on the track around the pitch; it was unbelievable.'

When speaking with Gordon Strachan for this book, he received the same question as his former teammates before him; his answer somewhat took me by surprise, but I couldn't help but smile at his response. 'I've got to say, I've only watched the Cup Winners' Cup final back once since the actual game itself. It was on a cold January morning a few years back when I had nothing to do. I was on my own that morning, and I just had an inkling to watch the game. After I watched it, I called big Alex who, at the time, was the manager at Aston Villa, and I said to him: "By the way, we were not that bad." I always thought we were just a hard-working side who got about the pitch, did this, did that and were very functional. Looking back on that DVD it made me realise how good we were. I didn't appreciate how good we were as a team. When I was watching the game there were so many incidents that happened that had slipped my memory, but the one I really remember was the free kick Real had right at the end of the game and Peter Weir standing in the wall moaning and groaning and praying to God! It's made me appreciate more what a good side we were.'

After the trophy presentation and during the lap of honour, John McMaster can be seen going around each player individually, hugging and congratulating them; he did the same with the backroom staff. Did that act epitomise the bond the team had back then? 'We all had each other's backs. We all knew each other's habits and we all knew if we were not well or doing the right things. There were no cliques in that dressing room whatsoever. We were teammates through and through; a band of brothers if you like. We all looked after each other and there were no cut-throats or pirates. It was different class, and I absolutely loved it. I fully understand why some of the boys felt depressed leaving that environment because we were all secure in there. It was just like going to work with your mates, and I loved my work. It was a fantastic time to play for Aberdeen.'

Once the post-match festivities had come and gone, and the Aberdeen support hit the streets of Gothenburg to celebrate, the Ullevi Stadium started to quieten down. The only thing that was left for the respective club managers to do was to meet the press deep inside the bowels of the stadium. For a legendary figure of the game, Alfredo Di Stefano, it was a time for reflection: 'Aberdeen deserved their victory. They are now one of Europe's top sides. Aberdeen were physically stronger than us and the conditions suited them better. The players who were most important to them were Gordon Strachan and Peter Weir. I was looking forward to the final being settled on penalties, but my players wanted to go all out for victory. I think I was right and they were wrong, because Aberdeen finished the stronger team in awful conditions. Aberdeen are giants.'

A truly delighted Alex Ferguson beamed with pride, and he said: 'We hammered them! It was a magnificent night for Aberdeen and for Scottish football. I admit Real had us worried after their equaliser because Stielike and Gallego gave us problems. The lads were glad to hear the half-time whistle, but we stayed calm, pushed Peter Weir further forward on the left, shut down Gallego and never looked back. I confess that I expected Real to play with four men in midfield, but they played three. Once we adjusted, they couldn't match us.' Fergie finished off by saying, 'My only concern was the game staying at 1-1 in extra time and going to penalties to decide the outcome. Real Madrid looked as though they would have been happy with that situation. However, we wanted to settle the game and John Hewitt certainly did that in great style. It sounds corny, but it's a dream come true for all of us at Pittodrie, but I had no doubt we could beat Real.'

The next morning while waiting to board the flight home, Ferguson spoke of the achievement and what it meant to him from a personal point of view. He said, 'It made me feel as if I have done something worthwhile with my life. Winning the Premier Division and the Scottish Cup were great experiences – but this was more than that. The Swedish press said that a new team had been born in Europe and that is a great tribute to us. We knew we had players with flair, but for others on the Continent to say so makes it all the better.'

For the injured Dougie Bell, he watched on from the stands with his wife who at the time was heavily pregnant. 'Looking back, it was probably better for me if I had actually gone down and sat on the bench to feel more part of it. It would have been great to have played in the final and got a medal. It was just as disappointing as it was Real Madrid – one of the biggest names in football – and I was playing well that season, but that is just the way it is. It's the most disappointing moment of my career without a shadow of a doubt.' As much as Dougie was disappointed to miss out on the game, he takes great comfort in the knowledge that he now feels very much part of the Gothenburg squad all these years later. 'I have to say that since we won it, all the guys and all the fans have been so good, and whenever there's a reunion I'm always involved, and I always get a nice mention and that means a great deal considering I missed the final. Even though I missed the game, all the guys make sure that I am made to feel part of it and remember the contribution I made in the other games.'

Real Madrid's Dutch sweeper Johnny Metgod was 25 years old when he faced Aberdeen in the 1983 Cup Winners' Cup final. By the time the game came around he was already a seasoned pro, having played over 250 club games in both Holland and Spain. John had formed a formidable partnership with Spanish international centre-back Paco Bonet and had a reputation as a tough-tackling defender who took no prisoners. John very kindly agreed to speak to me for this book, and despite the passing years was able to offer me a unique insight into the final from a Real Madrid perspective. I began our discussions by asking him what he knew of Aberdeen prior to facing the Dons in the Ullevi Stadium. 'Ever since I started playing, I was attracted to British football in general. I played for AZ Alkmaar against Ipswich in the 1981 UEFA Cup final, where we lost over two games. My interest for the British game grew after playing in those two games, so I knew quite a bit about Aberdeen. I didn't specifically know all the players or what they were like, but I had a fairly good idea as any professional should. Even before the final, when you play the semi-final you naturally look at the other tie as well; even more so because Aberdeen beat Bayern Munich in the quarter-finals. They then had to play Waterschei, which wasn't an obviously well-known side. I know they do not exist any more, but even back in those days they were not a well-known side but still, if you beat Bayern Munich, you are a force to be reckoned with; it's as simple as that.'

As we know now, Alex Ferguson and his assistant Archie Knox compiled detailed dossiers on each and every Real Madrid player; the effort was monumental. I was interested to know from John if Real Madrid manager Alfredo Di Stefano did the same and if any video analysis was offered as part of the research. 'I do not recall back in those days doing any sort of video analysis; not at

AZ and not at Real Madrid, and even later when I played with Nottingham Forest and Spurs. Obviously, they gave us an idea of the team we are going to play against, and the players; they prepared us in that sense, but for me it was very simple – you do not get to the final for nothing, and if you are playing in the final then you know one thing is for sure: that the other team are well capable of beating any side, no matter how small or how big you are, so you still have to play the game. It's a one-off game and in a one-off game anything can happen.'

For the preparation in Sweden, Alex Ferguson decided, upon the advice of Scotland manager Jock Stein, to stay away from the hustle and bustle of the city and reside in a more tranquil setting. Ferguson heeded that advice and did just that. For Real Madrid, the team prepared differently, by staying in the city. John recalls, 'It was very normal. In Gothenburg we stayed in one of the two hotels which were designated to us by UEFA. We went out for some walks and we trained in the stadium the night before the game. We had to be careful of the pitch which meant we were not allowed to train on the pitch for too long because of the weather. That was basically it. We didn't have time for anything else, so we just tried to focus on playing the game and on our opponents. We ate, trained, slept and focused on the game, and once in a while we went out for a walk; it was as simple as that.'

In the days leading up to the final, the weather remained calm and still, but that all changed come the afternoon of the game itself. By midday, the storms had gathered and remained for hours on end. I wondered, from a Real Madrid perspective, if there was any concern about the heavy rain? 'There was no concern in the sense that we thought that the game was going to get called off. Occasionally in Madrid we would get bad weather, but less frequently than they do in Scotland. But, to suggest that is why Aberdeen adapted better to the situation than us, I think that isn't fair because everybody sometimes must play in these conditions.

It was one of those games where you must adapt as a professional football player to whatever circumstances there are. It does sometimes make it a little bit more difficult, because if you cannot play football the way you want to play football, you have to find a way. The only thing I would say is, when it rained that much, and you want to try and play football on the deck, maybe under those circumstances, playing more direct was a better option. If you are not used to playing like that it does make sense, on occasions, to change your way of playing because of the circumstances on the night. If you try and play out from the back and you can see there are puddles on the pitch, that is risky. You do start to think that I am not going to do that again because it puts me in trouble. If we were to play normally and play a more direct game, I think it may have been more beneficial, but to say that was a big advantage for Aberdeen to win the game, I do not think it's fair on their overall performance.'

With the warm-ups done and with the Real Madrid players back in the dressing room awaiting the referee's signal to enter the tunnel, I asked John if he could recall the final instructions from Alfredo Di Stefano before the players stepped out. 'Basically, it was what he always said, which for me was difficult to understand, because I had only played in Spain for one year. He originated from Argentina and came to Spain, but the way that he spoke Spanish was very hard for me to understand. At the end of my first year, I was able to understand quite a bit more about what he was trying to say and do, but I had to listen and concentrate very hard as it was very difficult to pick up. He was always about the same thing: we are Real Madrid, we want to play football, we have to try and dominate the game in possession and if we don't have possession, we have to make sure that we work as a team to try and make it as difficult as possible for Aberdeen.'

With Aberdeen's bright and confident start to the game, was John surprised by how quickly the Dons came out of the blocks?

'No, not at all. If you look at Aberdeen before, in the normal league games but certainly in the European games, they always played as a team. They may have played well or not so well but it was always a team that worked their socks off and had a little bit of class and a little bit of quality in Gordon Strachan, in John Hewitt, in Eric Black, and in Mark McGhee. They always had players who, out of nothing, could create a chance or score a goal. We knew it was going to be a team performance that would eventually win the cup and we knew they were going to have a real go at us, right from the start of the game. We were able to weather the storm a little bit and then start playing our own game, but we always knew it was going to be difficult because they were working their socks off and they would never give up.'

Aberdeen had the best of starts, but only seven minutes after taking the lead, Real equalised thanks to Juanito's well-taken penalty. John admits that scoring so quickly after Aberdeen took the lead helped settle his teammates down. 'Probably a little bit. If you go 1-0 down in a final, it is never a good thing, but we had to believe in ourselves that we also had the quality to score goals or create chances. It was good to get the equaliser not long after Aberdeen scored, because the longer it takes, the more risks you probably have to take. After that it was just a matter of not giving away silly chances by making mistakes ourselves, which is exactly what we did for Aberdeen's winning goal. Juanito, in and around the halfway line, tried to nutmeg his opponent but failed. Aberdeen broke, the ball came in from the wing and they scored. That was something that we knew Aberdeen would try to do – hit us on the break!'

Half-time was a time for calm and reflection. On balance the game was evenly matched, but the sodden turf wasn't making for pretty, expansive football. John recalls the mood in the Real Madrid dressing room during the 15-minute break. Is it true there was a heated debate among the players? 'I do not recall anything different from any other game that we played in Europe or in the league. It was disappointing at half-time to be 1-1; that is how we all felt, and we thought we could do a lot better. Not that we had a lot of chances to be leading at half-time, but before the game we would have expected to be more in control of the game, dominating more and creating more chances. At half-time there was the usual talk of this not being good enough for a club like Real Madrid to play a final like that, and not being able to control the game as much as we wanted to.'

Into the second half and Aberdeen started to push further forward, as per Alex Ferguson's instructions at half-time, but the breakthrough never came. Real Madrid defended deep and when they did break into Aberdeen's final third, they found the formidable Alex McLeish and Willie Miller standing in their way. I wanted to know from John if he believed during the second half, that the longer the half went on, that extra time was creeping up on them. 'Oh yes! It was difficult for us to break them down. It was a game where we thought we could still nick it and I am sure they thought the same way; maybe they will make a mistake and we can hit them on the break and score. Usually in these sorts of games when it's all square at the break, and not much happens after the first 10–15 minutes of the second half, you can almost bank on it that there's going to be extra time, because nobody wants to take the risks any more and go for a winner. You can go for the winner but not by moving three or four players forward and take a gamble; that's not what you do.'

Full time, Aberdeen 1 Real Madrid 1. Extra time was upon us. In the period after full time and before extra time, was John able to recall Señor Di Stefano's mood? 'He was still the same, and he was still trying to instil in us the belief that we were able to do it, even though we were facing extra time. He knew it was tough on the night physically and it was very demanding. There was still a chance and we had to keep believing because we knew that we only needed one opportunity for Santillana to score a goal. He knew it was still possible, but the only way to achieve that was to believe in it and believe in the fact that we could still turn it around.'

With the clock now standing at 112 minutes, the next few seconds provided a moment that all Aberdeen fans everywhere will never forget – John Hewitt's winning goal. It is a moment that will never be lost over time, but for John, did he think, when he saw the ball hit the net, that it was game over? 'No, you never think it's game over, but it was going to be even harder than it was before Aberdeen scored their second goal. In that sense it was going to be a more uphill battle than it already was. In those tight games where there is a lot of tension and excitement, I think you rely on players to create that one opportunity for a striker or maybe for themselves. It was difficult at 1-1 but to then go 2-1 down makes it even harder.'

When researching for this section I found a rather poignant picture of John and Real Madrid teammate Juan Jose not long after the full-time whistle. Juan Jose is covering his face with his hands; it's a look of devastation. I asked John to try and explain his emotions in the moments after the game ended. 'The thing is, with a club like Real Madrid, they do not consider it an achievement to get to a final. The only thing that counts for a club like Real Madrid is to win it, to win trophies, to win cups and to win games. In that season we played in five finals: we played against Aberdeen, we played in the Super Cup final against Real Sociedad over two legs, which we lost. We played in the Copa del Rey final against Barcelona and lost that as well as the League Cup final against Barcelona, plus we also lost the league title on the last day when we played Valencia away. We only needed a draw, but we lost 1-0 which meant Bilbao won the league. If you sum that all up and you play for a club like Real Madrid, who are so used to winning and want to win, the only thing that counts is to win the cups and win the finals we play in. As you can imagine, that was quite a disappointing season. For another club in another country to get to five finals in one season would have been a really big achievement, but not for a club like Madrid. After the game, all we're thinking was that it wasn't our night. It wasn't a night where we dominated the 120 minutes of play and showed everybody how well we can play. We never got to that, and whether that is something that you can blame us for, or maybe it had something to do with Aberdeen who tried to stop us from playing the way we normally would play, I am not sure; it could be a bit of both.'

With the game now come and gone and with the power of hindsight, I wanted to know from John which Aberdeen players impressed him the most that night. 'It wasn't one or two players, it was a team performance: Alex McLeish, Willie Miller and then the midfielders as well as Eric Black and Mark McGhee. I think it would not be the right thing to pick out only one or two or three players from that team. For me personally, the reason why Aberdeen beat us was because it was a team performance, on the night, as a team; they were absolutely magnificent. They gave it everything that they had and up to a level they stopped us from playing the way we normally would do. They threw their bodies on the line when it came to stopping us from scoring; whatever was needed on the night they were doing that without too many problems, so that was the key for me. To single out any individual player from that team would be unfair. Every player from the Aberdeen team, in their own position, put in a winning performance.'

To finish off our chat about the final I did have one final question for John. Did he swap shirts with any Aberdeen player? 'I can't recall swapping my shirt with any Aberdeen player after the game, but what I do remember is facing Gordon Strachan again after he joined Manchester United and I joined

Nottingham Forest. It was very nice to see Gordon again and obviously he reminded me of the final in Gothenburg as you would expect.' John played one further season for Real Madrid before joining Nottingham Forest. John enjoyed three seasons in the Midlands before signing for Tottenham ahead of the 1987/88 season. He finished his career with Feyenoord back in the Dutch Eredivisie, winning the league title in 1993 and Dutch Cup on three separate occasions. He retired from playing in 1994.

The last words for this chapter can only go to one man – goalscoring hero John Hewitt. I asked him if he still has his shirt and medal from that wonderful night. 'On the night I actually wore two shirts because it was so cold. At the end of the game, I swapped my actual match shirt with Uli Stielike which is now in a glass cabinet inside the main foyer at Pittodrie. It had been sitting in a plastic bag in a drawer at home for years, and I asked the club one day if they would like to display it at Pittodrie, which they now do. The other shirt I had, which was the second shirt, I donated to the 'cash for kids' charity. My medal – well, that takes pride of place at home!'

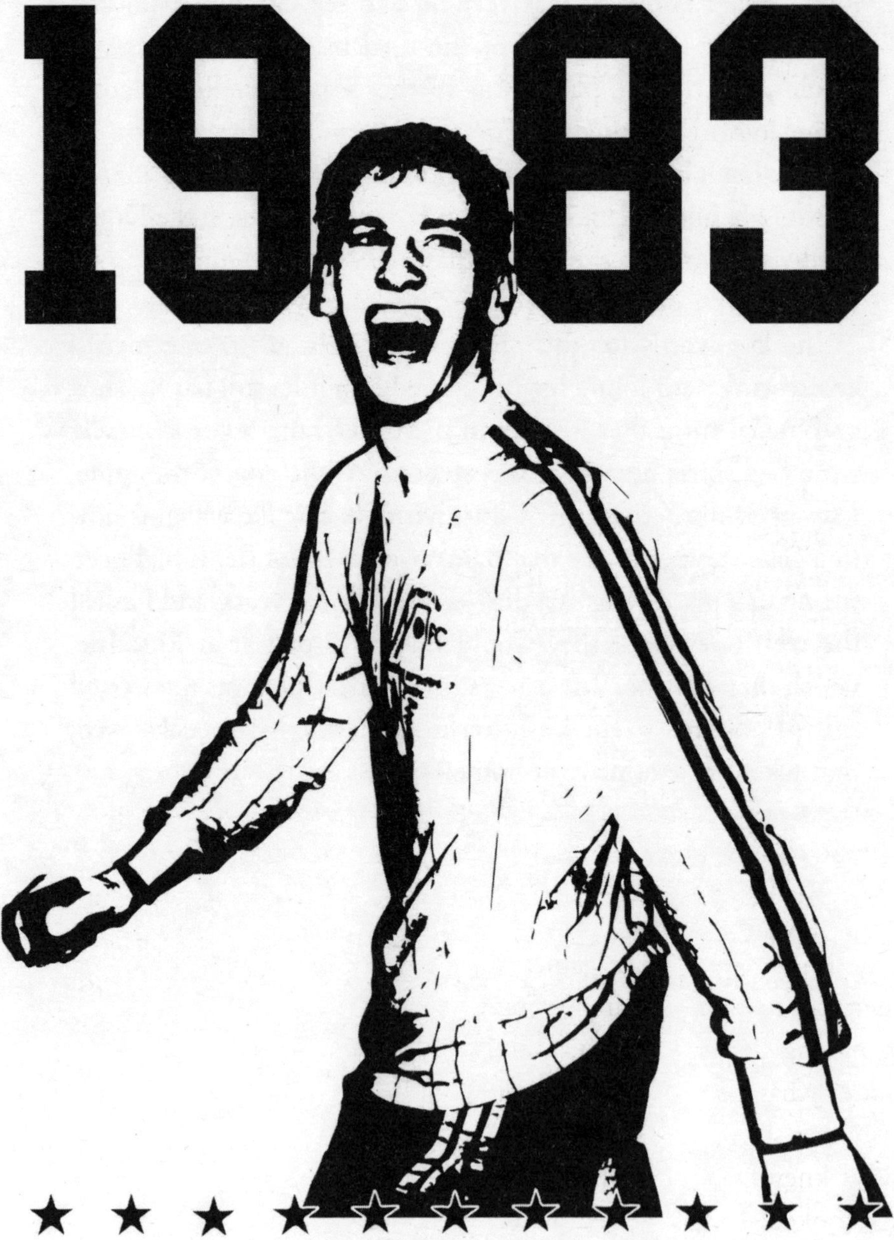
1983

NINE

SUPER CUP v SV HAMBURG

Revenge is in the air – that was the mood in the camp as Aberdeen prepared themselves to challenge for Europe's top club prize, the Super Cup. The Super Cup, which was first devised in 1972, would bring together the winners of the European Cup and the Cup Winners' Cup to determine which club was the best in Europe. No Scottish club had ever won the trophy before. Standing in Aberdeen's way were European Cup winners SV Hamburg, who two seasons earlier had knocked Aberdeen out of the UEFA Cup, much to the annoyance and frustration of the players and manager, because that loss was looked upon as a missed opportunity. In the early eighties, SV Hamburg were a team to be feared. From season 1978/79, for two successive campaigns, they finished runners-up in the West German Bundesliga and only 18 months previously lost to Nottingham Forest in the European Cup final in Madrid. Alex Ferguson appreciated the task ahead telling the local press, 'We couldn't have asked for a harder one.'

In the first leg at Pittodrie, Aberdeen were the masters of

their own downfall after two poorly conceded goals handed Hamburg the initiative for the return leg. Eric Black, who was making his European debut, opened the scoring before a horrible mix-up between Jim Leighton and full-back Stuart Kennedy allowed Horst Hrubesch through on goal to equalise. Andy Watson restored Aberdeen's lead before arguably the turning point in the game when Gordon Strachan missed a penalty with the score sitting precariously at 2-1; Aberdeen at that point had the Germans rattled. John Hewitt did add a third with nine minutes to go, but inexplicably, with three minutes left on the clock, and while down to ten men, none of the Aberdeen players had the presence of mind to kick the ball out of play to allow the waiting substitute Neale Cooper to enter the fray. Hamburg capitalised on the extra man and scored a second, much to the despair of the home crowd. Aberdeen won the game 3-2 but could and should have added to their tally after a dominant performance at Pittodrie. After the game, Alex Ferguson, despite the obvious disappointment at losing a late goal, was still very proud of his young team. 'I've heard an awful lot of moaning and groaning about missed chances, that missed penalty and the goals we gave away, but we can hold our heads up and say we won the game. Aberdeen beat Hamburg – that's a fact.' Gordon Strachan later assessed that the Aberdeen performance that night against Hamburg was the finest he had participated in.

For this chapter I spoke with former SV Hamburg defensive midfielder Bernd Wehmeyer, who between 1978 and 1986 played nearly 200 games for the West German club. During his time with Hamburg, Bernd was a multiple winner, having won the European Cup and the German Bundesliga on three separate occasions. He played in all four games against Aberdeen in the 1980s and recalls the UEFA Cup ties fondly: 'We knew Aberdeen had a strong team with really good players.

Back then it wasn't like it is today where you have so much information on your opponents; today that information is all available. Today, you can watch all the games on TV, but back then this wasn't possible. One of our coaches went to watch Aberdeen play and reported back, so we knew we were facing very tough games against them. We knew the atmosphere at Pittodrie would be very good, we knew that Aberdeen had fantastic fans and we knew about their style of play. In these games I was up against Gordon Strachan, man-to-man, and as you can imagine it wasn't so easy for me. He was a player who reminded me of Kevin Keegan who played for Hamburg at one time. Gordon isn't a tall guy, like Kevin. I am also not such a tall guy, but our coach knew I could run. It wasn't very often that we would play this style, but when our coach told me that we would play this way I knew I must be playing against a very special player. We would always play our game but in this case, we knew he was the mastermind in midfield for Aberdeen and we had to try and keep him out of the game, which isn't always 100 per cent possible. Aberdeen had other good players like Alex McLeish, Willie Miller and Mark McGhee, so we knew it was going to be a difficult game.

'The second goal was very important for us because it gave us hope for the game back in Hamburg. In the first game Aberdeen had a lot of pressure and it was a very tough game for us. Aberdeen had an excellent manager in Alex Ferguson, but we also had a great manager in Ernst Happel, the famous Austrian coach. We knew Aberdeen would put a lot of pressure on us, especially the night games, under the floodlights and with a crowded stadium; the atmosphere was fantastic. It was difficult for us to play our game because of Aberdeen's pressure. That is why our second goal from Horst Hrubesch was so important. It certainly helped us for the second game back in Hamburg. I crossed the ball for Horst to score our first goal; I managed to get a cross in from nearly the corner flag. Thankfully, we managed to win the game 3-1 and go through, but it was a tough match.'

For the return game in Hamburg a fortnight later, Aberdeen suffered a major blow the day before the game. Having left Dyce on the Tuesday morning, the lads had a light training session at the Volksparkstadion that evening, but during this session, winger Peter Weir tore a nerve in his back and was unable to play, despite the best efforts of the club doctor who even called out a specialist in the middle of the night to try and rectify the issue. On the night Aberdeen were unable to keep possession and lost their composure. It was no surprise that the big striker Horst Hrubesch headed home Hamburg's first goal to bring the tie level. Not long after the restart Hamburg were awarded a very dubious penalty, an incident that midfielder Neil Simpson remembers well. 'I never touched the boy. Felix Magath came across me and fell down; there was no contact. That put them ahead in the tie and gave them the momentum.' That penalty put Hamburg 2-0 up on the night and 4-3 ahead on aggregate, and not long after they added a third. The goal of the game though was reserved for substitute Mark McGhee who scored a superb goal from 18 yards to make the score 3-1 on the night, but trailing 4-5 on aggregate. That is how the game finished; Aberdeen were out. During a post-match television interview, West German legend Franz Beckenbauer was delighted to get through the tie. 'We were very satisfied with our performance because we won the game 3-1. It wasn't an easy game for us because the Aberdeen team played very well. After 3-1 we struggled a little bit to finally win the game, but we are very happy of course. Aberdeen is a very young team, the youngsters played very well so the future is good for this team.'

Aberdeen manager Alex Ferguson was gracious in defeat: 'I must congratulate Hamburg on a win they deserved. They were the better side on the night, so we have no complaints.'

That season SV Hamburg made it all the way to the final, losing 4-0 to IFK Gothenburg over two legs, home and away. The Germans did make up for that disappointment by winning the Bundesliga title for the fifth time and a year later won the European Cup for the first and only time in their history. That very same European Cup success for SV Hamburg, having beaten Juventus 1-0 in the final, coupled with Aberdeen's success over Real Madrid, meant the two sides would meet each other again on the European stage, but this time in the UEFA Super Cup final, to be played over two legs, home and away. The first game was scheduled for 22 November 1983 at the Volksparkstadion in Hamburg. For goalkeeper Jim Leighton, whose mistake led to Hamburg's equaliser at Pittodrie two years earlier, he wanted nothing more than to right those wrongs. He said in the days leading up to the first leg, 'We're looking for revenge against Hamburg and no one will be more delighted than me if we beat them. They knocked us out of the UEFA Cup two years ago and I still have nightmares about our last clash. They really turned it on over there and won 3-1 in the second leg. But I think I can promise there won't be the same differences between the two sides this time around. For a start we have grown up as a team and learned a lot since then.'

Midfielder Neil Simpson also firms up the sense of revenge ahead of the game: 'Fergie's message to us for that game was, "We owe Hamburg," because they knocked us out of the UEFA Cup two seasons previously. That was a huge opportunity missed as we should have beaten Hamburg back then! It was an opportunity for us to make things right, even though we were up against the European Cup winners; they still had big-time players playing for them: Wolfgang Rolff, Felix Magath and their goalkeeper Uli Stein. They were a quality side.'

Twenty-four hours before the game, in what was the last training session at the Volksparkstadion, captain Willie Miller sustained his hamstring. It was the first time that Willie had received that type of injury. Physiotherapist David Wylie jumped into action, but with no improvement overnight, Ferguson was now left with a selection headache. With only one hour until kick-off, Willie went through a vigorous fitness test on the park with David Wylie while Ferguson watched on from the sidelines. The decision was left to Willie – he gave both the nod and he played. Neil Simpson recalls the incident vividly. 'What I remember about that game was Willie Miller required a fitness test ahead of the game; if anybody else had pulled their hamstring they would have been out for ten days minimum, but not Willie! He got through the fitness test and played. It was a 50/50 game in Hamburg – they had a few chances and we had a few chances. I also remember Fergie was satisfied with the result and performance after the game.'

Defender Alex McLeish was so bristling with confidence that he expected nothing else but to add another medal to his already growing collection. 'By this point we had such a controlled arrogance that going to Hamburg and getting a 0-0 draw, we made it look easy! We had every belief after the first game that we would do them back home at Pittodrie; there was absolutely no doubt about that. With Real Madrid, we felt we were going into the unknown somewhat, but now that we had overcome that hurdle to win the Cup Winners' Cup, everybody in our dressing room was convinced we would win the Super Cup!'

A workmanlike display in Hamburg for the first game is testament to Aberdeen's new-found maturity. Chances in the game were few and far between but Aberdeen did create the best opening when Mark McGhee cut in from the right wing and danced his way past a host of defenders, and with only the keeper to beat, he inexplicably struck the ball against Uli Stein's outstretched right leg – it would have been the goal of the season. For Hamburg, who always carried an attacking threat, they struggled to break down Aberdeen's regimented back line. When the Germans did break through, goalkeeper Jim Leighton stood firm, saving twice from Dieter Schatzschneider and Felix Magath in quick succession. The Dons finished the game strongly and on the front foot but couldn't find that all-important opener over 90 minutes, and the game finished 0-0. After the game, a satisfied Alex Ferguson met the press and had this to say, 'We defended as I had hoped, and we were aware of Hamburg's strengths. Our midfield had to stay focused as they have real quality in there, but we were ready for them. We still have to win the tie, but this result gives us a marvellous platform to finish the job in front of our own supporters.'

Naturally, for SV Hamburg this wasn't the result they desired or needed ahead of the return leg. Having played against Aberdeen in both UEFA Cup ties two years previously, defensive midfielder Bernd Wehmeyer was better placed than most to fully appreciate the difficulty that lay ahead, and he explains: 'We were disappointed to draw 0-0 because we knew from the games two years before how difficult it would be to play away in Aberdeen. We had many games at that time including the Intercontinental Cup final in Tokyo. The team that played against Aberdeen for the Super Cup final wasn't the same team that played two years previously in the UEFA Cup and it wasn't the same team that won the European Cup only a few months before when we beat Juventus in Athens. After the European Cup final both our main strikers, Horst Hrubesch and Lars Bastrup, left the club. Our manager at the time, Günter Netzer, wanted to make our team younger, but to be honest this didn't work for us. We replaced Horst Hrubesch, who would score goal after goal, with a young striker called Dieter Schatzschneider from Hannover, who scored many goals in the second division in Germany. We also signed Wolfram Wuttke from Schalke, but they couldn't replace Hrubesch and Bastrup. They were both very good players, but the mentality that Horst Hrubesch had especially was missing, and Lars Bastrup was a very quick player who was very good on the counter-attack; this was missing from these two new players, so it meant the team wasn't as strong as it was when we won the European Cup back in the summer of 1983. We were disappointed to only draw the first game in Hamburg as we knew how tough the game would be at Pittodrie.'

Aberdeen had to wait nearly a month for the return leg at home, but in that time the Dons had gone undefeated in the league, having beaten Dundee United, Motherwell and Hibs while drawing 0-0 with Celtic in between. The Dons had also progressed to the semi-finals of the League Cup having beaten Dundee 3-1 at Dens Park. During this time, Alex Ferguson's trusted lieutenant Archie Knox left to take up the manager's role at Dundee. Ferguson took sole charge of the side until he appointed Willie Garner in February 1984. For the match itself Ferguson made two changes from the first leg in Germany. Freshly signed Stewart McKimmie replaced Neale Cooper at right-back and John McMaster replaced Doug Rougvie at left-back. It was an opportunity for those who missed out on Gothenburg to hopefully witness Aberdeen win a European trophy on home soil, and that night the ground creaked and swayed as every last seat was taken up by a passionate home support.

In his programme notes on the night of the match, Alex Ferguson explained why the club paid Dundee £90,000 for McKimmie's services: 'The investment necessary to bring Stewart McKimmie from Dundee is all part of the plan to ensure that top-class football remains at Pittodrie for at least as long as I am in charge of playing affairs. This signing has been made vital because of the long-term absence of Stuart Kennedy, a full-back whose quality and contribution to the team is very difficult to replace.' It would prove to be the best of introductions for the 21-year-old! Stewart McKimmie played the first of his 39 European games for the Dons against SV Hamburg in the Super Cup final; it was only his second appearance for the club after signing from Dundee.

Stewart spoke to me for this book and recalled his emotions ahead of kick-off: 'I was nervous before every game, but it was a good nervous because I think if you are not nervous there must be something wrong. I was nervous until the referee blew his whistle to start the game but as soon as the whistle went, I forgot about my nerves. I got on with the game and concentrated on the job in hand against my immediate opponent and what I had to do in the game. I went into a great side – I have said this previously – and anybody could have slotted into the right-back position in that side. They made it so easy for me. I could never have imagined I would have played in that game two weeks earlier while at Dundee and fighting against relegation, wondering if I would receive a new contract. Before I knew it, I was playing in a Super Cup final against Hamburg who were the European champions, I could have never imagined that. Then, I am in and part of the team. The players around me were so good that it made it easy for me. I look back now and watch the games and see the videos and I get more emotional now than I did back then because maybe at the time I didn't appreciate what I had just achieved. I have played in a European final, won the league title and Scottish Cups, but it isn't until I stopped playing and look back that I think I actually did quite well and achieved much in the game – back then it was my job! That's how I treated my career – it was my job.'

There was such a demand for the game that a television broadcasting deal was confirmed six days before the match. For fans back home the game was shown live on Grampian TV and Scottish Television and for those abroad the pictures were beamed into places such as West Germany, Libya, Portugal, Holland, Algeria, France, Thailand, Malaysia, Singapore, Brunei, Hong Kong, Pakistan, Malta, Qatar and Abu Dhabi. This deal though did bring one amusing complaint from a committee member of the Perth branch of the Aberdeen Supporters' Club who said, 'We have been conned into paying £5 for a ticket for the game, because Aberdeen said the game wasn't being televised live. Aberdeen will lose a lot of support from Perth and Forfar. I'm going back to supporting Celtic!!!!'

Alex Ferguson was determined that his Aberdeen team would go all out for the win and add another prize to the already glistening trophy cabinet. He had this to say ahead of the game: 'I am convinced we are going to see a great game tonight. We will be facing Hamburg's strongest team and we will have to work as hard as we have ever done if we are to beat them. The lads will be exhausted by the end – but hopefully it will be an enjoyable exhaustion. This game is as important as any cup final we have taken part in. This time though, we have a reputation in Europe, and we must try to live up to it.' He went on to say, 'We have got to start off in top gear and make sure Hamburg do not get an early lift. We gave Bayern Munich a goal in the opening minutes last season and we had to chase them after that point. And we must be equally sure there are no gift goals handed out to Hamburg this time. They got more than their share when they were here a couple of years ago.'

Midfielder Neil Simpson had other thoughts on his mind pre-match, and he explains. 'I had not been playing particularly well up until that point. I was going through a slight loss of form but thankfully Fergie always picked me for the bigger games. I was playing OK during the first half but nothing amazing, so when I scored my goal in the second half it felt like a huge weight had been lifted off my shoulders which meant that for the second half of the season, I was able to rediscover my form and played well again. I didn't overly celebrate when I scored because maybe it was just how I was playing at the time, so I think I felt relief more than anything else. The celebrations at the end of the game felt a little muted because it was not like we received the trophy up in the stands; we were waiting for the trophy then suddenly it was just a plaque we received! It was almost like, "Oh, is this it?" Don't get me wrong, it wasn't a major disappointment that it was just a plaque, but it would have been nice to receive an actual trophy that we could all have held aloft.'

Neil Simpson's opener came just at the right time, two minutes after the restart. For the opening period Hamburg enjoyed the bulk of possession but never at any time did they look like scoring. At half-time Alex Ferguson gave the lads his instructions: 'Get the ball played quicker into the last third of the park to get our full-backs to sit tighter on their midfield.' The goal started from a great tackle from Alex McLeish down Hamburg's right flank, and from there Peter Weir drove into Hamburg's final third and delivered a telling cross into the box. John Hewitt sliced his initial effort, but at the second attempt created the opportunity for Neil to score. Aberdeen made it 2-0 on 64 minutes when, from a driven, inswinging Peter Weir corner, the ball made its way to Willie Miller who had drifted in unnoticed at the back post, and he drove the ball back across the six-yard box for a grateful Mark McGhee who only needed to cushion the ball home. For the remainder of the game Aberdeen never looked in any danger of losing their grip on the tie, and the final whistle was met with scenes of joy once again. The team received a rousing ovation from the 22,500 capacity crowd as Willie Miller received the Super Cup or plaque as it was back then from the head of the Dutch Football Association. In 27 European ties at Pittodrie, this was the 12th time that Aberdeen had denied their opponents a goal. The Super Cup triumph was Aberdeen's 27th win in 55 European games.

In what was an astonishing sequence of events, Peter Weir recalls that night with a huge amount of fondness, not for the fact that he added another medal to his growing collection, but for the fact his wife gave birth to a baby boy – without his knowledge!! 'After we won the game, we're all lining up to collect our medals when club secretary Ian Taggart came over and offered his congratulations. At the time I had absolutely no idea that my wife's waters had broken at 4.45 p.m. back home in the Bridge of Don. Thankfully, my brother-in-law arrived at the house just afterwards and was able to get her up to hospital. Here is me thinking Ian was congratulating me on a fine game I had just played but he was congratulating me on having another baby son. Stuart was born at 7 p.m. I had absolutely no idea! You must imagine the scenes in the dressing room after the game when the lads found out I had just become a dad again – they were throwing baby powder all over me. Honestly, it felt like I was in a dreamland. After I had cleaned up and made my way out the stadium, I went up to the hospital to try to go and see my wife and new baby son, but they would not let me past the main entrance to the hospital because it was after visiting hours! Here is me banging on the doors and eventually the night porter came around who was a big Aberdeen fan, and he sneaked me in, so I was able to get a few minutes with my wife and Stuart. Honestly, that was an absolutely magical night.'

After the game, a beaming Alex Ferguson met the press and looked back on another glorious night for the club. 'It was the start of the second half that really killed off Hamburg. I told them at half-time to step up the pace a bit and they did a marvellous job. I thought we competed well in the first half, but it was very tight. In the first half we allowed them too much room on the flanks. However, that was sorted out at the interval, and when the first goal came it changed the complexion of the game. Having travelled halfway around the world in the past week, we had to find out about their stamina, and although they showed they are a good side, it was obvious they were toiling near the end. I think you can say I enjoyed the game.'

For Hamburg it was one disappointment after another. The Germans had been knocked out of the European Cup by Dinamo Bucureşti in the second round, they had lost the Intercontinental Cup (Club World Cup) against Brazilian side Gremio only nine days previously, and now they had lost in the Super Cup final. I wanted to know from Bernd Wehmeyer if the long trip to Japan had taken its toll on the Hamburg players. 'Oh yes, for sure it did. Before the Intercontinental Cup in Tokyo, we had to play a Bundesliga game and left immediately for Japan. We only arrived a day before the final and we didn't have the time to acclimatise whereas Gremio had arrived one week before the game. We had some injury problems due to many games in a short period of time. We had a few injuries ahead of the game in Aberdeen. Manfred Kaltz missed the first game, but he did start against Aberdeen for the return game but had to come off. Thomas von Heesen was also missing for the second game. We knew when Aberdeen scored their second goal that it would be very difficult for us to get back into the game. At the end of the day Aberdeen were the better team and deserved to win. It's good to look back at this game and remember the special atmosphere created at Pittodrie because the crowd are so close to the pitch. It was a fantastic experience to play in a small, packed stadium. I enjoy looking back on those games.'

It was no surprise that the Germans didn't hang about and headed directly to the airport, and the only comments came from Hamburg general manager Günter Netzer who apologised to waiting reporters by only saying, 'I'm sorry, the bus is waiting.' And according to one report an unnamed SV Hamburg player was allegedly overheard saying, 'I wish we could play in atmospheres like that all the time.'

For Neil Simpson, the magnitude of Aberdeen's victory only became apparent having had a good night's sleep! 'The achievement for me personally started to sink in when I was reading the match report in the newspaper the next day because many of the headlines read "Kings of Europe". We also won the Adidas Team of the Year when we were ranked the number one club in Europe just before the game, so it was an incredibly special period for us. Fergie was delighted with us in the dressing room after the game, but his attitude was like it always was – "This is what I expected you to do!"

Before the year was out Aberdeen collected another award having been voted 'the best team in Europe' in an annual award hosted by Adidas and renowned football magazine *France Football*. Manager Alex Ferguson flew to Paris for the event and collected the award, and he said afterwards, 'It's a tremendous honour to be voted the best team in Europe when you think of some of the other cracking sides who were in the running. It's always nice to receive recognition for your efforts on the field. Beating Real Madrid to win the Cup Winners' Cup last season put Aberdeen firmly on the map and being voted Team of the Year helps to promote our name even further.'

In the space of 224 days Aberdeen had won the Cup Winners' Cup, the Scottish Cup and now the Super Cup. As well as the trophies taking pride of place in the boardroom, Aberdeen FC's bank balance was now £200,000 better off thanks to ticket sales and additional monies earned from the television deal. It was the perfect end to the perfect year.

1984

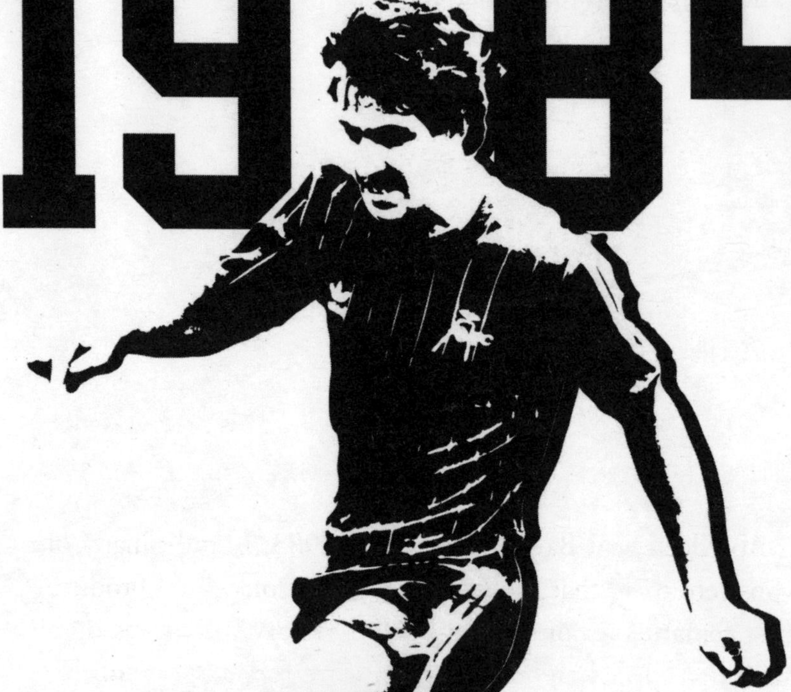

TEN

UJPEST DOZSA

After Aberdeen beat Bayern Munich in 1983, I doubt many of us who were there that night believed the Dons could produce another remarkable come-from-behind victory which was on a par with that special night at Pittodrie. Fast-forward 12 months, and they did, against little-known Hungarian outfit Ujpest Dozsa. Aberdeen entered the Cup Winners' Cup for the second successive season after winning the Scottish Cup, while aiming to be the first club ever to retain the trophy. Aberdeen had negotiated their way through the early rounds after Akranes of Iceland and Beveren from Belgium were dispatched without too much fuss. There were scenes of jubilation ahead of the Beveren game as it was announced only hours earlier that Alex Ferguson had agreed a new five-year deal to manage the club, making him the highest-paid manager in Scotland on a reported annual salary of £250,000 plus bonuses. There was something in the Pittodrie air that night which inspired the lads on the pitch, who put in an excellent all-round performance by winning the game 4-1 to reach the quarter-finals.

The draw for the quarter-finals was a favourable one for the Dons considering Barcelona, Manchester United and Juventus all lay in wait. It proved to be another evening spent biting fingernails down to the bone after a tumultuous 90 minutes of football under the lights at Pittodrie, but one never to be forgotten. Aberdeen's schedule for the month of March included two league games, a Scottish League Cup semi-final second leg, a Scottish Cup quarter-final and the two games against Ujpest – there was always something to look forward to as spring blossomed across the north-east.

The travelling party headed to Budapest for the first leg knowing they had not been beaten in 29 games. It was an astonishing record, but like all good things, they must come to an end at some point. That's exactly what happened in the Megyeri úti Stadion. Twenty-nine thousand ardent fans stood shoulder to shoulder that night and helped create a superb yet intimidating atmosphere in a stadium that had a remarkable resemblance to the Praterstadion in Vienna, albeit on a smaller scale.

In the days leading up to the game, Ujpest manager Miklós Temesvári spoke to the local press and offered these thoughts: 'I don't think we could be better prepared. As far as we are concerned it will be a case of trying to transmit those thoughts into actions. I don't believe we are as good a team as Aberdeen, but I didn't think we were as good as Cologne – and we beat them in the last round.' Alex Ferguson sat with the written press the night before the game and stated the importance of coming away from Budapest with something to play for ahead of the return leg. He said, 'I have already said to the players that no-scoring draws are not good enough for us away from home in Europe. We want a place in the semi-final draw and if we can take a step towards it by winning in Hungary, then that's all right with me.' Fergie finished off by saying, 'But, we must not be complacent and take anything away from Ujpest as they have the type of players who will need some close attention. If we lose our concentration, it could prove fatal and give us an uphill job at Pittodrie.'

That night, 7 March 1984, Aberdeen went in search of their 100th European goal, but the lads were responsible for their own downfall having missed three glorious chances to get back into the game after Ujpest took the lead thanks to a brilliantly executed free kick by Sándor Kisznyér just after the break. First up, Doug Rougvie missed from within the six-yard box when it looked easier to score, then Gordon Strachan rounded the keeper and with the goal at his mercy, somehow managed to smash his goalbound shot against the post. The miss of the night though goes to Mark McGhee. With goalkeeper József Szendrei lying on his back inside his own net after making a remarkable clearance from a poor back pass, he somehow managed to stop McGhee's follow-up with his legs from two yards – it was a jaw-dropping miss! Aberdeen were to rue those misses as Ujpest doubled their lead with only eight minutes left, so it was a sore one to take with Alex Ferguson in particular raging with his side's inept performance over 90 minutes. As soon as the team bus arrived back at their plush hotel on the banks of the River Danube, Fergie disappeared to his room and was only seen again the next morning. He was still in a bad mood!

For this chapter I spoke at length with former Aberdeen striker Mark McGhee, who gave me a unique insight into both games, and we started talking about Alex Ferguson's mood at full time in the away dressing room. 'I will never forget it because it wasn't so much a hairdryer but more akin to a pyroclastic blast! I once did a foundation module for the Open University and it was all about plate tectonics and I have always remembered that, and that is why I use that expression to describe Fergie's reaction that night. His face was literally two inches from mine while he was screaming at me because I had missed that sitter during the game; he absolutely blasted me! I just remember for that chance I had that the ball came back off the bar; the pitch was really muddy but the ball was there to be put in the back of the net, and while the keeper is lying in the back of the net after making his save, I have come in ready to strike but the ball got stuck in the mud and somehow the keeper stuck his arm out and stopped the ball from going over the line, so they were able to scramble it away. With the game ending 2-0, Fergie felt with that goal that I should have scored he would have been more comfortable with 2-1, because then he knew there was a game on against a team which we should not have lost 2-0 to.'

For the Dons to progress to the semi-final, history would have to be rewritten as never before had an Aberdeen team recovered from a two-goal deficit in a European tie. That was all about to change though on 21 March 1984. Ahead of the match, Alex Ferguson wrote in his programme notes that despite the toughness of the occasion facing Aberdeen, he recalled losing 3-0 away in Düsseldorf yet winning the home leg 2-0. It wasn't enough to turn the tie around that night, but he finished off by writing, 'That result will do me by the end of normal time tonight – and then we will see what might happen.' Did he have a crystal ball in his possession in the days leading up to the game? Fergie was adamant that his side would make up for the poor first leg showing by saying, 'I look forward to the prospects of seeing Aberdeen reassert themselves with effort and imagination to conquer the challenge. As far as I am concerned, we are just one step away from a place in a major European competition semi-final, and it's something which I refuse to surrender just because we have two goals to recover.'

Mark recalls the thoughts of Fergie in the days leading up to the game. 'He was never one for dwelling on things, and it wasn't about what had gone on before. He was only focused on almost trying to script what in the end happened on the night

– get a goal in the first half, get a goal in the second half and see where we go from there, because we have that length of time to win the game. We don't have to win it in the 90 minutes so he tried to take some of the pressure away from us. That was his approach to the game – making sure we knew we had 120 minutes to try and win the game if we could get the two goals back, which he was confident we could do.' Mark also recalls the thoughts of the players going into the game. 'I would say that we were determined more than anything else, and we wanted to make up for the result over there; we were determined to get through. We were confident we would give it a go, but I think it's fair to say that you can never be confident we were going to turn that one around – we were determined, and I think that was the big difference.'

Aberdeen started the game brightly but were unable to break down what was a stubborn Ujpest defence, and it was obvious that the Hungarians had come to Pittodrie to sit in and protect their two-goal lead. The Dons had to wait until the 37th minute to break the deadlock when Mark McGhee powered home a brilliant Gordon Strachan cross. That goal was Aberdeen's 100th in European competition. The Dons went into the break a goal to the good but still trailing in the tie. Alex Ferguson and Archie Knox had 15 minutes to rally their troops, which Mark explains further. 'They both kept repeating the same message: we have 45 minutes to get a goal. They both reminded us that we only needed one goal, not two, just one and see where it takes us. At the same time, they reminded us to keep the door shut at the back and nullify any threat that they might pose early doors. Sir Alex reminded us that we must not take risks, and we do not go out for the second half with some sort of abandon to our play. Fergie made sure that we were all conscious of that by not throwing the kitchen sink at it, which could open us up to possibly concede.'

With Aberdeen leading 1-0 but with the clock ticking down, the Dons desperately went on the prowl for an equaliser which would take the game to extra time, but not at any time did that concern Mark and his teammates. 'That never entered our heads because those nights tended to be a bit of a whirlwind. We were so focused on getting that goal that we never took the time to check where the clock was sitting – I can never recall worrying that there was only x minutes to go in a game. It was always about keeping going – keep going, keep the pressure on them; keep getting chances and get the goal until we made the breakthrough.'

Ferguson gambled and threw Willie Falconer on for John Hewitt. Willie recalls the instructions from the boss as he stood waiting to enter the field of play. 'Mark McGhee was playing through the middle that night so he put me out on the left and told me to get past the full-back and get the cross in as early as I could. I can still recall the cross that I put into the box for Mark to score what was our equaliser right at the end of the game. That was a huge moment for us. The atmosphere at Pittodrie for that night, and every European game I had been involved in, was unbelievable. When Mark scored that goal, the whole place lifted. Thankfully, that night worked out well for me. Sir Alex was delighted but, to be honest, you could never tell how he would react. There were times after games, and he would go through every individual player, or he and Archie would come in and you could see that they were happy enough with the result and performance. That night I think it was just the relief that we had been able to get through to the semi-finals after being 2-0 down from the first leg. I even received a well done and a wee pat on the back which was nice!'

Mark's equaliser came with only two minutes left on the clock. From a Neil Simpson throw-in, deep in the corner, he played a driven ball to Willie Falconer who in turn did brilliantly to create the room inside the 18-yard area to drive a ball across the six-yard box. Mark was on hand to stroke the ball home; he couldn't miss! He turned away with his right arm pointed forward and he was quickly surrounded by his delighted teammates; the game had been rescued right at the death. Mark explains the emotions of that moment: 'I had thought about it for years and I had never actually been able to properly put into words the emotions I felt until I heard the Neville brothers talk about the players' relationship with Sir Alex. They got it spot on – they said it was personal and they were right! When I went out and played for him and if I didn't play well or missed a chance, the only person that I really cared who I was letting down was him. Most of the time that was part of his genius, that he didn't always leave you feeling that he was angry with you, but he left you feeling that he was disappointed with you. It's that feeling when you disappoint your parents. The feeling is ten times worse than making them angry, so my emotion was that I had lived for those past couple of weeks between the games knowing I had let him down, and the one thing that I didn't want to do was exactly that. When I scored the second goal, I felt like I had helped us get a step closer to the victory; I felt like I had given us an opportunity to win the game.'

Mark McGhee's winner, three minutes into extra time, was met by a noise reminiscent of John Hewitt's winner against Bayern Munich. Pittodrie erupted once again! That goal completed Mark's hat-trick, his second for the club overall and very much made up for that horrendous miss in the first leg. Mark would go on to finish joint-top goalscorer in the competition that season with five goals, a record he shared with Shakhtar Donetsk pair Viktor Grachev and Sergei Morozov. 'At the time, unlike other goals that I had scored, for example in the cup final, it was almost like a feeling of euphoria. There had been a lot said by Sir Alex in the dressing room after the first game; he slaughtered us! After the first game back in the hotel, Gordon Strachan and I, who shared a room together, felt angry about the defeat and more determined that we would bounce back. Gordon and I spoke for hours about that defeat after the game in the hotel. We had dwelled on that game and that result for the entire period up until the return leg. It wasn't like others where you can set it aside and get on with everything else that you need to get on with when it comes to other games, because at that stage of the season, we had plenty of big games to contest. The Ujpest game had bugged us, and it was on all of our minds, so when that third goal went in the feeling was one of euphoria as we knew then that we would go on and win the game.

'What I have always recalled is Archie Macpherson's commentary on the full-time whistle in great praise of Willie Miller's performance – Sir Alex was a little like that too. I have watched the coverage back and Archie began his post-match summary by saying something along the lines of, "Well, if anybody typifies the Aberdeen spirit," and don't forget I have just scored a hat-trick, so of course I am sitting there expecting Archie to say, "it's Mark McGhee," and the camera pans towards Willie and he says 'Willie Miller"! Sir Alex almost took the same attitude. Just because I had scored a hat-trick, there was no way he was going to let me off the hook. It was almost like he was thinking, "Well, you put yourselves in that position in the first place from the first leg and you were not good enough in the first game." He didn't give us much quarter; he was still slaughtering us.'

Afterwards a beaming Alex Ferguson admitted watching his troops was a 'nerve-wracking experience' and went on to say, 'We knew, however, that was liable to be the case, and the players stuck to their task magnificently. This was a real test of character for my players, and I'm delighted the way they handled it.' His counterpart Miklós Temesvári kept his team in the dressing room for a good half an hour after the game, and when he did eventually appear to speak to the press, he conceded the better team won on the night. 'I would like to say that Aberdeen were a much better team than us. I said before we met them that they were one of the best in Europe and that's still the way I feel.'

When researching for this book I was surprised to learn that Mr Temesvári was critical of the home support when he said this about the Aberdeen fans: 'I thought they were still quiet and didn't do enough to help their team.' He had also mentioned ahead of the game that Aberdeen would receive no assistance from the home fans. Having been lucky enough to be in attendance at Pittodrie that night, I will take umbrage with Mr Temesvári's comments as the noise created by the home fans to help their team get across the line was as good as I had ever heard. You will just have to trust me when I tell you it was spine-tingling stuff, especially when Mark McGhee headed home Aberdeen's winner. The place went mental! Mark has often wondered if the atmosphere that night was comparable with the Bayern game. 'I think it was but equally, Bayern Munich are Bayern Munich. When you play these big teams there has to be another dimension, an extra edge to dream about playing in Europe and how the fans feel at that time; we wanted to play against the big teams and therefore the game against Bayern painted a bigger picture for us. It was a bigger statement whereas against Ujpest it was a game that had to be dealt with and on the night it was a fantastic performance, result and outcome which was limited to that night – it didn't have global repercussions like the Bayern result did. Nobody was thinking, "My God, Aberdeen have beaten Ujpest Dozsa; hardly anybody would have noticed, but when we beat Bayern Munich everybody in the world started to wonder who Aberdeen were."

A second successive European semi-final beckoned! Sadly though, despite their best efforts, the Dons went out of the competition to a Porto side who had too much in their locker for

Aberdeen over two legs. Aberdeen right-back Stewart McKimmie recalls the disappointment felt at the time. 'For the Porto game I think everyone underestimated just what a good team they were, not so much Aberdeen Football Club and Alex Ferguson but more the supporting public. I remember playing over there and the atmosphere was amazing. There were near enough 65,000 fans inside the stadium that night; they had such passion, the fans, and it was an amazing experience. We lost the game 1-0 and we probably didn't deserve to win that game to be fair, but we kept ourselves in the tie which was the main objective. For the home game at Pittodrie there was massive expectation on our shoulders, and everybody expected that it would be a foregone conclusion; the public maybe expected us just to turn up and we would win the game. Porto were very well organised, very athletic and had very good football players. Unfortunately, we lost a late goal; I was off the park at that moment because I picked up an injury and came off. The guy who I was marking, Vermelhinho, picked the ball up and scored and that put us out of the competition, which was hugely disappointing because we did believe we had a massive opportunity to get to the final.'

That game against Porto would prove to be the last time Aberdeen competed in a European semi-final. They came ever so close two seasons later but for a late away goal at Pittodrie by IFK Gothenburg's Johnny Ekström. Aberdeen went out of the European Cup at the quarter-final stage on away goals, having not lost a single game in the competition! After that soul-destroying exit at the venue of our greatest ever triumph right up until the new millennium, Aberdeen failed, like they did in the seventies, to progress beyond the second round of any European competition. There were some frustrations along the way including three away goals defeats against Feyenoord in November 1987, Rapid Vienna two years later and most annoyingly against Bohemians from Dublin in what was described at the time as one of the worst European results in Aberdeen's history. Stewart McKimmie played in the majority of those games during the late eighties and nineties, and he recalls: 'Feyenoord are a massive name in Dutch football and Rapid Vienna were a quality side from Austria. We were playing against top players and established teams from their respective countries. Holland as a country was renowned in world football and Austria was still emerging as a football nation. It was hugely disappointing to lose these games on the away goals rule.'

In season 1993/94, Aberdeen were drawn against Serie A side Torino, and that tie produced one of Pittodrie's most famous goals when Lee Richardson smashed one home from 20 yards. It was a gallant effort by the Dons, but the quality of the Italians proved too much in the end. Stewart recognised the effort put in by the side over the two games. 'In Italy, I think we surprised ourselves because when you go to play against teams from Italy, you always think you are going to be up against it. We played brilliantly in the first 20 minutes. It was disappointing to lose a two-goal lead but, despite the defeat, it was still a decent result over there which I think was better than we were first expecting. When we got them back to Pittodrie and went 1-0 up, at that point, the away goals rule kicked in and we were winning the tie. Maybe again we underestimated how good the Italians were. They may have underperformed in Torino whereas we played very well, and we may have put some added pressure on ourselves after Lee Richardson scored because there was a fantastic opportunity to get through. I don't think we should have been so disappointed at going out because we matched them which was probably unexpected going into the games.'

The following season Aberdeen were drawn against little known Latvian side Skonto Riga – what happened next proved to be one of the worst results in the club's history. It's an experience Stewart has not forgotten, 'We had some players playing in these games that didn't have much European experience. We may have disrespected them a little, we are talking about a Latvian club so there may have been a feel that just because it was a team from Latvia we were expecting just to turn up and win. I think we may have underestimated them, very much like what we did with Barry Town. I appreciate we beat Barry Town but we struggled against them at Pittodrie. There could be an argument to suggest that we may have thought that we were better than we actually were and that we should be walking over these types of teams. It's important to earn your victory and I think we went along just expecting to win.'

So, why, in Stewart's opinion, did Aberdeen fail to progress beyond the second round of any European competition after season 1986/87? Why did the flames go out of our European campaigns for so long? 'There were a lot of changes in personnel at the club, especially the managers. If you look at some of the bigger teams that we played against during the successful years, we had an established team, whereas when all the changes in management happened, they started bringing in players from some of the smaller clubs who had very limited experience, if any, of playing in Europe. I do not understand why we treat European games differently, especially the away leg, because I am a believer at the end of the day that a game of football is just a game of football! Regardless of whether you are playing home or away, why should we play more defensively away from home? What is the difference? We are playing the same side that we did back at Pittodrie, so why change the tactics to accommodate the away leg? When we lost games on away goals, I couldn't understand why we would have to go out there and play a more defensive game. We didn't go out there to win the match, we went out there not to lose the match! That is a big difference in attitude. We tried to keep it tight and then if we lost a goal, that was it, the plan went out of the window. If I were the manager or the coach of a team playing in Europe, I would not change my tactics; I would play to our strengths. There is no point having your strikers just chasing back all game. There is an argument to suggest that we showed too little respect to the smaller clubs and too much respect to the bigger clubs. I just wish we had played the Aberdeen way and the Aberdeen way back then was to play attacking football.'

Stewart played his final European game for Aberdeen against Brøndby in the UEFA Cup on 29 September 1996. Aberdeen lost 2-0 on aggregate over two legs with all the damage inflicted in the first leg at Pittodrie. The Dons would not compete in Europe again until the turn of the new millennium, but the less said of the Bohemians Dublin defeat on away goals the better! Two seasons on from that humiliating exit, Aberdeen redeemed themselves somewhat with two excellent performances against German Bundesliga side Hertha Berlin. In what was the club's 100th game in European competition, Aberdeen didn't have any answers to Hertha's steady back line, and the first leg finished 0-0. Between legs, Aberdeen won both of their domestic games in the Scottish Premier League and headed to the German capital in buoyant mood. In what was an ill-tempered match, Hertha won the match thanks to a last-minute header by Michael Preetz who broke the hearts of the 2,000 travelling Aberdeen support. It would be another five years before the Dons would compete on the European stage again, but it was so worth the wait.

20.07

★ ★ ★ ★ ★ ★ ★ ★ ★ ★ ★ ★

ELEVEN

DNIPRO

Writer Arthur C. Clarke once said, 'The only way to discover the limits of the possible is to go beyond them into the impossible.' Those sentiments couldn't be truer as Aberdeen faced a long trip to the outer reaches of the Ukraine to face a Dnipro side who held the Dons to a scoreless draw at Pittodrie in the first leg of the UEFA Cup first round in September 2007. It was a daunting task, but the Dons took a great deal of encouragement from the opening game. It wasn't beyond the realms of possibility that they could progress with the right application on the night. For the first leg Aberdeen were returning to European football for the first time in five years, but having recorded only one win from six at the beginning of the season, the form of the side was a concern. Dnipro on the other hand had made a solid start to their domestic campaign and sat second in the Ukrainian top flight coming into the game.

Manager Jimmy Calderwood was experiencing European football for the first time as a head coach and was very much looking forward to the task ahead. Preceding the first leg at

Pittodrie he collected his thoughts on the game for his column in the match-day programme: 'There is no doubt it's a massive ask as Dnipro have a number of international players in their squad, and we all know the quality of Ukrainian football. Technically, they will be extremely adept with a lot of movement but as we've seen on occasion recently, football is a strange game and, for our part, it's all going to be about performance.

Jimmy added, 'Obviously Sandy Clark and I have watched Dnipro in action and, as good as they are, like any team, they do have weaknesses and it's up to us to try and exploit them. While I would have preferred to have had the away leg first, you must accept what you're given and the most important thing for us tonight is that we play our own game, keep a clean sheet and hopefully gain an advantage at the other end!'

Aberdeen applied themselves well at Pittodrie but rued several missed chances and had to settle for a frustrating 0-0 draw. Midfielder Derek Young was a product of Aberdeen's youth system and spent seven seasons with the club before leaving for spells with Dunfermline, St Johnstone and Partick Thistle. In the summer of 2007 Derek rejoined the club to work under Jimmy Calderwood once again. Derek took his place in midfield that night against Dnipro and recalls his thoughts after the opening game at Pittodrie: 'We were a little bit down because we thought we had done enough in the first game to snatch a victory before we headed over there. We had made a couple of decent chances to score and overall we thought we had played well and kept them at bay. However, we knew their team had one or two very good players who had been watched carefully by bigger clubs in Europe who were looking to buy them, which was a sign they had been playing well. Going over there we knew we had a chance, and we knew we were solid enough at the back because we had been having a decent season, so we knew there was a chance of doing something over in the Ukraine. We were prepared to go over there, although we knew these places could be a million miles away from what we had been used to, and that's what it ended up being.'

Jimmy Calderwood remained upbeat after the game, and he said, 'We played really well and created good chances. For long phases of the game, we dominated a good team. We had to play at pace, and we did that well.' He finished off by saying, 'I think we are capable of scoring over there. They will have to open up and we have a bit of pace about us.' For Aberdeen to progress, the club's history books would have to be rewritten; never before had the Dons progressed in a European competition having drawn the first leg. The travelling party set off from Dyce Airport on a specially chartered flight on the Wednesday morning with the game scheduled for 24 hours later. Upon arrival in Ukraine's fourth largest city, the lads rested before heading to the stadium to go through a light training session. Central defender Zander Diamond, who started every game for Aberdeen during that UEFA Cup campaign, recalls an indifferent training experience. 'We knew we had to take something from the game in Ukraine to qualify. It was a one-off game and I have always remembered the dirty tactics the Ukrainians played on us in a poor attempt to unsettle us. When we had our training session in the stadium the night before the game, we could see people setting off smoke bombs and throwing them over the wall into the stadium; they must have set off a fire in a tyre factory or something. It was an incredible sight. There were guys there who were kidding on they were journalists. They were not journalists at all; they were there just to throw a microphone in our face to try and unsettle us once again. The guys who were there for the half-time entertainment were rehearsing on our side of the pitch and Jimmy C went berserk, so he shifted us all to the opposite goal. As we moved so did the entertainment people. Jimmy was doing his nut!'

Derek Young also recalls the trip over. 'We flew out on the day before the game; we all met at Aberdeen Airport and flew out from there. We knew some of the staff had been out here beforehand to check things over for us and had reported back that we would be playing in an old run-down stadium with no roof on it, completely open to the elements. Thankfully, the pitch was OK. When we arrived, we headed directly to the hotel, but we had been warned not to wander too far from the hotel and to only go out for a walk as a group which was absolutely fine – the lads just got on with things because we knew we were there to do a job. After the walk we came back to the hotel, rested for a couple of hours before having a meal and then headed to the stadium on the bus for a training session. I was surprised by the state of the stadium – it looked so old and it looked like it was falling to bits. Our dressing room felt like it was miles away from the pitch, and we had to walk down one long corridor and then another before walking out on to the pitch.

'I remember when we first walked into the dressing room, we couldn't quite believe our eyes. There were chairs spread about all over the place, all different sizes and different heights! There was also an old, leather couch which was pushed to the side, and we all walked in wondering if this was the actual changing room! I don't know if Dnipro were playing games with us or not, but I can imagine they had a plush, modern dressing room and they stuck us in their community room! When we walked out for training, we heard loads of noise from one side of the stadium but on the outside, hundreds of their fans had gathered and were setting off pyrotechnics and flares. We were warming up before the actual session thinking this is nuts, and then the smoke from the fireworks started drifting across the park. We were all choking on the smoke and I recall all the lads looking at each other wondering what on earth was going on! This was just the fans outside trying to intimidate us. It wasn't ideal, but we had to get on with it.'

The players and management were under no illusion that it would take a monumental effort to get a result in Ukraine, but Jimmy Calderwood had every faith in his players. He gave his usual pre-match instructions to the boys, which striker Darren Mackie, who was making his first start for the Dons since August, remembers vividly. 'He told us to just go out and give it everything that we've got, there's nothing to lose, and all the pressure is on them. Go out and give absolutely everything, and we will see what happens. He was particularly good at getting us all fired up. He would go around us individually while we were warming up, trying to get our confidence as high as possible before the game. He would put an arm around our shoulders and say, "Come on, I need a big performance from you," and it seemed to work often. Every guy on the pitch that night was outstanding. Everybody did their job and we all gave 100 per cent – that's what we needed that night.'

Derek Young also remembers the pre-match instructions. All the lads knew that the task ahead was going to test not just their physical capabilities but their psychological strength too. 'The manager told us the team in a meeting back at the hotel after our training session. Jimmy had us well prepared because the Dnipro team we played at Pittodrie was nothing compared to the team we played over there. Dnipro were more open, and they were flying down the wings and retaining the ball much better than the first game. At Pittodrie we were right up against them and winning the ball back. Jimmy knew that they would come at us and told us to sit tight and don't get caught out of position; just make sure we covered each other and most importantly not to lose an early goal. Michael Hart played behind me at right-back; I was playing right midfield and we had done well at Pittodrie. We had linked up well and restricted their left-back as he hardly made any runs in behind all game. We said to each other as we walked out on to the pitch for the return game that we must try and do the same again, but within minutes of the game starting, Michael and I knew we were going to be in for a long night because their left-back was on his bike down the flanks for the entire game. I can remember we had spoken about this before the game and there were a few times he got in behind and delivered one or two crosses but thankfully we were able to clear them without too much bother. If we won the ball, they attacked us straight away and gave us no room or time on the ball; it was so different from the game at Pittodrie. I knew we were going to be in for a long night only after five minutes!'

Twenty-seven minutes into the game came the moment that any Aberdeen fan will not forget in a hurry. From a quick throw-in, Richard Foster made space to deliver a cross with his left foot which Darren Mackie had already anticipated. He takes up the story: 'I was just making sure I was in the middle of the box, because as a striker that's where you need to be, and you're just hoping that the cross finds you. Fozzie is obviously thinking about putting it in and around the six-yard line and he has put it on a tee. He couldn't have delivered a better cross and, thankfully, it was right where I wanted it to be to throw myself at it. I was just doing my job, getting in the centre of the box, and hoping the ball came to me. Everything happened so fast. You are trying to make room for yourself in the box and get away from your marker; it's just that movement. A lot of the time you get attracted to the ball, but the defender that night has been attracted to it, and all I have done is peel off him. I have always been decent with my head and it was just a case of throwing myself at it. I knew if I made a good connection it was going in. There was an instant sense of pure elation. It was a massive release of ecstasy and all the boys were buzzing, and I was aware of the noise coming from the small band of Aberdeen fans behind the goal. It's hard to put into words. It was just an amazing feeling knowing we were now leading the tie and they had to score two goals. It felt like we had one foot in the group stages. I appreciate the moment more so now because, when fans ask me about it, they can remember where they were at that moment so, yes, it's genuinely nice to remember it that way. It's fantastic to have played a small part in Aberdeen's recent history.'

As the move developed, Derek Young bust a gut to make his way into the Dnipro final third, and as Richard Foster broke free, Derek had already anticipated the move and followed Darren Mackie into the danger area. It's a moment that has not slipped his memory. 'With the way we were set up we had plenty of pace in the side. Richard Foster, Darren Mackie, and I was quite quick myself, so as soon as we won the ball, we had to judge whether we could go at full pace or not, and that's all about game awareness. We managed to get the ball up the left-hand side and Richard Foster managed to get the ball out of his feet and started running at the boy and then fired a ball into the box; it was a great cross, right on the top of Dazza's head. I was also coming in the back of Dazza so there were two of us in the box ready to meet the ball, but Darren has dived in and managed to score a brilliant goal for us. What a relief that was. I can honestly say I can never remember feeling so good about a goal, even one that I had scored myself. We then knew we had something to hold on to, and we all knew if we kept it the way it was what was at the end of it; none of us had ever played in a UEFA Cup group game so we knew how big the carrot was at full time. I honestly do not know how we managed to hold out, but we did.'

That priceless goal was Darren Mackie's 50th goal for Aberdeen, and it was also his most significant. Aberdeen went into the break a goal to the good. Half-time couldn't come quickly enough as Derek Young explains: 'We came in at half-time into that bloody dressing room and we are all looking at each other thinking how the hell are we a goal to the good because it felt like we had hardly touched the ball in the first half! I can remember Jimmy Calderwood warning us this was going to be a battle from now until the end of the game. He reminded us that we had something to hold on to and not to make a daft run for the sake of it. He went on to say that if we were struggling to keep a hold of the ball, just to stick it high up into the stand. When we walked back out on to the park, we all reminded ourselves of the importance of sticking together and the need to get the result; we needed to make it happen! I can recall one moment during the second half when Scott Severin, Barry Nicholson and I were grouped together, and Barry asked me if I had touched the f**king ball yet! All he said was, "I'm just f**king kicking people; I'm just chasing people." We were all just dying! Whenever I received the ball in right midfield I would try and play a one-two and get down into one of the corners, or even knock a ball down there and chase it down, but as soon as I turned my back to see if I had any support from my teammates, they were all deep, holding a line. I know they missed a couple of good chances and we were defending like our lives depended on it, plus let's not forget that Jamie Langfield was having the game of his life – what a game he had that night.'

Dnipro needed to score twice to progress so the pattern of the second half didn't come as much of a surprise with the home team peppering Jamie Langfield's goal. Aberdeen's back line stood firm until the 75th minute when a fortuitous goal by Andriy Vorobey gave Dnipro a lifeline. It was going to be a long 15 minutes, but in the centre of defence Zander Diamond was having the game of his life. 'When Dazza scored we knew we had something to hold on to. If we all did our job that night, we knew we had a chance. When they equalised, I do not know for the life of me how they didn't score a second; balls were coming off the woodwork, Jamie Langfield was making save after save and we were blocking shots left, right and centre.'

Derek Young continues, 'I know that our coaching staff had

done their research on all their players and told us which of them could play on their left foot, who was strong on their right foot, and who could run with the ball, etc. They were very good at providing that sort of information. One of their lads played in an attacking midfield role and I could hear the two Jimmys shouting to us, "Keep him on his left, he's right-footed, keep him on his left." I gave the two Jimmys the big thumbs up to acknowledge their instructions. One minute later this boy gets the ball to his feet about 25 yards out, so I have shown him on to his left foot and he hits a ripper from 20 yards which flew just wide – what a hit it was! Half of our boys turned to the touchline to ask what the f**k was going on!! "You told us to keep him on his left," was the main complaint towards our bench! I swear they must have got the boy mixed up with somebody else! This happened again about a minute after Dnipro equalised. The instructions came from the bench to keep the lad on his right foot as he's all left-footed and again the boy hit one with his right foot which smacked off the bar! When the lads and I get together and talk about the Dnipro game we all have a really good laugh about that. As the clock ticked down, we were trying everything to waste time. If any Dnipro player came near us, we would go down and roll about; that was us giving them a taste of their own medicine from the first game.'

Aberdeen held out for the draw and progressed to the group stage. Dnipro threw everything they had at the Dons, but the lads held strong. It was an astonishing defensive performance from Jimmy Calderwood's men. For his exploits, defender Zander Diamond was dead on his feet. 'I have always remembered the end of that game because, as much as I was exhausted, I was completely elated as well. I have a brilliant photograph of me with the Aberdeen fans in front of the big clock. I love that photo! When we all got back into the dressing room, Jimmy C told us all that this was the highlight of his career to date. At the airport I was so tired, plus I was a little sore as I played that night with a couple of injections in my groin. I was feeling it somewhat. All the fans who were waiting on their own flights home had filled the bars and the stories were flowing which was brilliant fun! We were all hoping for a good draw so, when the draw was made, I do not think anybody was disappointed; it was a great group! Nobody gave us a chance that night, but we proved them all wrong.'

Derek Young also recalls the emotions as the referee blew for time up. 'When the full-time whistle blew it was such a rush of emotion. I actually think it took a good couple of minutes for it to sink in as we were all done – it felt like all of our bodies had caved in. I wish there were photographs to portray the mood in the dressing room after the game because everybody came in and patted each other on the back and congratulated each other, but within moments everybody just slumped down into their seats and the place fell very quiet because we were all so exhausted. Even the manager, Jimmy Nicholl and Sandy Clark were exhausted because those three are usually very animated on the touchline so I could see how tired they were. The flight home was ridiculously quiet because everybody was so tired. The manager had told us that we could have a drink after the game, but I was so tired I just wanted to sleep. I remember speaking with Jimmy and having a laugh with him because only 12 months previously I was playing for Partick Thistle in the Ramsdens Cup and now a full year on I am just away to play for Aberdeen in the UEFA Cup group stages which was almost ridiculous. I look back and don't care how the game went; I do not have a problem with that at all. It was a brilliant night and an experience I will never forget.'

That night Aberdeen had created history by progressing on away goals for the very first time. The scenes up on the terraces from the travelling support were just as impressive. Darren

Mackie's goal was quickly nicknamed the '£1 million-pound goal' with the club benefiting greatly from that UEFA Cup campaign. Jimmy Calderwood was quick to praise the efforts of the lads after the game. He said, 'It's a great performance. They're a good team, but we got the break by getting the goal and held on. Maybe we're not as bad as people think.' Once everybody was showered and all the post-match obligations had been completed, the Aberdeen party headed straight back to the airport where they were met by several joyous Aberdeen fans. It proved to be a memorable trip for so many, but the official flight home was as quiet as you would expect – the lads' exertions having taken their toll – and nearly all of them slept the 2,574 km journey back across Europe and onward to Dyce Airport. The UEFA Cup group stage lay in wait.

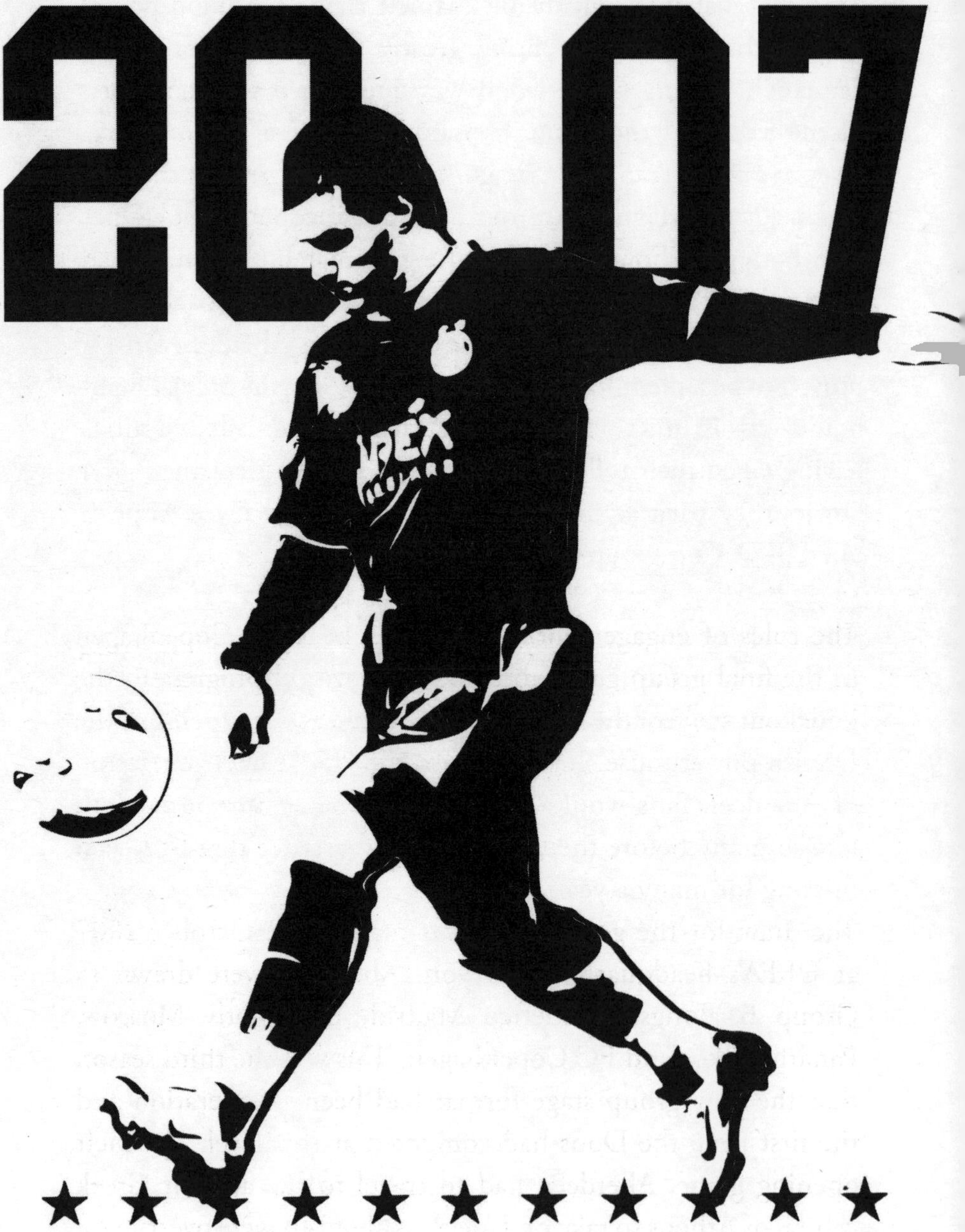
2007

TWELVE

FC COPENHAGEN

The rules of engagement were simple: beat FC Copenhagen in the final group game and Aberdeen would progress to the knockout stage of the 2007/08 UEFA Cup at the expense of the Danish powerhouse. It would turn out that a new generation of Aberdeen fans would enjoy a memorable European night like so many before them; it was an experience that had been missing for many a year.

The draw for the group stage was made on 9 October 2007 at UEFA's headquarters in Nyon. Aberdeen were drawn in Group B alongside Atlético Madrid, Lokomotiv Moscow, Panathinaikos and FC Copenhagen. This was the third season that the new group stage format had been in operation and the first time the Dons had competed at this level. For their opening game, Aberdeen had to travel to the ancient Greek capital of Athens to take on Panathinaikos but were overrun on the night and left the field of play having lost 3-0. Two weeks later Aberdeen welcomed Russian giants Lokomotiv Moscow and their 73 travelling fans to Pittodrie. Despite taking the lead thanks to a Zander Diamond header, the Dons conceded late into stoppage time at the end of the first half and with not much else to report from the second half, Aberdeen had to settle for a point.

The Dons travelled to Spain next to face the might of Atlético Madrid, knowing they faced an uphill task in the Vicente Calderón. Aberdeen put on an excellent display over the 90 minutes and were unlucky to go into the break a goal down. A soft penalty on the hour condemned the Dons to a 2-0 defeat, but the lads left the Spanish capital with their heads held high. Then came FC Copenhagen and scenes that had not been seen for many a year. Aberdeen went into the game bottom of the group, knowing nothing but a win was required to progress to the knockout stage. In his pre-match press conference manager Jimmy Calderwood urged his players to 'create their own piece of history'. He said in his match-day programme notes: 'It's absolutely fantastic that we are in the position that we find ourselves in this evening where we know exactly what we have to do to continue our European adventure – namely record a victory against a very good Copenhagen side here at Pittodrie. It is indeed a measure of how far we've come, and all credit to the players for making it possible.' The players didn't disappoint.

For midfielder Jamie Smith, who had been struggling with niggling injuries and had only started three out of 13 games since the new campaign began, it was fast becoming a frustrating period. But, for the 27-year-old, his hard work and perseverance in the gym paid off when Jimmy Calderwood gave him the nod to start the game against Copenhagen. 'During the week in training the gaffer asked me how I was feeling – I was feeling good. I had been working hard with John Sharp, our physiotherapist, who is undoubtedly the best physio I have ever worked with. He had a fantastic knack for managing people and treating them accordingly. He was extremely qualified and talented in the medical field, so I worked a great deal with him to get fully fit. The gaffer asked me if I was ready to go and if I was feeling good. I said to him, "Absolutely." So, two days before the game we had an eleven-a-side training session where we could generally sense who was going to start the game. Wednesday was a more relaxed session in preparation for the following night. The gaffer had a fantastic way to motivate people. He got the best out of the players that he had. Remarkably like Martin O'Neill in a sense as Martin was also an amazing motivator; you could argue almost like an old-school manager, and you would run through a brick wall for them. That style of management is almost like a lost art in football these days. There's so much tactical analysis, and there are plenty of data points which are involved in football, but that old ability to actually manage people, to get the best out of players, is certainly not as prevalent as it used to be.'

Pittodrie that cold December night was packed, and there wasn't an empty seat in the house. The Red Army cranked up the levels as the game kicked off. There was a cacophony of noise as the vuvuzelas rang out across Pittodrie, and the round of 32 waited with bated breath for the victorious team. The opening gambit was one of caution by Jimmy Calderwood's troops as Copenhagen quietly stamped their authority on the game. Despite the dominance of possession, the Dons' back four held firm, only allowing one or two meaningful chances to be created by the Danes. Jesper Christiansen, in the Copenhagen goal, was only troubled in the opening 45 minutes by the biting wind. How did Jamie and his teammates feel at the break with the score reading 0-0? 'Almost opposite to what I mentioned before about risk-taking; we played very conservatively. I thought we were too focused on trying to deny them the opportunity to create chances. In football, if you are scared to lose, you are never going to win, so I felt we played far too conservatively in the first half, and we didn't take any risks. They were very organised, which is exactly what we expected. They had many international players and they created a couple of chances which, maybe, they should have taken on the breakaways so, for me, we went about our business too quietly. To go in at the break 0-0 knowing that we just required the one goal, you could explain it almost like a game of cat and mouse. We knew we couldn't just be gung-ho and start bombing forward as there had to be an element of protecting our goal. Yes, we scored four goals, but the guys at the back, starting with Jamie Langfield, were solid, which gave us the platform and the foundation from which we could go and get the result that we wanted.'

To turn a game on its head can take a moment of brilliance, some luck or an unfortunate mistake. For that game Aberdeen fans gaped in wonder as Jamie served up one of the finest goals ever seen at Pittodrie. Three minutes after the restart, from a long Jamie Langfield boot up the park, big Lee Miller flicked the ball on and, out of nowhere, Jamie hit one on the volley from distance. The ball sensationally looped up and over the despairing Jesper Christiansen in the Copenhagen goal and hit the back of the net. To coin a commonly known phrase on a European night at the old ground: 'Pittodrie goes berserk'. What an unbelievable strike to open the scoring. Jamie recalls, 'Back in my first season at Aberdeen I remember scoring a goal in the second half up at Inverness from about 25 yards. It flew right into the top corner. I recall at half-time during that game Sandy Clark said to me, "Wee man, you score in training, you bang them in all the time but now it's time to take that into an actual game on a Saturday." During the half-time chat in the Copenhagen game, I remember feeling disappointed with my own first-half performance. I felt there were a couple of times when the ball was in the final third of their half that we were not creative enough with the ball, and that we were not taking enough risks. I said to myself at half-time: "Do you know what, the first opportunity I get I'm just going to have a pop and see what happens." As it turned out, it certainly worked in my favour. It was a goal-kick from Jamie and big Lee [Miller] flicks it on. It fell nicely for me, but I do not think their central defenders anticipated what I was about to do, so they never at any point closed me down. I had no idea how far away from goal I was, but it was a case of letting the ball bounce. It took a slight touch off my hip and then I just thought I am going for it, so I just hit it! It was certainly a ballsy hit, that's for sure, but as I mentioned before, high risk – high reward!'

Jamie continues, 'It's like a golf shot. You just know when you've played a good shot – it's like you can almost not feel the ball hitting the club. It was a little bit like that as the ball came off my foot. It bounced up perfectly and my body shape felt right. I knew I wanted to get the ball up in the air as I was so far from goal. I also needed to take it quite quickly as I recall Jim Leighton saying to me that for him Duncan Shearer was a nightmare in training as he would always get his shots off really quickly and it never gave Jim the time to set himself to make a save; it was always really fast, quick shots coming at him all the time from Duncan. So, from that, after the ball took a bounce, I set myself to hit it first time on the volley to try and surprise the goalkeeper; it came off my foot well so, as soon as I hit it, I pretty much knew it had a good chance.'

If the opening goal was good, the second one was just as impressive. From a long, looping Lee Miller ball, Jamie ran in on goal but, this time, the ball dropped to his weaker left foot – surely he wasn't going to attempt another volley? He did and connected just as well as his opening goal. The ball flew into the net past the despairing Christiansen in the Copenhagen goal. Pittodrie again went mental. It was obvious Jamie's opening strike gave him the confidence to try it again. He agreed. 'Absolutely. Without attempting to throw in an old cliché, football is a game of confidence; you see it at the highest level. When players are confident playing at the highest level they are going to go out and try things which are not quite orthodox. When you get success trying something it gives you a boost to think to yourself; "OK, I'm going to try something else here." That's exactly what I did for the second goal.'

It is obvious by the reaction of Jamie's teammates, the fans and the bench what the second goal meant. The Dons now had a firm grip on the game – the round of 32 was now firmly in their sights. Jamie had performed minor miracles with two memorable goals so, how did the emotions differ when the ball hit the net for a second time? 'I think it was different. When I saw the net ripple for the first goal, I knew it was the goal that we were looking for; it was the goal we needed. It was relatively early at the beginning of the second half, so the feeling was more elation. The best feeling in football is when you score a goal, especially in a big game, and the first goal was elation coupled with adrenaline. For the second goal, I was a little calmer, partly because of the situation I was in when I scored the goal. First goal was: long ball, flick on, hit, whereas the second goal I certainly had more time to think about it. There was certainly a feel of elation, but it was different, especially as it was such a big game.'

So, with two goals expertly put away, which one did Jamie prefer, the opening goal or his left-footed volley? 'It would be easy for me to suggest the first one. The second one, from a technique point of view, was more difficult due to the fact that I had more time. The situation was quite different. I was running at speed, so I knew I had to wait and let the ball bounce, and then wait for it to come down. When you do that, there is always the risk of allowing a defender to come and make the tackle. The second goal was certainly more difficult than the first. There are times in football when your instincts take over and you simply get a feeling that you have to produce something almost out of nothing and that allows you to have a certain action, or certain response, so I would have to say the second goal purely down to the situation we were in at the time.'

With a passionate home support acting as the 12th man, the confidence was oozing throughout; the players and fans alike gelled into one to help reach the goal of making the knockout stage. The Dons now held a commanding position, so did Jamie think at this point in the proceedings that they had too much for Copenhagen? 'Just with the atmosphere alone inside Pittodrie that night, the fans were unbelievable; they were so loud from beginning to end. Considering it was a very cold night they came out in their thousands. The whole atmosphere inside the stadium felt almost infectious. The whole team received a lift from them which helped put us on the front foot. Michael Hart, Richie Byrne and Andrew Considine were all so eager to get forward, maybe a touch gung-ho at times for Jimmy's liking, but we were so keen to get on that front foot. Two-nil is always a difficult scoreline because, if you are an average team, there is always the danger you can lose the game. If you are up 2-0, and you are a good team, there is every chance you will see out the game. If you are a good team, there is every chance you will go on and score more. I am not suggesting we were one of the best teams in the history of football – not even close to be honest – but we very much had a spring in our step that night. With the atmosphere as good as it was, we wanted to play our part.'

With the fans playing their part and the side commanding a two-goal lead, Jamie had a glorious chance to score a hat-trick and further cement the Dons' position in the game. The ever-alert Michael Hart broke up what looked like a testing Copenhagen counter-attack and fed the ball through to Jamie, who found himself in a one-on-one with the keeper. Inexplicably he hit the side netting when it looked easier to score! He explains: 'It's just typical, isn't it? We manage to get ourselves in a strong situation, we are over the final hurdle and on the brink of success and we fail; typical Scottish mentality you could argue! I've watched it back a few times and I'm certain I was offside so I'm using the excuse that I knew I was offside and I decided to just put the ball out of play!' Jamie laughs. 'With that chance, and being caught up in the whole atmosphere, my first instinct was to just absolutely rip it high and hard to make sure it hit the net. I just wanted to put my laces through it and smash it as hard as I could. I am not suggesting there was a moment of doubt, it was more clarity, but I knew I had to be more composed to place it near the front post as the goalkeeper was probably expecting me to go across the goal. I decided to try and hit his near post as I doubted he would expect that. Typically, I didn't even hit the target; I should have just gone with my instinct and smashed it.'

In the end it mattered little as the Dons continued to force the play. A third goal was scored in the 71st minute. Lee Miller used his strength to outmuscle his immediate opponent and fired a teasing ball across the six-yard box. Unfortunately for Copenhagen defender Mikael Antonsson he couldn't sort his feet out quickly enough and diverted the ball into his own net. Surely at that point Jamie believed the game and the round of 32 had been secured. 'That was probably the goal that in my own mind – as I certainly do not want to speak for my teammates – meant we were going to have a good night! I felt we had cleared the final hurdle. Some of the lads thought I had scored the third goal as I was at the back post waiting to tap it in, but the Copenhagen defender was obviously only trying to do his job and ended up putting into his own net. That was the moment I think we knew the level of what we had accomplished that night. For the fourth goal it was a good move. It was Lee and young Chris Maguire down the right-hand side. Chris puts a great ball across the box to find Fozzie [Richard Foster] at the back post. It was almost like the third goal regarding the ball getting whipped across the goal, but this time, it was one of our boys putting it into the back of the net.'

Quite remarkably the Dons had beaten all the odds and progressed to the knockout stage. I think it's safe to say that with the scoreline being somewhat precarious at the break, I'm not sure many Aberdeen fans would have envisaged such an astonishing 45 minutes of football like the one just witnessed. It was breathtaking! It took a while to catch one's breath so how did the emotions for the players play out at full time? Jamie explains: 'In football you need to try and be calm – you cannot let the highs get too high and let your lows get too low, if that makes sense. Don't get me wrong, we were all extremely excited, and all absolutely buzzing. The stadium was buzzing, all the background staff, the folk that worked in the stadium, whether in the marketing department or up in the restaurants, everyone felt the fantastic atmosphere that was generated that night inside the stadium. To play a small part in that was just fantastic. Aberdeen is a great club with loads of history, and I loved my time there, so to play my part on a night like that was certainly one of great satisfaction. The gaffer was playing it cool as he always did. We knew he was excited, and, at times, he could get very emotional as he wore his heart on his sleeve which, for the most part, made him such a good manager. I think those moments can pass you by quite quickly and soon we would all forget about it, but I didn't want that to happen. I did my utmost to take it all in, to soak it all up, you could say.'

The Danes had been put to the sword, obliterated in a 45-minute period executed to perfection. In a season of ups and downs, the lads had pulled a rabbit from the hat. It was an obvious question to Jamie: Why do you think you were able to pull off such a spectacular performance? 'It goes back to a couple of things I mentioned before. We had a good team with a good bunch of players; we had a team that on any given day could get a result against the best teams out there. When you look at the following game against Bayern Munich which, unfortunately, I couldn't play in as two days before the game I pulled my calf muscle, the lads that played that night were magnificent. Those games under the floodlights at Pittodrie we could compete against anybody. I also believe the gaffer, Sandy and Jimmy Nic knew how to get the best out of us. They were proper managers, proper leaders of people, and that helped make a huge difference on that night. It was a big plus point for the team back then.'

Manager Jimmy Calderwood described the result as 'the best night of his football career'. He went on to say, 'It really was a great performance from the lads. It was a wonderful night, it's wonderful, and we have something to look forward to, but all credit to the lads.' When Copenhagen head coach Stale Solbakken emerged from the away dressing room to speak with the press, there was a sense of resignation in his body language, and he said, 'The disappointment is as deep as it can be. We made a couple of mistakes and didn't play as a unit after 2-0. But all credit to Aberdeen, they were very professional.'

The memories of Aberdeen's golden era had been rekindled thanks to a magnificent performance by the class of 2007, and there is an argument to suggest that the Copenhagen game remains the last meaningful victory at Pittodrie on a European stage. Next up for the Dons, memories of days gone by. Los Geht's!

2008

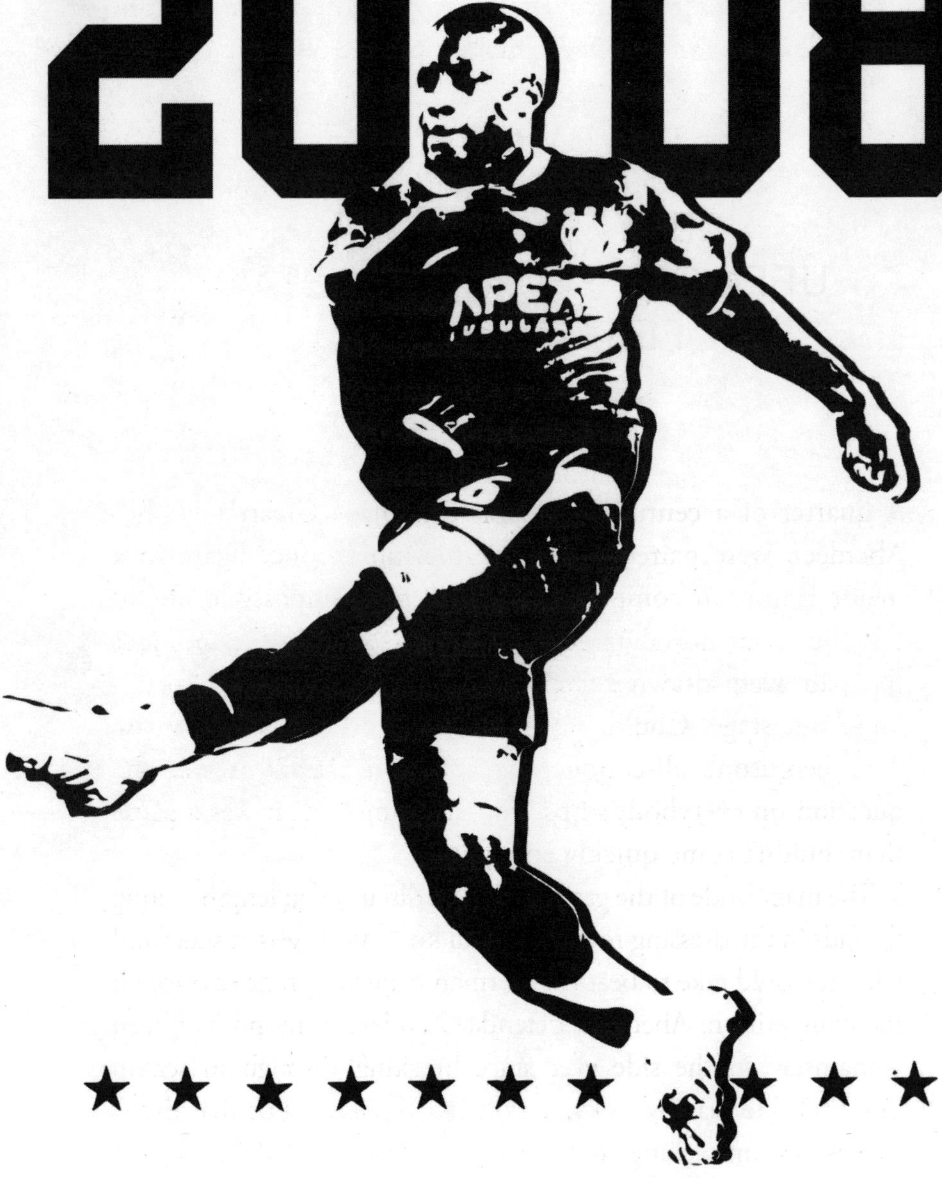

THIRTEEN

BAYERN MUNICH
UEFA CUP KNOCKOUT STAGE
FEBRUARY 2008

A quarter of a century on from 'Pittodrie's Greatest Night', Aberdeen were paired with Bayern Munich once again in a major European competition. It was nigh impossible not to feel the air of nostalgia gripping the game from the moment the pair were drawn together for the 2007/08 UEFA Cup knockout stage. Could Jimmy Calderwood's charges emulate Alex Ferguson's all-conquering side from 1983? It was the question on everybody's lips. For the home fans it was a game that couldn't come quickly enough.

The magnitude of the game had been discussed at length among the lads in the dressing room. They all knew what was at stake and what it would take to beat the German giants to progress through the competition. Aberdeen defender Zander Diamond had been a mainstay in the side ever since breaking through in season 2002/03. He was by now an experienced player but that didn't stop him from seeking advice from those who had played against Bayern 25 years previously. 'Willie Miller was always around us and joined us on European trips so, occasionally, I would pick his brains but, because we were so immersed in the occasions, Jimmy had us fully prepped and prepared. The Gothenburg legends would turn up for some games, which was brilliant, and once or twice I spoke to them, but I mainly spoke to Neil Simpson; he always told me that Pittodrie will be rocking for a European night and, even though it is different times, he was convinced that I would love the occasion. He reminded me that the stadium would be three-quarters full before we even came out for our warm-up and that helped energise the stadium. That night, for the Bayern game, it felt like the whole city was inside Pittodrie; it was unbelievable. The night before, when Bayern trained, Chris Maguire and I sneaked into the ground to watch them. We had the fob for the players' entrance, and we managed to get into the Richard Donald Stand and, from one of the boxes, watched them train. Their training was effortless, and it was fantastic to watch, but there was an intensity to it which made it so fascinating to watch. That was the level we all strived to get to.'

Manager Jimmy Calderwood had charged his lads with leaving their own indelible mark on the history of the club, but he knew the task was a massive one. In his usual pre-match press conference with the nation's finest sports writers, he said this of Bayern: 'With their own high standards they are used to being in the Champions League all the time. Bayern are probably favourites to win the tournament, but big teams have lost on their day so hopefully they have a bad day and we have a very good day.' He added, 'If we defend like we have for most of the season, apart from the European games, we're going to get hammered. Hopefully, we have learnt from that.' Despite two heavy defeats against Dundee United and Celtic in the space of five days, Pittodrie was packed to the rafters and several of Aberdeen's Gothenburg greats were also in attendance; there was a real buzz about the place. In the dressing room, the lads prepared like it was just another game.

Midfielder Josh Walker had only joined Aberdeen on loan from Middlesbrough three weeks previously, and the 18-year-old had only played three games for the Dons when Bayern came calling. Josh recalls the relaxed atmosphere in the dressing room ahead of kick-off. 'When I first arrived at the stadium the mood in the dressing room was one of just like any other game. All the lads were having a laugh and a joke and not taking anything too seriously, which is very normal. It's during the warm-up on the park when you really start to switch on; the warm-up was really good because everybody was so focused, and it was obvious to me all the lads were bang on it! I can recall going back in after the warm-up and looking round the dressing room at the lads' faces and it was nothing but pure concentration and focus. It was quiet in there because all the lads were fully aware that we would have to play out of our skins that night just to survive. Do not forget we were playing, arguably, one of the top three teams in the world at that time. It was a game we all had to be fully focused on.'

Coming into this game Bayern Munich suffered from an abundance of missing players, all superstars in their own right: Franck Ribery, Oliver Kahn, Mark van Bommel, Daniel Van Buyten and Willy Sagnol, but the team that manager Ottmar Hitzfeld picked to play Aberdeen that night would still put the fear of God into any opponent. They included Bastian Schweinsteiger, Toni Kroos, Miroslav Klose, Luca Toni and Zé Roberto to name but a few. Josh felt no fear. 'Throughout my career I have never looked at anyone I am to play against; I have never paid any attention to whom I am standing next to except shaking hands with my opposing captain whenever I have skippered the side. I am just so focused and looking forward to the game that I do not pay any attention to these guys. When we walked through the tunnel and reached the pitch, that is when the atmosphere hit us; the noise and the smell of the flares is noticeably clear in my mind. I had never been in a situation like that before where I couldn't see our fans in parts of the stadium due to the smoke coming from the flares. It just hit me, it was like, "Wow, this is it!" That is when the goosebumps appear all over the body and the adrenaline kicks in. Despite not needing to be lifted, you cannot help but be lifted by the atmosphere. It gave us such a massive boost pre-kick-off. I was already high as a kite anyway, but that really was "Wow, here we go!"'

Aberdeen started the game brightly, and there was a freshness to their approach which had been clearly missing against Dundee United and Celtic. To the surprise of some, the Dons were matching their illustrious opponents man for man. The Dons had a strong penalty claim turned down in the opening stages before Bayern's Christian Lell warmed the gloves of goalkeeper Jamie Langfield after his 30-yard piledriver required careful diversion past the post. With 24 minutes played, Aberdeen picked up a free kick inside the centre circle. Josh strategically placed himself just outside the 'D'. 'In my head I wasn't thinking a goal is about to come from this. All I was thinking was that the Bayern defence will deal with it and clear it and I will have to win the second ball. I was trying to judge where the ball was going to go from Scott Severin's free kick. I remember Zander Diamond winning a header, Lee Miller getting a touch and then the ball dropping to Sone [Aluko] near the edge of the box. I then started to gradually move forward while screaming for Sone to lay the ball off for me. Sone is such an intelligent player that he was able to see me and then read where I would need the ball laying off so I could hit it first time. So many players may have just laid it off as a normal pass and I would have had to take a first touch which meant I would have struggled to get my shot off. Sone just rolled it to the side which made it perfect for me to just whip it in. As soon as it left my foot, I knew it was going in. I was almost celebrating before it hit the back of the net. I can still remember after Sone laid it off, Bayern's central defender

Martin Demichelis coming out towards the ball, and I knew I had to bend it round him. I knew as soon as it left my foot it was going in because I could see the gap the goalkeeper had left, and that's what I was aiming for when striking the ball.'

It was a brilliant strike, composed and calculated as it could ever be. The movement on the ball was perfectly judged by Josh as it curled beautifully past the despairing dive of Bayern goalkeeper Michael Rensing. As the ball hit the back of the net, Josh recalls his emotions. 'It was insane! It was crazy. If someone had said to me, considering the season I was having up until December, and then by February that I would be playing against Bayern Munich in the round of 32 of the UEFA Cup and scoring against them I would have been saying, "You're having a laugh!"' Josh chuckles. 'The emotion was almost surreal. I had feelings of relief and a sense that I was actually good enough to play at this level because, when you're injured for a sustained period, you do start to have doubts. I knew afterwards that I could go on and be a good player. I had all these feelings in the seconds after I scored and then, at the same time, as I am jogging back to the halfway line, I am thinking to myself that we're only 25 minutes into the game! As much as there was a sense of excitement, we knew we had to get right back into it because Bayern would come straight back at us.'

Bayern did exactly that! Only five minutes after the Dons took an unexpected lead, the Germans rallied and equalised. Miroslav Klose atoned for an earlier miss when he nipped in front of Zander Diamond and fired home from a Luca Toni flick-on. Despite the obvious disappointment, as the lads set themselves for the restart, the more senior players offered a rallying cry to get the boys going again. Josh for one was grateful to be surrounded by such experience. 'We had such a good spine in that team with Zander Diamond and Andrew Considine through the middle of defence. I had great experience playing alongside me in Barry Nicholson and Scott Severin, and then we had big Lee Miller playing up top. Those players I have mentioned were massive on the night for us, and when you see players like that helping us through the game and offering encouragement all the time, it's a big help to the younger lads like myself and Sone. I think we stepped up in that game as well which, I believe, helped kick them on in the game. We all complemented each other that night, that's for sure.'

With Bayern equalising, the neutrals may have fully expected an onslaught but, with the Dons more than holding their own, any sort of aggression was comfortably suppressed. Some believed Bayern had a complacency to their style of play that night which was rightfully punished by the Dons when Sone Aluko quite brilliantly restored Aberdeen's lead. Josh was directly behind the play as Sone took possession of the ball just outside the 18-yard box and set himself to hit the ball on the volley. Josh takes up the story: 'It was a brilliant finish. For him to have that composure on the edge of the box to just lift it over the defender and then strike it first time on the volley was superb. Folk have said that the keeper should have saved it but, for me, Sone has hit the ball so well, and so early, that the keeper has been caught off guard; I do not think he was expecting the strike at all. When we went 2-1 up, I could sense more belief in the lads. Any team can go 1-0 up against another team when you bring a bit of luck into play, but when Bayern equalised most of the ground may have been thinking that Bayern will steamroll us now. But then, to go 2-1 up in the first half was phenomenal! We all just thought, "This is our night."'

Aberdeen went into the break leading 2-1, and they received a rousing reception as the lads made their way back to the dressing room. Jimmy Calderwood, Jimmy Nicholl and Sandy Clark got the lads in, sat them down and began their half-time team talk. The initial instructions were quick and to the point and that was the norm for Jimmy Calderwood. He made his way around each individual player to offer personal encouragement and one final pep talk before the lads made their way out for the second half. 'The instructions were quite simple really. Jimmy just said to us that he wanted "more of the same". He wanted us to keep believing in ourselves, keep up the work rate and run ourselves into the ground. Jimmy said to me personally that he wanted me to keep matching their runs in midfield and try my best to get on the ball, pass the ball, but also keep the ball when we needed to remain in possession. He also gave me instructions that if we lost the ball, I had to get tight on people and try and keep the play condensed. I remember thinking to myself that this could be a brilliant night.'

The atmosphere continued to electrify the Pittodrie night sky as the second half kicked off. Ten minutes after the restart, Spanish referee Eduardo Iturralde González exasperated the home support when he awarded Bayern what appeared to be an incredibly soft penalty. Much to the annoyance of the home crowd he turned away a similar appeal for Aberdeen in only the first minute of the game when Andreas Ottl appeared to have handled the ball from a Sone Aluko cross inside the 18-yard box. No matter what, the penalty was given, and Hamit Altintop duly scored at the second attempt. 'Their penalty knocked us slightly as it was quite early in the second half. There is no doubt it was handball, but it was incredibly soft. I have no doubts that Alan Maybury didn't mean to handle the ball as his arms were down by his side. I think the problem was that Alan was so close to the ball and it's just one of those where the ball came up and struck his arm. With the game going to 2-2 folk again may have started to think that Bayern would go and score three, four or five, but they didn't! I think at that point our own level of football wasn't as good as it had been for larger parts of the game in the first half, but you could see how tenacious we all were! I am not saying that we were overrunning Bayern but, at times in the second half, we had them running about trying to keep pace with the game. It certainly wasn't a one-sided game that night.'

Aberdeen more than held their own against the Germans and deservedly came away from the game with a very creditable draw. Chances were few and far between in the closing stages as Jimmy Calderwood's men closed out the game. Josh Walker ran himself into the ground for the cause and was substituted with only a few minutes left on the clock. For his exertions he received a standing ovation from the Aberdeen fans. He recalls, 'I was absolutely wrecked!' I was dead on my feet because, prior to coming to Aberdeen, I had played truly little football; just the odd reserve game here and there while I was trying to get fit again. The game against Bayern was only my fourth game and I felt completely shattered; mentally as well as physically! I also remember feeling ecstatic because my calves were starting to cramp up after all the running I had done during the game. I had so much nervous energy during that game because I am up against Bastian Schweinsteiger and Zé Roberto who are making runs without me even seeing them; I needed to have eyes in the back of my head because these guys were everywhere. They were dropping short and spinning longer, they were clipping balls between each other, and all this had to be matched. I was really delighted with the way that I played and absolutely over the moon to receive a standing ovation from the crowd.'

After the game, manager Jimmy Calderwood was full of praise for his team, describing the 90 minutes as a 'wonderful performance'. His counterpart, Ottmar Hitzfeld, was content enough to suggest his side 'are now favourites to go through'. Josh recalls the mood in the dressing room. 'Jimmy was delighted after the game. He was also a little frustrated that we couldn't see the game out. I think if we could have held them off for a little bit longer before they scored from their penalty, I think we could have held on. I think maybe it wasn't meant to be but, saying that, to be able to draw 2-2 with a side of the calibre of Bayern Munich who, at that time, were one of the best teams in the world, I think we did very well.'

Aberdeen travelled to Munich a week later for the return leg, but despite the promising showing against Bayern, the form of the side was alarming. Having progressed through the Scottish Cup at the expense of Hamilton at the beginning of February, Aberdeen would not win another game until 15 March. The away leg in the Allianz Arena came in the middle of what was a mini slump for Jimmy Calderwood's men. It was imperative for the Dons to make a good start, but with only 11 minutes on the clock, Bayern took the lead thanks to Lucio's free kick. Aberdeen dug in but with ten minutes to go until half-time, Bayern scored a second thanks to Daniel Van Buyten's header. There was a more composed feel to Aberdeen's play in the second period, and Darren Mackie did have the ball in the Bayern net, but his effort was frustratingly ruled out for offside against Lee Miller. The Bavarians put the game to bed in the 70th minute when Lucas Podolski made it 3-0 and six minutes later added his second and Bayern's fourth when he headed home from an outswinging corner. The large travelling support did have something to cheer on the night when Steve Lovell headed home a mere consolation with eight minutes to go. It was just reward for a determined second-half showing. Only a minute later Bayern scored a fifth when Mark van Bommel fired one home from 18 yards; there is an argument to suggest that the scoreline was somewhat flattering to the home side, but Bayern went through, winning 7-3 on aggregate.

To close this chapter, I will leave you with the post-match thoughts of Aberdeen manager Jimmy Calderwood who, after the game, faced the press and expressed his disappointment. He said, 'We tried to play football, and when we settled, we had a few chances. It was a bit harsh, and I felt sorry for us and the fans because we didn't deserve that. It has been a wonderful adventure in Europe, and for it to end in this stadium against Bayern is absolutely no disgrace.' How right he was!

FOURTEEN

GRONINGEN

While researching this book I came across a quote which I thought was quite apt for this chapter: 'Never underestimate the underdog; the underdog has everything it takes to become successful.' This resonated with me as I pieced together two of Aberdeen's more recent successes in Europe: Groningen in season 2014/15 and Rijeka one year later. Both games came in the Europa League qualifying rounds and will go down as two of the best results and performances attributed to any Aberdeen team from down the years.

After competing in the UEFA Cup in season 2007/08, Aberdeen didn't qualify for Europe again for six long seasons. Having finished third in the Scottish Premier League in Derek McInnes's first full season in charge, the Dons entered the Europa League qualifiers full of hope. Latvian minnows Daugava Riga were cast aside 8-0 on aggregate in the preliminary round; for the second round the Dons now faced Dutch side Groningen. Like Aberdeen, the Dutch outfit had also not played in Europe for seven seasons; they qualified having beaten AZ Alkmaar 3-0 in the end of season play-offs. Groningen had strengthened their squad during the summer, adding Curaçao international striker Jarchinio Antonia to their books while retaining the services of both Filip Kostic and Tjaronn Chery, despite much transfer speculation surrounding the two. Both would have to be watched carefully during the 90 minutes. Groningen went into the first leg in confident mood – some may argue, with too much confidence!

For this chapter I spoke with Aberdeen defender Andrew Considine who surprisingly sat out the first leg at Pittodrie, and he explains the reasons why: 'I had played most of the pre-season games leading up to that game, but we played Arbroath in our last game before meeting Groningen and the manager pulled me to one side and told me he wanted to play Jonny Hayes at left-back in the Arbroath game to experiment, and it went quite well for the team and Jonny. We won the game comfortably and from an attacking point of view it was good to watch, so I had an inkling this would happen. When it came to the match-day against Groningen, Derek McInnes told me he was going to start Jonny, but that I would be a sub. He wanted to attack down that side because they had a lad called Tjaronn Chery who wasn't much of a defence-minded player so he felt we could exploit that and get down that side of the pitch. He wanted Jonny to double up with Niall down that side. When I think about the first game there wasn't too much in it, and I think both sides were a little tentative over the 90 minutes. I was disappointed not to play because you want to play on the biggest stage against the biggest teams from across Europe.'

Aberdeen didn't have long to prepare for Groningen having knocked out Daugava Riga; seven days to be precise. The coaching staff's preparations began in earnest as dossiers on Groningen were quickly edited together for the players. There was no resting on any laurels, and the gears went up a level as Andrew remembers:

'We would have team meetings on a Monday, Tuesday and the day of the game. There is a big red board in the dressing room and the manager had reports on all of Groningen's players as well as information on the subs who he expected would probably come on in the game. On that board included all their stats and positions as well as height and weight details which were all readily available for us to look at. The meetings on a Monday and on a Tuesday would be more aimed at the ins and outs of Groningen's possession and on the Wednesday, he would name his team and try and predict Groningen's team and how we would go about our way of playing. There was a lot of tactical mind games going on before big games like that.'

Midfielder Niall McGinn also spoke to me for this book, and he echoes his teammate's thoughts when it came to preparation for the Groningen game. 'It's difficult for the European games as we didn't have too much time off, because if you win you are straight into preparations for the following Thursday night. We would normally get a day off on the Friday and then we would report back on the Saturday to start preparing for the Thursday game and getting down to the nitty-gritty. It was good that we were drawn against such a high-profile team like Groningen because the research needed for dossiers was readily available. It was a big attraction for us and obviously the bigger the team, the more exciting the tie becomes.'

As well as Andrew and Niall offering their thoughts for this book, I was particularly pleased to speak to former Aberdeen assistant manager Tony Docherty, who gave me more of a unique insight into how he and manager Derek McInnes prepared their side for the games against Groningen and Rijeka. 'The Doc', as we like to call him, cast his mind back to the days prior to the first game against Groningen and how the preparations kicked into gear. 'Between Derek McInnes and myself we had agreed that one of us should travel over to

Holland and go and watch Groningen play, so the decision was made that I would go over. Groningen were in the middle of their pre-season and they gave me access to all areas. It wasn't long after the Riga game that I flew over and fair play to them because they were so accommodating. I was able to watch them train and watch one of their pre-season games. I called Derek and told him that the impression I was getting from them was that we were a little bit of a "diddy" team. They said come over, have a look at the facilities, watch us train – no problems at all they said! I played up to that by putting on a daft wee schoolboy act by pretending I was in complete awe of the club and the facilities but in the back of my mind all I was thinking was, "Right, you're going to get it." By the time I got back to Aberdeen we had compiled a very strong dossier on them. Tom O'Neill, our chief scout, had managed to get over again after I came back and watched them play, so we saw them twice live. We had video analysis and a full dossier to present to the players. We had done extensive homework on them, that's for sure. We had always done that during our European run, and we kept a close eye on the progression so Russ Richardson (head of recruitment) and Tom worked tirelessly in the background to give us as much information as they could on our opposition. It was all new to us, so it was brilliant and very exciting – great times.'

The lads couldn't have been more prepared for the game, as the due diligence was as detailed as it could have been. The Doc explains more the thinking behind the tactics deployed on the night of the game. 'Derek always had a game plan and I remember in the Scottish press he was criticised for that same plan, but we knew after watching them that Groningen were a top team. There was an element of "it's just Aberdeen" from them because we had not played in Europe for so long. Derek had a game plan, particularly for the first game, and we went

4-2-3-1. The reason we did that is because we still wanted attacking options down the sides with Jonny Hayes but with Barry in the side, because we thought that Groningen wanted to come here and win the tie in the first leg. We went a little pragmatic which Derek was brilliant at. His game plan was excellent and he conducted all the team meetings. He was criticised in the Scottish press for not going for it by putting on David Goodwillie and going two up front and try and get the win at home, but as much as we were tempted and as much as the fans wanted that, we knew it was going to get won over two legs if we didn't concede in the first game. There was a plan in place to make sure that when we went over there, we were still in the game and it was important not to get carried away or get too excited because we didn't want to fail at the first hurdle having not played in Europe for so long.'

The game finished 0-0, and it was a close-fought affair with Aberdeen dictating the tempo of the game, but neither side was able to make the breakthrough. It was all to play for in the return leg in Holland seven days later. In the dressing room after the game, Andrew recalls the mood of the management team: 'I think in any sort of European game at home you are hoping to win and to at least grab a goal, if not a couple of goals, to take away for the second leg, so I think he was happy they didn't score an away goal because that is always tough to claw back. I think he was reasonably happy, but I think deep down he was really hoping we could have nicked a goal.'

For Niall McGinn, a 0-0 first leg scoreline was a respectable result; it was after all only half-time. He recalls the mood in the camp after the game. 'It was good because we learned so much for playing them first at Pittodrie as we got to see how talented they were. Thankfully, we didn't concede which was pleasing and I always felt, with the team of players we had, when going away from home we always believed we could score. Whenever teams come to Pittodrie, more times than not, they always sit behind the ball, but a team like Groningen for example were always on the front foot. They played nice football but we always felt we could match them and thankfully when we went over there, we did just that.' For manager Derek McInnes, he was nothing but upbeat after the game as he reflected on his team's performance: 'We set out to win the game that's for sure, and to be honest we're not totally satisfied or disappointed with the performance. We knew Groningen would be a tough opponent, but I feel we are more than capable of going over there and scoring a goal or two. I have no doubts about that.'

Second leg

A week later Aberdeen made the short trip to Holland for the return leg. The mood in the camp was one of quiet optimism. In the hours after the first game at Pittodrie, a host of Groningen players gave post-match interviews to the accompanying Dutch press, and the comments attributed to those players did nothing but give Aberdeen the extra incentive to get through the tie. Winger Filip Kostic said, 'We go home happy; we have done 80 per cent of what we need to get through.' Captain Maikel Kieftenbeld added, 'I only see Groningen winning in Holland.' Ahead of the return game Aberdeen manager Derek McInnes was more gracious saying, 'I don't believe the opposition will be taking us lightly, and if they do they will be out of the tournament. There is mutual respect, and you won't get any of my players dismissing Groningen as they are a good side.'

Aberdeen remained respectful throughout and refused to be drawn into a war of words ahead of the return leg, but in the confines of the dressing room the words uttered by the Groningen players had not been missed by the lads. Niall McGinn says, 'As players we are aware of these things, so it was down to us to just do our talking on the pitch. As a group of players and management together we did all have a sense that they thought they had come to Pittodrie and held us, and they would then get us back to their own patch with a great support and obviously turn us over three- or four-nil. That gave us the incentive to keep them quiet and thankfully it all turned out the right way. They certainly ate their words that night – that's for sure.'

Andrew Considine returned to the side for the return leg, with Barry Robson missing out. This tactical change allowed the more attack-minded Jonny Hayes to get further forward. Andrew explains further the reasoning behind the move for the return game in the Euroborg Stadium: 'We knew we would have to defend a lot more than we did in the first game and defend waves of attacks, which is what we ended up doing. One of their centre-backs, Eric Botteghin, is a tall, strong player but wasn't that mobile, so if we were going to attack the instructions were to get the ball down mine and Jonny's side – that was our out ball. We knew we were going to have to defend for most of the game but if we could turn the ball over quickly and get Jonny bombing down the left and get balls quickly into the box to try and disrupt their centre-backs, that was the thinking behind trying to exploit their weaknesses.'

The Doc explains further the thinking behind the tactics ahead of the second leg and how, ultimately, Aberdeen got it spot on over in Holland. 'For the return game we played the same shape, but were more counter-attack-minded with Andy in at left-back playing just behind Jonny Hayes. We went all-out counter-attack and it paid off because in the early stages they threw everything at us. I just remember thinking, "Come on, lads; just get through this spell." The view was to push Jonny higher up and, making sure we countered against them, we had Peter Pawlett with his pace supporting Adam Rooney with Jonny and Niall out wide, and Willo Flood and Ryan Jack in behind with Shay and Andy supporting them. We knew we had to play like an away side and try and get the away goal. We cleared one off the line but not long after we countered and the counter worked because Jonny won us a penalty. It was exactly what we hoped would happen and Adam being Adam slotted it away. I can clearly remember the boos from the home crowd, and I think that was the first time they realised that they had a game on their hands, and we thought that we were on to a winner there if we could nick another goal.'

Aberdeen started the game well with ball retention very much part of the agenda. Groningen did start to come into the game more and more after a few minutes and had one effort cleared off the line, but just when the Eredivisie side started to get to grips with the game, Aberdeen counter-attacked and won a penalty thanks to some brilliant play by Jonny Hayes who was brought down in the box. Adam Rooney steadied himself for the spot kick. Andrew steadied himself from the centre circle; was he feeling confident? 'Adam didn't miss many penalties during his time with Aberdeen so I was very confident he would score. Once we went two up, we knew we were in the driving seat. To be honest, Jamie Langfield in goal didn't have too much to do; maybe a little more at the end of the second half when they were really piling on the pressure. He made one or two good saves but other than that he didn't have that much to do in the game. I have to take my hat off to all the players from the strikers to the defenders, because as a team we defended very well that night.'

Adam's teammates had no doubt that he would step up and slot the penalty away. Niall McGinn expected nothing less. 'He did his normal run-up and hit the ball; Adam would practise penalties for hours on end so we all fully trusted him. Once we got the penalty, I knew he was going to score, and I sensed then that this could be a special night; thankfully, it all went according to plan. We played some really nice football that night. We obviously came under a lot of pressure which is totally normal, but what a result – it was unreal! The first goal silenced the crowd a little which really helped us. I remember the Aberdeen fans were magnificent that night and I could hear them all the way through the game.'

Having scored his sixth goal in European competition already, Adam Rooney turned provider for Niall McGinn to double Aberdeen's lead just after the half-hour mark. Adam controlled the ball brilliantly before attempting to lob it over the advancing Groningen keeper, but the ball rebounded off the bar and fell nicely to the feet of winger Niall McGinn who tapped home from six yards. 'That was just me being Adam Rooney; he got in ahead of the back four and attempted to lob the keeper and all I thought was, why not, just follow it in and thankfully it fell at my feet and I scored a very important goal which helped us get through to the next round. I've been delighted with my contribution in Europe over the past few years but scoring that second goal in Groningen was very special.'

As the Dons pressed the Groningen back line deep into their own half, the Aberdeen bench sensed another goal wasn't far away. The Doc recalls Aberdeen taking a two-goal lead. 'I remember for the second goal that it came from another breakaway and Adam hits the bar and the ball falls to Niall; it felt like an eternity before he put it in, and I remember looking up and seeing all the Aberdeen fans. Oh my God, they all went mental! The first goal was received by boos from the home crowd, but the second goal was met with silence apart from the Aberdeen fans who all went nuts. From there we just wanted to get into half-time at 2-0.'

Aberdeen were on their way much to the jubilation of the 1,100-strong travelling support. Groningen regrouped and went again, and were rewarded for their pressing play when they pulled a goal back just before the break. That goal changed the complexity of the mood at half-time as Andrew explains: 'The manager gave me a bit of a doing because I played a ball into central midfield to Peter Pawlett in the hope that he would control it and turn and glide through the Groningen midfield as he normally did, but he lost the ball and they played it out wide, got the ball in and that move resulted in their goal. During the break, the manager reminded me to clear my lines and get the ball down into the corners; I didn't realise that there were only two minutes to go until half-time when we lost our goal, but thankfully we had the away goal advantage which meant they still had to do a fair job on us in the second half, but it did change the half-time team talk.'

Having scored, Groningen went into the second half knowing they required a further two goals to progress; this was very much in the forefront of The Doc's and Derek McInnes's minds as they walked back to the dressing room for half-time. 'Their captain scored with just a minute to go to half-time. Jamie Langfield, who had been brilliant for us, could maybe have kept it out; that changed our half-time chat because Derek and I only moments before had been discussing what we would say at half-time with the score at 2-0 and even considering making a change to see the game out. We knew they would throw everything at us in the second half because they needed two goals to go through. We brought on Barry Robson and David Goodwillie but at times we were almost like a back six because, as I mentioned, they threw everything at us.'

With the Dons leading 2-1 on the night, but with the added advantage of two away goals, the lads knew Groningen required a change of gear if they had any ambitions of turning the tie around. For the start of the second period Groningen boss Erwin van de Looi made a tactical change and introduced more pace to his side. Andrew Considine recalls, 'For the second half they brought on Jarchinio Antonia for their captain who in the days leading up to the game had been very disrespectful to us in the media – he had basically written us off for the game! This lad Antonia I can remember was rapid! He was so quick, and he was down on my side, so as you can imagine I didn't overly enjoy that! There were times when Jonny was almost underlapping me to try and help me out because this lad was so quick. We did have our backs to the wall, so the manager changed the formation slightly. I moved in one and Jonny came into almost a left-wing-back role to combat Antonia's speed. We had to defend waves of attacks; we didn't create much at all in terms of attacking in the second half but overall we defended so well that night, they were brilliant.'

For Derek McInnes and The Doc, both knew the lads would have to defend as if their lives depended on it. Groningen threw the kitchen sink at the Aberdeen back line, but they all dug deep and held on for a famous victory, much to the satisfaction of The Doc. 'Jamie made a couple of brilliant saves; Mark Reynolds made a couple of brilliant blocks and we just dug in. Russell Anderson was another who was absolutely outstanding that night; we were deep and defending deep, but I do recall thinking during the game that we were actually OK, that we were all right and could see it through. We weathered it; it was a brilliant night! See when that final whistle went it was brilliant. We went back to the hotel as we were not due to leave until the next morning and what a night we had. There was this feeling that we were such huge underdogs going into this tie and their players, coaching staff and manager had underestimated us. At the end of the game Derek shook hands with their coach and said to him, "You didn't think we were good enough to beat you." The guy was completely flummoxed. Their comments after the first game didn't surprise us because they fully expected to beat us at home after drawing 0-0 with us at Pittodrie. Those words did inspire us, no doubt. There was great satisfaction from Derek McInnes that night because after the first game their manager didn't even come into Derek's office after the game which is the norm for travelling managers to do. I think there was an element of disrespect from them towards us, so I know Derek took a huge amount of satisfaction from beating them.'

Aberdeen held on and progressed to the next stage. It was a remarkable victory considering this was the first time the club had won a competitive game on Dutch soil. The back line remained resolute throughout with Ryan Jack and Willo Flood adding an extra layer of protection to ensure no gaps were exploited by the Dutch. Aberdeen kept Groningen at bay and never looked in danger of losing their grip on the tie. The full-time whistle was greeted by a chorus of boos and whistles from the home fans but utter jubilation from the Aberdeen support, high up in the stands. Once the players arrived back in the dressing room, after taking their applause from the fans, the mood was one of celebration. Andrew Considine remembers the moment well. 'The place was bouncing; it was unbelievable. There was almost a sense of disbelief that we had gone over to Holland and beaten one of the best teams in their league over two legs. As I mentioned before, their manager and captain had both been disrespectful to Aberdeen; they basically said we had no chance of winning the game over there, and they were treating it almost like a pre-season warm-up game, so in the end they got what they deserved!'

For The Doc it was a night that he looks back on with a great deal of fondness and pride. 'It was a brilliant night and a brilliant night for the club. That was a particularly good season but the squad that we assembled after bringing in Willo Flood and Barry Robson, we knew they had a bit of steel about them, and my God did we need that during that second half, but they epitomised the spirit we had. Derek was so motivated to beat this manager. There was real pride in the win and it is right up there with one of my best Aberdeen memories.'

Manager Derek McInnes was full of praise for his side afterwards, expressing nothing but delight for a marvellous victory, and he said, 'It was a special night for the supporters to come and see their team win. I always feel, whether we are underdogs or the favourites, we always put in a shift. It's a big result to be honest, but no more than I expected. I always believed we could win here.' The gaffer wasn't the only one delighted with the victory. Niall McGinn said, 'It was a huge win, and that game and the Rijeka game are up there with two of the greatest performances and results during my time with Aberdeen. They were both very special nights; I am so happy to have been part of it, that's for sure.' Aberdeen would next face Spanish La Liga side Real Sociedad, but after two brave performances the quality of the Spaniards proved too much for the Dons and they bowed out of Europe having lost both games.

FIFTEEN

RIJEKA

One season on, Aberdeen, like the previous campaign, would have to navigate their way past several Europa League qualifying games if they had any ambition of reaching the lucrative group stage. The Dons nervously manoeuvred their way past Macedonian outfit KF Shkëndija before facing the much-fancied HNK Rijeka. The Croatians had not lost in European competition at home for 12 games. The first leg was set for the pretty Croatian city on 16 July 2015.

Aberdeen qualified for the Europa League having finished runners-up to Celtic in the Scottish Premier League. In the close season manager Derek McInnes strengthened his squad by recruiting on-loan goalkeeper Danny Ward from Liverpool and threw him straight into the qualifiers. In his usual pre-match press conference McInnes explained that he expected nothing but the toughest of ties. 'Rijeka are in the same bracket as Real Sociedad. They have a high calibre of player and they have experience of top European matches. They will be a tough nut to crack but that's not to say we can't win. Many people in Scotland won't have been too aware of Rijeka when the draw was made. We have worked tirelessly to get as much information as we can about them. The standard of their league is strong, and it's clear they have a strong pedigree.'

Andrew Considine admits the research had to begin in earnest and dossiers studied carefully. 'I didn't know much about Rijeka if I am being honest, and in the build-up to the game we spent a good deal of time looking at videos and watching their formations and tactics, but I didn't know a great deal about them.' Winger Niall McGinn was another who was grateful for the due diligence that had been done on the Croatians by the scouting department ahead of the game, and he explains further: 'It was a common theme for the European games, especially because we didn't know a great deal about our opponents. In the dossier, each player would have a picture and their stats including their strengths and weaknesses. Once you see that some of these players have international caps, it makes you sit back and realise that we are going to play a very good team. We had a couple of international players at the time, but when I looked through the dossier, I could see they had a host of international players including those who played at under-21 level, so we knew we were coming up against serious opposition. We knew they had not been beaten at home for many European games, so we knew the task was an enormous one. We never thought for a million years we would go there and win 3-0.'

Ask any player and they will tell you that the preparation for any big European game must be of the very highest standard, and this can take on many forms, from the scouting reports to the travel planning and accommodation. Andrew Considine said, 'The club looked after us very well for that trip, as they do for all of our European games. We stayed in the city of Split, which isn't too far away from Rijeka. The hotel was fantastic, located by the water, and the food was excellent. The only uncomfortable thing I do recall was the heat, because it was in the low thirties and I remember training at the ground the night before the game and as soon as we stepped on the pitch it was stifling hot. There is a huge rock behind the stadium, and we could feel the heat radiating off the rock; it was so hot! The heat was going to play a factor, but thankfully our surroundings were first class.'

The Doc said, 'The hotel was magnificent, we stayed right on the coast and it was glorious, but it was so hot, it was roasting! Derek had his family with him for that trip which made him much more relaxed. He knew we had beaten Groningen the season before and he knew we were growing in stature, and I think having his family there influenced him. We had a confidence about us that night because we were trying a new system and we had all the answers within our squad.'

For the coaching staff, hours of thought and preparation went into this game. After much deliberation, the manager made a bold move, and The Doc explains more: 'The way that the travel worked out meant I couldn't travel out to Croatia to have them watched, so our head scout Tom O'Neill went. We managed to have them watched three times which meant we had really done our homework on them because we knew this was a level up from Groningen. We gave the boys many match reports to read through as part of their homework, plus we had our usual team meetings. We were very aware of how they played but, on the night, we completely changed our shape. Normally we would play a 4-2-3-1 with Jonny and Niall on the sides with Adam up front; that was our trademark, and that's how we got all of our success. With the experience we now had in Europe we looked at Rijeka and Derek came up with a brilliant game plan of how to play against them – we still call it the Rijeka shape! After that game, many other teams copied our way with that shape.

We had seen the way they played and the way they attacked, so we played Ash Taylor, Paul Quinn and Andrew Considine with Jonny Hayes and Shay Logan as the wing-backs with Ryan Jack and Graeme Shinnie sitting in front, which meant we were counter-attack protected but we had pace in front of that with Peter Pawlett, Niall McGinn and David Goodwillie. We came in for some criticism for that, but David was more of a link player than Adam Rooney. Adam was a finisher, so we knew we needed a link player to link it to get the pace of Peter Pawlett, Jonny Hayes and Niall McGinn going by him. Derek put so much thought into that formation, and we trained and played practice games based on the way Rijeka would set up. We did it to deal with their threat and again try to be pragmatic, but with our own counter-attacking threat.'

It took Aberdeen 20 minutes to get into their stride. It was no surprise that the home side dominated possession and pressed the Dons back deep into their own half. Winger Niall McGinn knew a shift would have to be put in, up and down the flanks, in an attempt to offer support and occasional respite for his wing-backs. He explains further: 'I think it's your automatic instinct, especially when a team has so much possession and they are moving the ball about so quickly and you're playing in a hot environment, to get back and support. Rijeka were used to their own surroundings whereas we were not. That water break came at such an important time; the manager put his points across which gave us more confidence to get forward more. I put the corner in for Andy to score and we grew in confidence from there. When I look back on that night, what might get lost a little due to the result was the performance of goalkeeper Danny Ward; he was absolutely brilliant for us that night as he came out and caught crosses and helped slow the game down for us. There isn't a better feeling when you are an outfield player, when you are coming under a great amount of pressure, that your keeper catches everything and helps calm everything down; it's massive for the team and gave us an extra incentive to get high up the pitch, take your break and regroup. It gave us the time to reorganise and get back on the front foot. Danny was so important that night as well as the goals we scored because we scored them at good times in the game.'

Then came the moment which arguably changed the pattern of the game. With 20 minutes on the clock and the lads feeling the heat not just from the climate but the constant pressure they had been under, a welcome water break was called for by the referee. The Doc looks back on that pivotal moment in the game: 'Our director of football operations Steven Gunn had fought with the match officials to allow a water break during the game because the heat was ridiculous. The night before the game we could hardly train, so we were very conscious of the heat. We were not sure if we were going to get these water breaks because Rijeka had opposed it slightly. That water break was massive for us because it meant we could get the team in and all we did was make a small tweak; no change of formation but all we did was ask Shay to get closer to his immediate opponent and that tiny tweak allowed our game plan to flourish. The first 20 minutes we got our backsides felt, we really did! In terms of atmosphere, it was the best game I have ever been at. The stadium was so picturesque with a huge rock behind the terracing which amplified every shout from the crowd; it was so unique. Their crowd, like Groningen, had been ramping it up and after the brilliant start they made we did think they could murder us here!'

Andrew Considine also appreciates that the water break came at a good time as Rijeka's pressure was starting to tell: 'We were backs to the wall for the opening period and they hit the woodwork a couple of times, and Danny Ward also had one or two saves to make in that period. Once the water break came, the manager changed the midfield which in turn helped settle us down and we reduced their chances significantly. When we managed to score, that was a huge moment for us. It was almost a sigh of relief, but it also gave us the belief to actually go out and win the game. In the build-up, Rijeka had been disrespectful to us in the media. I appreciate they had an impressive home record in Europe and had beaten some big names along the way, and they obviously must have thought, how will a team like Aberdeen come over here and beat us.'

Having settled down and starting to get a foothold in the game, Aberdeen forced a corner. The work that had been done beforehand now kicked in. The Doc explains the corner routine which led to Aberdeen's opening goal. 'We had worked on that corner beforehand. We had watched their defensive set-up at corners and put the sheet up in the dressing room to remind the boys of it. Like the formation, so many teams copied us with this routine after the game so we would work out and then work back in again. For the timing to work, Niall McGinn, who was taking the corner, would put his hand up and then count to five which gave us five seconds to get out and then around and attack the ball. Andrew was the target at the back post, and it worked a treat.'

Andrew and his colleagues at the back, Paul Quinn and Ash Taylor, fully expected the home side to now step up a gear as they went in search of an equaliser. The game plan was working as Andrew explains. 'We had clearly ridden our luck in the first 20 minutes because they came out all guns blazing, and we did think this could be a long night, especially if they score early. We had ridden the storm and we knew if we could hold on to that one-goal lead, we would be fine. We had the boys with engines in midfield: Ryan Jack and Graeme Shinnie, who can run all day. We knew these guys playing in front of us would protect us. David Goodwillie did a great job for us that night as well by winning us free kicks on the halfway line which gave us boys at the back some respite. They were starting to take chances by committing men forward which potentially leaves gaps and space behind for us to exploit. It was a great night's work.'

For the start of the second half, Rijeka pressed as they went in search of an equaliser, but seven minutes after the restart the Dons doubled their lead in quite spectacular fashion. Andrew Considine talks me through Peter Pawlett's sensational diving header. 'Peter's goal was brilliant! It's always a special moment seeing Peter scoring a headed goal as it does not happen that often. I have seen a few diving headers in my career that have been monumental for us, like Darren Mackie's one against Dnipro, but I tell you what, Peter's one against Rijeka is right up there with the best of them. I think what made it more special was because of the distance from goal he was. I know Kenny McLean added a third, but for most of the second half it was backs to the wall defending. We did reduce them to very little as they tried to press the game, but between me, Paul Quinn and Ash Taylor, we were dealing with everything. It was a team effort and another outstanding night of football for us.'

For Niall McGinn he had the perfect vantage point to see Peter Pawlett's header, and he recalls that moment as he saw it: 'Shay's cross was a good cross, but it wasn't a brilliant cross because it didn't reach that area between the six-yard box and the 18-yard box. Pete, though, made it look like a great cross because of his finish. I am not taking anything away from Shay because he did whip it in. My first instinct was, "Wow, what a finish; what an unbelievable header; how's he done that from there?" All the goals came at good times because we were soaking up pressure. Andy's and Peter's headers and then Kenny's strike for the third – that was also a very important goal.'

For goalscorer Peter Pawlett it's a game and a moment that will live long in the memory, a moment to savour. 'What I recall more than anything is getting played off the park for the first 20 minutes, but then we had a welcome water break, and everything changed after that! During the break, Derek and The Doc told us all to just "settle down". The gaffer reminded us that we had managed to get through the opening period without conceding, so all we needed to do now was relax and start playing. The gaffer changed the shape a little bit, tinkered with the tactics slightly, and that is when the game started to turn in our favour. When Andy Considine opened the scoring, we then had something to hang on to. When you have something to hang on to your mindset changes – if your runner makes a run, you track him all the way and little things like that. Thankfully, I was able to score my goal which put us two up; I must be honest, I surprised myself with that header from the edge of the 18-yard box. I remember sitting in the dressing room after the game thinking, "Wow, what a win." Rijeka had not been beaten in Europe in 12 home games and we had just beaten them 3-0! They were a top team; that is a night I will not quickly forget – a brilliant night.'

Prior to Aberdeen taking a two-goal lead, half-time proved critical for the coaching staff. Instructions had to be relayed and all had to be reminded of their jobs and responsibilities as The Doc recalls: 'At half-time all we did was reinforce the message and kept the same shape. We reminded them of the distances between us and their immediate opponents, and when we get it what our out pass is going to be, and when we go at them, we really go at them. Our second goal was brilliant but wee Shay Logan surprised me because he must have thought he had turned into Lionel Messi for 30 seconds! He had a break down the right, did a small stepover and curled a cross towards the 18-yard line. What a goal that was by Peter, what a brilliant header. That goal gave us an almost relaxed feel to our play. Like Groningen I remember the boos ringing out all over the stadium, especially for the first goal, but for the second there was almost a silence to them and then when we scored the third goal, which was another brilliant goal, I expected the stadium to empty but nobody left; all the Rijeka fans stayed behind to watch. The boys told me afterwards that they loved playing the final 15 minutes because by that time Rijeka were done.'

Midfielder Kenny McLean added a third with a quarter of the game to go. The Dons cruised through the remainder of the game as the Croatians looked like a broken team. Andrew Considine remembers the mood in the dressing room after the full-time whistle. 'Utter joy! The manager made a big point about how disrespectful they had been towards us and told us that this will go down as one of the best results in the club's history if we can come here and win. The boys were exhausted but the smiles on everybody's faces was amazing to see. We knew that it was only half-time as we had to welcome them back to Pittodrie for the second leg, but it was a massive result for us.' Niall McGinn also looks back on that moment in the dressing room at full time with a great deal of fondness: 'We all came in and just looked at each other and thought, "Wow, did that just happen?" Rijeka had put out some big teams over the years on the European stage – that was one of the best performances I have been involved in. On the night everything clicked – it might have been that magic water on 20 minutes!' The astonishing result made for a very enjoyable trip home as Andrew Considine recalls. 'It was busy. There were some travelling fans with us as well as board members and the chairman, and everybody was as high as a kite because everybody recognised what a fantastic result it was for us. Winning 3-0 meant unless we were to completely capitulate at home, there was no chance they were going to go through. We all recognised what an amazing result it was and made for a brilliant flight home.'

Having now beaten two of Europe's best sides on their own patch I was intrigued to know from The Doc if the emotions of beating Rijeka differed to those of beating Groningen 12 months previously. 'It was different because the Groningen victory was game over, it was done; there was the emotional feel to it – we beat you, you underestimated us – whereas the Rijeka victory was more about us growing on the European scene. We knew we were getting better and better, so the feeling was more of satisfaction. Croatian people are mad for their football, they are so passionate, and they got behind their team massively that night, but what I do remember is that when we got on the bus to leave the stadium to go back to the hotel, the crowd had all stayed, they lined the bus and they applauded us on the way out to the main road. I remember feeling quite emotional about that because this was almost like a football mecca and you could see that they appreciated what we had done that night. First, they booed us when we scored the opener, there was a silence for the second goal and when the third goal went in it was all about respect. It was an ovation all the way until we reached the main road – that was a special moment.'

For manager Derek McInnes it was one of his proudest moments in his short time as Aberdeen manager. 'To win a game here 3-0 is a fantastic result, but the conditions were torture at times as it was a battle of endurance. It's a job well done from everybody tonight and immensely satisfying. We should enjoy it and feel good about ourselves. It shows what can be done with players because Rijeka are a good team. The level of teams that they've managed to see off would suggest that was a very good job from everybody at Aberdeen.' Just for the record Aberdeen welcomed Rijeka to Pittodrie for the return leg a week later and, after an almighty scare where the Croatians took a two-goal lead, Aberdeen showed their mental strength by getting back into the game thanks to goals from

Niall McGinn and Jonny Hayes. Aberdeen went through 5-2 on aggregate. Sadly, that was as far as the Dons went as they succumbed to Kairat Almaty in the final qualifying round, going out 3-2 on aggregate.

CLOSING LINES

To bring this book to a close I thought it would be quite apt to use a quote from our greatest ever manager, Sir Alex Ferguson. This quote was taken from his very own documentary film *Sir Alex Ferguson: Never Give In* which was released in the spring of 2021. In what was a very moving and poignant moment in the film, Sir Alex said these words: 'Winning was always based on my own attitude to failure; you have to treat losing as part of the progress. Throughout my life a defeat or a failure sparked something inside me that I did something about it. As human beings you have to understand that adversity is part of your life. When it happens, you find yourself.'

It's a quote that resonates. Aberdeen Football Club has played a huge role in my life, and for years Pittodrie was my second home. I grew up in an era, the likes of which I doubt I will see in my lifetime again. I am grateful for the memories and time spent enjoying those moments with my parents, who have now both passed. When I think of them, I fall back to a time that was magical and enchanting. It was my childhood. I can still see my parents in my mind, hugging each other after we defeated Bayern Munich, and then again, when soaked to the skin, as the full-time whistle blew in Gothenburg. Those moments came from a team and a manager who never gave up, who believed the impossible could become possible. They all had the desire and the belief to win, win at all costs. To become immortal in the eyes of the fans, those very same players had to use the pain of defeat to drive them forward, to learn, to become better and to form a bond that was unbreakable. At the time of writing Aberdeen are entering a new era and venturing into a European competition, the likes of which we have never seen before. I ask this: call upon Gothenburg, call upon Dnipro and Bayern Munich and Copenhagen, don't work against it, work with it and don't ever be blinded by nostalgia. Lest we forget – we have what money can't buy: a soul, and a team spirit built in family tradition.